Few books on poverty and education manage to achieve what Parrett and Budge do here: Marry an equity-informed, evidence-based framework for understanding why class disparities exist with an accessible, action-oriented approach for eliminating them.

If you're ready to stop fiddling with simplistic strategies and embrace a holistic, transformative approach, start here.

—Paul Gorski, founder of the Equity Literacy Institute
and author of *Reaching and Teaching Students in Poverty:
Strategies for Erasing the Opportunity Gap*

This is one of the best books I have read. Every educator should read it to gain a deeper understanding of poverty—and how to disrupt the cycle of poverty that impacts communities across the nation. Parrett and Budge offer research, connections with educators doing the work, and practical strategies that can be implemented in any system. This work is an integral part of our school-based training.

—Tiffany Anderson, superintendent,
Topeka Public Schools, Unified District No. 50,
Topeka, Kansas

ASCD MEMBER BOOK

Many ASCD members received this book as a
member benefit upon its initial release.

Learn more at: **www.ascd.org/memberbooks**

2ND EDITION

TURNING HIGH-POVERTY SCHOOLS INTO HIGH-PERFORMING SCHOOLS

2ND EDITION

TURNING HIGH-POVERTY SCHOOLS INTO HIGH-PERFORMING SCHOOLS

WILLIAM H. PARRETT
KATHLEEN M. BUDGE

ASCD

Alexandria, Virginia USA

1703 N. Beauregard St. • Alexandria, VA 22311-1714 USA
Phone: 800-933-2723 or 703-578-9600 • Fax: 703-575-5400
Website: www.ascd.org • E-mail: member@ascd.org
Author guidelines: www.ascd.org/write

Ranjit Sidhu, *CEO and Executive Director;* Stefani Roth, *Publisher;* Genny Ostertag, *Director, Content Acquisitions;* Julie Houtz, *Director, Book Editing & Production;* Darcie Russell, *Editor;* Judi Connelly, *Senior Art Director;* Mary Duran and Masie Chong, *Graphic Designers;* Cynthia Stock, *Typesetter;* Kelly Marshall, *Manager, Production Services;* Shajuan Martin, *E-Publishing Specialist;* Isel Pizarro, *Senior Production Specialist*

PAPERBACK ISBN: 978-1-4166-2900-9 ASCD product #120031
PDF E-BOOK ISBN: 978-1-4166-2902-3; see Books in Print for other formats.
Quantity discounts are available: e-mail programteam@ascd.org or call 800-933-2723, ext. 5773, or 703-575-5773. For desk copies, go to www.ascd.org/deskcopy.

ASCD Member Book No. FY20-6A. ASCD Member Books mail to Premium (P), Select (S), and Institutional Plus (I+) members on this schedule: Jan, PSI+; Feb, P; Apr, PSI+; May, P; Jul, PSI+; Aug, P; Sep, PSI+; Nov, PSI+; Dec, P. For current details on membership, see www.ascd.org/membership.

Library of Congress Cataloging-in-Publication Data
Names: Parrett, William, author. | Budge, Kathleen M., author.
Title: Turning high-poverty schools into high-performing schools / William H. Parrett and Kathleen M. Budge.
Description: 2nd edition. | Alexandria, Virginia : ASCD, [2020] | Includes bibliographical references and index. | Summary: "Learn how educators combine research with proven practices and actions to disrupt the adverse effects of poverty on students' academic achievement and lives"—Provided by publisher.
Identifiers: LCCN 2019051597 (print) | LCCN 2019051598 (ebook) | ISBN 9781416629009 (paperback) | ISBN 9781416629023 (pdf)
Subjects: LCSH: Poor children—Education—United States. | Children with social disabilities—Education—United States. | School improvement programs—United States. | Academic achievement—United States.
Classification: LCC LC4091 .P36 2020 (print) | LCC LC4091 (ebook) | DDC 371.2/07—dc23
LC record available at https://lccn.loc.gov/2019051597
LC ebook record available at https://lccn.loc.gov/2019051598

29 28 27 26 25 24 23 22 21 20   2 3 4 5 6 7 8 9 10 11 12

To our grandchildren
Lukas, Kennedy, and Adley Jo.
You remind us that until the world
is better for *all* children,
it will not be better for you.

2ND EDITION

TURNING HIGH-POVERTY SCHOOLS INTO HIGH-PERFORMING SCHOOLS

Foreword

Early in my career as a school administrator, I was standing in front of the faculty to present data about the achievement of our students. I was working the room to engender a dialogue about what we were going to do about the gaps in the numbers. The numbers, frankly, suggested we weren't serving many of our students very well. This was the early 1990s and the education field was embarking on the era of standards, just post-publication of *Nation at Risk*, and beginning to incorporate data on student performance in conversations about improvement. Our school, though facing circumstances nowhere near as difficult as many of the schools chronicled in this volume, worked with a student population that was among the poorest and most racially and linguistically diverse in our small city district.

As I stood at the overhead projector and began to present the data on student achievement, some hands started to go up in the back of the room. The questions went something like this: "I know many of our kids struggle, but they come to school way behind other kids. How can you expect us to teach those kids to the same level as kids who have two parents, get breakfast every morning, and have adequate support to get their homework done every night? We just can't do it all!" Note that I'm sparing you the lengthier diatribe from a concentrated group of faculty members. This group, despite stating mainly good intentions for trying to do the right thing for our students, couldn't get past the difficult circumstances and learning needs our kids brought with them to school every day. Unfortunately, despite my efforts, the conversation deteriorated into blaming the kids and their circumstances instead of talking about owning the problems that we saw in our data and engaging in efforts to shift practices to be more powerful for the kids. Looking back, it was a failure of my early leadership for sure, but the episode was an example of how our beliefs about what is possible for children's learning hamper our efforts to teach all kids.

The confused wisdom of *some* of my educational elders (not all, let me emphasize) in the room that day, regrettably, was that what we needed to be most effective in ensuring adequate learning growth in our students was *better students*. Latent in the dialogue among a *few* (again, I emphasize) of our mostly white, mostly middle-class teachers was that we would do a lot better if we only had fewer of "those" minority kids. In this case, they were referring to kids from immigrant families from Southeast Asia who came to school without English as a first or second language and who had begun populating the apartment complexes in our immediate neighborhood. And if those few teachers could just have the pleasure of teaching a batch of kids from better circumstances, who looked and talked more like they did, by golly, they'd do a heck of a job of educating them.

Wrong-headed thinking, for sure. I want to believe that the profession has traveled far from that early 1990s faculty meeting conversation. Certainly, the book you are about to read is predicated on an argument that absolutely and completely refutes the claims I heard from some of my faculty that day. Building on long-standing work done by scholars studying how schools manage to teach virtually all children well, what Bill and Kathleen have rendered is an analysis and an accompanying tool kit for understanding how schools all over the United States manage to realize outstanding student achievement results among high-poverty, high-minority populations.

This volume reinforces foundational ideas that compose a sort of recipe for success in serving all children's learning needs. The recipe begins with the experiences of schools that prove that regardless of race, socioeconomic background, language, family situation, or [pick your descriptor], all children can learn. It continues with educators who believe our students can learn, approach teaching with the idea that students will learn if taught well, and seriously make an ongoing effort to improve and align our practice with best thinking and examples in the field. And the final ingredients are when teaching of this kind is realized across a whole school (or system), which occurs when leadership at the school and district is squarely focused on supporting the improvement of teaching in an ongoing, routine way.

This simple recipe for educators is incredibly complex to implement, yet powerfully rendered here. Much of my career in education has been dedicated to teaching and to the research that supports ways to make these simple ideas come to life in practice. Bill and Kathleen synthesize learning from research and practice that specifically highlights the moves that leaders take in schools and systems that have realized significant growth in learning for all kids, regardless of their race, language, or socioeconomic status.

I wish I had this book in my hands to give to my faculty that day back in the early 1990s. For all educators and practitioners reading these ideas now, take them to heart and put them into practice.

Michael Copland
Deputy Superintendent
Bellingham (WA) Public Schools

Introduction:
We Can Do This

> We have much more to learn from studying high-poverty schools that are on the path to improvement than we do from studying nominally high-performing schools that are producing a significant portion of their performance through social class rather than instruction.
>
> —*Richard F. Elmore (2006, p. 943)*

On a snow-slushy, gray day in March, where winter had lingered a little too long, we talked with the principal and a group of teacher leaders at Peterson Elementary in Kalispell, Montana. The hours of interviews flew by as they told us about the importance of loving their students, reaching out to families with empathy, professional learning necessary to meet their students' needs, and additional challenges. From improving literacy instruction and addressing inequitable homework practices to developing multiple strategies for responding to the stress and trauma students were experiencing, they described the collective commitment and action it took to transform their school.

The educators at Peterson are at once ordinary and extraordinary. They are not superhuman, and there is still work to be done in their school. What they are is courageous. What do we mean by this? They are committed to doing what is in their sphere of influence to disrupt poverty's adverse impact on student learning. We found other educators, in locales far different from Kalispell, who are the same. Taken together, they fortified our faith in the power of a committed group of individuals to accomplish whatever they set their minds to do, contributed to our conviction that opportunity gaps can be narrowed (or even closed), and substantiated our view that the transformational work of turning a high-poverty, low-performing school into a high-performing school, although considerably complex, is absolutely doable.

High-performing, high-poverty schools are *models of the possible*. They are places where the belief that transformation is possible has been proven correct and where students who live in poverty experience success. These models and experiences lead to optimism, hope, and self-efficacy. If you are an educator, policymaker, parent, or simply someone who cares about improving public schools, we hope you'll heed Richard Elmore's words that we've quoted in the epigraph. He is correct: there is much to learn from these schools. Even if you are not working in a high-poverty school, the same lessons can be applied to disrupting poverty's adverse influence on learning *wherever* students living in poverty go to school. We are excited to share with you what we have learned from high-performing, high-poverty schools in the past decade and particularly from the 12 schools profiled in this second edition.

How to Use This Book

High-poverty schools do not become high performing by tinkering their way to success. A former superintendent of a high-poverty rural district described the district's efforts to confront underachievement like this: "We could not continue to do what we knew would, at best, only minimally raise student achievement . . . and for only some of the kids. We had to fundamentally change the way we did business."

We have written the second edition of this book, *Turning High-Poverty Schools into High-Performing Schools*, to continue supporting schools in "doing business differently." Those who work in high-poverty schools can benefit from the information we provide here, as can anyone working in a school where an achievement gap exists between students who live in poverty and their more advantaged peers. For your school to become high performing and to close achievement gaps, you must apply the theories, research, and practical ideas in this book to your unique context. Throughout the book, we have provided tools to help you do just that.

Chapters 1 through 4 lay the groundwork for informed conversations among colleagues and future action planning. Although an individual can gain valuable knowledge by reading this book, we encourage all school stakeholders—administrators, teachers, teacher leaders, coaches, and the like—to learn together. These chapters provide information about poverty and carry the optimistic message that schools can and do make a difference.

Chapters 5 through 9 show how educators in HP/HP schools have built leadership capacity and collective efficacy, fostered the necessary learning environment, and improved learning. We describe how their actions influenced the school's culture in terms of values, beliefs, and norms. We discuss what educators *started* doing or improved—you'll see this in the "taking action" chapters (Chapters 5–7)—as well as what they *stopped* doing or worked to eliminate (Chapter 8). Each chapter includes a rubric that you can use to assess your school's current situation and guide your reading and discussion.

We also include several inserts highlighting the practical applications of strategies that have been successfully used in HP/HP schools. Look for the following:

 Uncommon Sense, which presents novel approaches to problem solving. For example, one school started an after-school dinner program for kids who participated in the after-school tutoring program, which many students took advantage of before riding the late bus home. We call this out-of-the-box thinking "uncommon sense."

 School Culture Alert, which signals or makes concrete and visible the values, beliefs, and norms operating in these schools.

We conclude with Chapter 9, in which we revisit the interactive, dynamic nature of the components of our Framework for Collective Action and challenge all of us—educators and other stakeholders—to confront the reasons we have not yet ensured that every high-poverty school is high performing. We present districts that focused on creating clusters of high-poverty, high-performing schools, as well as others that embraced a more unified approach.

What's Your School's Story?

The two self-assessments that follow—Assessing Our Ability to Take Action (Figure 1) and Assessing Our Willingness to Take Action (Figure 2)—will enable you to reflect on your unique situation as a school, a department, a grade-level team, a collegial cluster, or an individual. We hope these assessments will help you in two ways: by generating data related to your school's readiness to undertake an improvement effort and by guiding your use of the resources and information provided in this book.

These assessments elicit beliefs about people's *ability and willingness* to work with students who live in poverty, together with their beliefs about

Figure 1   Assessing Our Ability to Take Action

Please rate each statement from highly unlikely (−3) to highly likely (3).

1	I can name at least five ways poverty adversely influences students' lives and learning.							My colleagues can name at least five ways poverty adversely influences students' lives and learning.						
	−3	−2	−1	0	1	2	3	−3	−2	−1	0	1	2	3
2	I know the percentage of students in my school who live in poverty and who, of those students, are underachieving.							My colleagues know the percentage of students in our school who live in poverty and who, of those students, are underachieving.						
	−3	−2	−1	0	1	2	3	−3	−2	−1	0	1	2	3
3	I can name three to five specific strategies used by high-performing, high-poverty schools to develop the leadership infrastructure necessary for improvement.							My colleagues can name three to five specific strategies used by high-performing, high-poverty schools to develop the leadership infrastructure necessary for improvement.						
	−3	−2	−1	0	1	2	3	−3	−2	−1	0	1	2	3
4	I can name three to five specific strategies used by high-performing, high-poverty schools to develop a safe, healthy, and supportive learning environment for students and adults.							My colleagues can name three to five specific strategies used by high-performing, high-poverty schools to develop a safe, healthy, and supportive learning environment for students and adults.						
	−3	−2	−1	0	1	2	3	−3	−2	−1	0	1	2	3
5	I can name three to five specific strategies used by high-performing, high-poverty schools to improve student learning, support adult learning, and "work smarter" as a system.							My colleagues can name three to five specific strategies used by high-performing, high-poverty schools to improve student learning, support adult learning, and "work smarter" as a system.						
	−3	−2	−1	0	1	2	3	−3	−2	−1	0	1	2	3
6	I can explain how educators' mental maps can perpetuate underachievement.							My colleagues can explain how educators' mental maps can perpetuate underachievement.						
	−3	−2	−1	0	1	2	3	−3	−2	−1	0	1	2	3
7	I can list at least three counterproductive practices, policies, and structures that perpetuate underachievement.							My colleagues can list at least three counterproductive practices, policies, and structures that perpetuate underachievement.						
	−3	−2	−1	0	1	2	3	−3	−2	−1	0	1	2	3
8	I can describe how counterproductive mental maps, practices, policies, and structures are confronted and eliminated in high-performing, high-poverty schools.							My colleagues can describe how counterproductive mental maps, practices, policies, and structures are confronted and eliminated in high-performing, high-poverty schools.						
	−3	−2	−1	0	1	2	3	−3	−2	−1	0	1	2	3
9	I can describe the beliefs, values, and norms that constitute a school culture conducive to mitigating the adverse effects of poverty on learning.							My colleagues can describe the beliefs, values, and norms that constitute a school culture conducive to mitigating the adverse effects of poverty on learning.						
	−3	−2	−1	0	1	2	3	−3	−2	−1	0	1	2	3

Figure 2   Assessing Our Willingness to Take Action

Please rate each statement from highly unlikely (−3) to highly likely (3).

1	I believe I make a difference in the lives of my students, despite the challenges some of them face.							My colleagues believe, as teachers, they make a difference in the lives of students, despite the challenges some of those students face.							
	−3	−2	−1	0	1	2	3	−3	−2	−1	0	1	2	3
2	I believe I am professionally responsible for learning.							My colleagues believe they are professionally responsible for learning.							
	−3	−2	−1	0	1	2	3	−3	−2	−1	0	1	2	3
3	I believe all students can meet high academic standards in my classroom, despite the challenges some of them face.							My colleagues believe all students can meet high academic standards in their classrooms, despite the challenges some of them face.							
	−3	−2	−1	0	1	2	3	−3	−2	−1	0	1	2	3
4	I believe learning more about how poverty adversely influences life and learning would help us better meet the needs of students who live in poverty and who are underachieving.							My colleagues believe learning more about how poverty influences life and learning would help us better meet the needs of students who live in poverty and who are underachieving.							
	−3	−2	−1	0	1	2	3	−3	−2	−1	0	1	2	3
5	I believe working more collaboratively would help us better meet the needs of students who live in poverty and who are underachieving.							My colleagues believe working more collaboratively would help us better meet the needs of students who live in poverty and who are underachieving.							
	−3	−2	−1	0	1	2	3	−3	−2	−1	0	1	2	3
6	I believe our school has an organizational climate that encourages innovation, risk taking, and professional learning.							My colleagues believe our school has an organizational climate that encourages innovation, risk taking, and professional learning.							
	−3	−2	−1	0	1	2	3	−3	−2	−1	0	1	2	3
7	I am open to new ideas.							My colleagues are open to new ideas.							
	−3	−2	−1	0	1	2	3	−3	−2	−1	0	1	2	3
8	I believe in our ability as a school to succeed in making changes, even changes of a significant magnitude.							My colleagues believe in our ability as a school to succeed in making changes, even changes of a significant magnitude.							
	−3	−2	−1	0	1	2	3	−3	−2	−1	0	1	2	3
9	I feel a sense of urgency about meeting the needs of students who live in poverty.							My colleagues feel a sense of urgency about meeting the needs of students who live in poverty.							
	−3	−2	−1	0	1	2	3	−3	−2	−1	0	1	2	3

their colleagues' ability and willingness to do so. They will provide information about the gap, if any, between those two perceptions.

Although the questions in the assessments are designed to help you evaluate your school's readiness to benefit from change, this doesn't mean that if a school appears unready to change, it should do nothing. Rather, assessing readiness helps schools tailor their actions to the needs of their staffs. For example, if staff members score more positively in terms of willingness than ability, this would indicate a need to initiate conversations and professional development to build knowledge and skills. If they're more able than willing to do this work, the school would need to address the factors that are influencing that low level of willingness so that the educators step up to the challenge of successfully educating their students who live in poverty.

A Word About—And to—Our Readers

This book is for every adult in the school community who is interested in better serving the needs of children and youth who live in poverty. These adults include those in the roles of administrators, teachers, teacher-leaders, instructional coaches, specialists, media specialist/librarians, counselors, coaches, paraeducators, cafeteria staff, custodians, bus drivers, security staff, and front office staff. It takes everyone working *collectively* to turn a high-poverty school into a high-performing school.

1 Turning Any High-Poverty School into a High-Performing School

One of the biggest issues in improving schools is the perpetual search for the next bell and whistle. Educators who visit us and see our kids with both hands up—our way for students to communicate their ideas and responses to their teachers—want to grab onto things like that. The simple questions they should be focusing on are "What are you putting in front of your kids? Is it aligned to the highest level of rigor? Is it going to get the kids to the end in mind by the end of the school year?"

—Eric Sanchez, executive director, Henderson Collegiate PK–12 Schools, Henderson, NC

What Will It Take?

Most students who drop out—more than 1 million a year in the United States—leave school between the ages of 14 and 16 after enduring years of schooling in which frustration, embarrassment, failure, and minimal achievement were daily realities. Many simply lose hope, seeing little reason to stay in school. Of the roughly 84 percent who do make it to graduation, only slightly more than one-third of that group (41 percent) graduate prepared for the demands of the workplace or higher education. Overall graduation rates are even more dismal for Hispanic (76 percent), African American (79 percent), and Native American (72 percent) students. These rates reflect the failure of public schooling to work for a significant number of our children, our most precious resource (Stark & Noel, 2015).

Dwarfing the number of students who leave early is the number of kids who remain in school and graduate woefully underprepared for postsecondary education or the workplace. More than 3 million U.S. students enrolled in grades 9–12 in 2018 will not graduate on time with their classes

(Stark & Noel, 2015). Combined, the number of students who drop out and the number who are unprepared for life beyond graduation illustrate the crisis that continues to plague the United States.

Not all students who drop out or who underachieve live in poverty, but many do. Despite recent modest progress in student achievement at the elementary and middle school levels, most of our high schools continue to demonstrate little success in closing long-standing achievement gaps between low-income and more advantaged students.

Why do so many people continue to be ambivalent about recognizing, let alone addressing, the continued reality of significant achievement disparity in our public schools? Are the daily needs of children who live in poverty and who are not reaching their potential too immense for most of us to grasp? Are their lives too distant from our own for us to see? Are we too embedded in an unspoken reality of classism and racism, as many argue? What will it take to educate the whole child if that child lives in poverty?

Questions to Ask—And Answer

Our children are the victims of this legacy. They suffer the consequences of a widespread unwillingness on the part of policymakers and education leaders to address three key questions:

1. Why are some high-poverty schools high performing and others are not?
2. What do we need to do to significantly improve our lowest-performing schools?
3. What can we learn from high-performing, high-poverty schools that can help students who live in poverty achieve at higher levels, regardless of where they go to school?

Asking and answering these questions could result in improved educational outcomes for virtually every child living in poverty. Federal policy through the authorization of the 2015 Every Student Succeeds Act (ESSA) continues to require states to identify and provide comprehensive services to their lowest-performing schools (the lowest-performing 5 percent of the state's Title I schools), as well as targeted services for low-performing subgroups of students in other schools. However, far too little has been done to create the conditions that research has demonstrated are necessary to ensure that most, if not all, low-performing schools and their students will significantly improve. In this second edition of *Turning High-Poverty Schools into High-Performing Schools*, we urge all educators and policymakers to study the successes of high-performing, high-poverty schools and to apply and act on this evidence in their own states, districts, and schools.

Leadership Is Essential

In 2007, Barr and Parrett were among the first to synthesize emerging research regarding how low-performing, high-poverty schools become high performing. They identified eight practices that significantly improved a low-performing, high-poverty school:

- Ensuring effective district and school leadership;
- Engaging parents, communities, and schools to work as partners;
- Understanding and holding high expectations for poor and culturally diverse students;
- Targeting low-performing students and schools, looking initially at reading skills;
- Aligning, monitoring, and managing the curriculum;
- Creating a culture of data and assessment literacy;
- Building and sustaining instructional capacity; and
- Reorganizing time, space, and transitions.

Barr and Parrett further concluded that the first practice mentioned—ensuring effective district and school leadership—linked to successful use of the other seven practices. In fact, 16 of the 18 studies that Barr and Parrett synthesized concluded that leadership, often collaborative and distributed, was essential to improve school practices or receive the district-level support necessary for high-poverty schools to become high performing.

A Framework for Action

Building on the contributions of Barr and Parrett (2007), the continuing work of the Education Trust, and that of other scholars and organizations, we initiated a study to develop a greater understanding of the impact and inner workings of leadership in HP/HP schools. This study resulted in the publication of the first edition of this book in 2012. Drawing from the research base, we developed a framework to capture conceptually the function of leadership in these schools, a Framework for Action. We then selected a small, diverse group of schools against which we could "test"—or, in research terms, *member check*—our framework. Each school selected demonstrated significant and sustained gains in academic achievement for at least three years; enrolled 40 percent or more students who qualified for free and reduced-price meals, using federal eligibility guidelines; reflected racial, ethnic, organizational, and geographic diversity; and were willing to work with us. In addition, the Education Trust, the U.S. Department of Education, and individual state departments of education had recognized these schools for their significant improvements in closing achievement gaps.

The leaders and educators we interviewed confirmed what the growing research base on HP/HP schools had identified and what was reflected in our framework: leadership—collaborative and distributed—served as the linchpin of success. This included the crucial role the principal and often a small group of teacher leaders and instructional coaches played in *developing systemic, shared leadership capacity* throughout the school, which was a catalyst for the creation of a *healthy, safe, and supportive learning environment* and an *intentional focus on improving learning*. Their actions in each of these areas also led to changes in the school's culture. The leaders and educators further noted that beyond influencing the classroom and the school at large, they *developed relationships and formed partnerships* with the district office, students' families, and the broader neighborhood and community to reach their goals.

The Framework Updated: The Framework for *Collective* Action

Following publication of the first edition of this book, we continued to visit and study HP/HP schools across the United States, as well as schools in Canada, the United Kingdom, Japan, South Africa, and Belize. We also had the opportunity to work with ASCD to study and video-document the factors that led to success in four HP/HP schools in three states. This research afforded us multiple opportunities to not only learn from these schools, but also validate or disconfirm elements of the framework. In this edition, we have revised the title of our framework to clearly assert the need and importance for school leaders, teachers, and all other educators and staff to work together; hence, the addition of the word *collective* to the title of the framework.

Our more recent study, which resulted in the publication of *Disrupting Poverty: Five Powerful Classroom Practices* (Budge & Parrett, 2018), sheds light on how teachers create classroom conditions to disrupt poverty's adverse influence on their students' learning. Our interviews of more than 40 effective classroom practitioners, over half of whom grew up in poverty, extended what we had learned in the original study.

Across states, nations, and cultures, we have found the primary tenets of the Framework for Collective Action to be consistent with factors that drive the transformation of low-performing, high-poverty schools to high performance. Moreover, we spent considerable time since the publication of the first edition in working with, supporting, and learning from many schools and districts in their quest to improve. These opportunities have also informed our research.

Based on this work and on our most current study of an additional 12 HP/HP schools, we have modified the Framework for Collective Action to acknowledge that the ubiquitous presence of a *relentless sense of urgency to better serve all students* is part of the cultural fabric of HP/HP schools. We have also acknowledged the importance of *building collective efficacy*—that is, a staff's shared belief that through their collective action they can positively influence student outcomes.

In the Framework for Collective Action (Figure 1.1), we illustrate the complex interactions among the three arenas in which educators work

Figure 1.1   A Framework for Collective Action: Leading High-Poverty Schools to High Performance

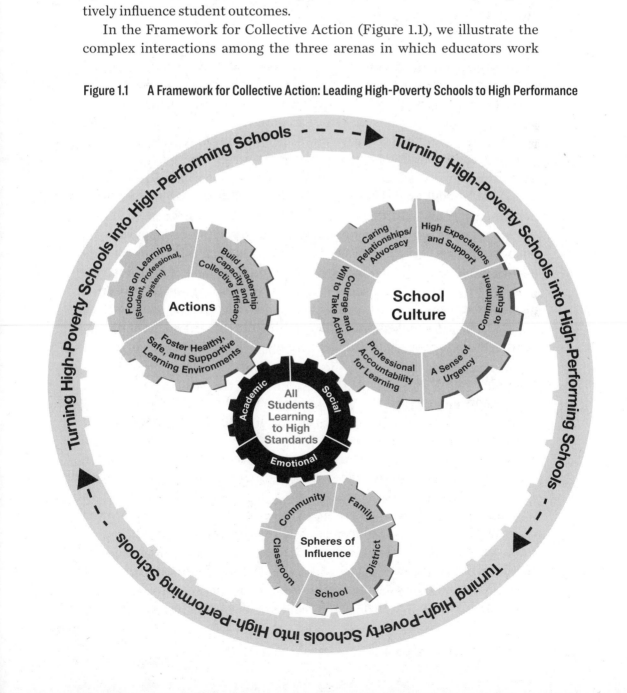

to support deeper levels of academic, social, and emotionoal learning by fashioning them as three gears: Actions, School Culture, and Spheres of Influence. These three gears connect to a central drive gear, All Students Learning to High Standards, which represents the core mission of high-performing, high-poverty schools. The inclusion of two new factors in the framework—a sense of urgency and collective efficacy—are elaborated in Chapter 4, as is the new placement of the drive gear.

Disrupting the Cycle of Poverty

An effective school can rescue a child from a future of illiteracy, save hundreds of students from the grim reality awaiting those who exit school unprepared, and directly affect and improve our society. To do so, however, it must have leaders and educators who are oriented toward social justice. They ask questions that cause themselves and others to assess and critique the current conditions in their schools. They identify whose interests are being served by the current conditions—and whose are not. Their professional practice was consistent with what others have identified as *social justice leadership* (Dantley & Green, 2015; Dantley & Tillman, 2006; Scheurich & Skrla, 2003; Theoharis, 2009; Wang, 2018). Their vision for the school and their professional practice centered on students who, for whatever reason, were not succeeding and focused on inclusive practices ensuring that all students had equal opportunities for powerful instruction. They confronted structures, policies, practices, and mental maps that perpetuated inequities and thus created more equitable schools in which expectations were high, academic achievement as well as social and emotional learning improved overall, and achievement gaps were closing.

A Focus on Excellence, Equality, and Equity

The educators we interviewed and those in other HP/HP schools aim for three ideals: excellence, equality, and equity. What do we mean by this? First, these educators understand the distinction among the three words, as well as the possible tension among them. Excellence is the expectation in HP/HP schools—and it's not sacrificed to attain the other two goals of equality or equity. These schools are not places where curriculum is watered down, standards are lowered, or the pace of instruction is slowed to ensure equality in outcomes (e.g., where everyone gets an *A*). Rather, these schools strive for equality in outcomes (e.g., all students meet high standards or all students graduate ready for college) by committing to equitable opportunity for learning. In the case of students who live in poverty who are not learning to their potential, providing such opportunity often necessitates *equitable*, as opposed to *equal*, distribution of resources (time, money, people). In HP/HP schools, all students do not get the same thing— all students get what they need to succeed.

A Focus on Academic Achievement

Although many high-poverty schools are criticized for focusing too much on standardized testing, which has been perceived as narrowing the curriculum and emphasizing the "wrong" things, this was not the case in the schools we visited. They focused on multiple indicators of high performance, including (but not limited to) increased attendance, improved graduation rates, fewer discipline violations, increased parent and community involvement, improved pedagogy, and improved climate. All these factors contributed to or were indicators of improved academic learning and improved social and emotional learning.

At the end of the day, however, there can be no social justice without addressing academic achievement. These schools both increased academic achievement overall and closed achievement gaps, but as the framework in Figure 1.1 indicates, doing so involves more than simply focusing on raising standardized test scores. Our approach in writing this book is to clarify how schools can transform to better meet the needs of children and adolescents who live in poverty, as opposed to "fixing" these students so they better fit in the current system of schooling.

Place-Conscious Social Justice Leadership

Scholars (Rodriguez & Fabionar, 2010) who have studied the effect of poverty on students and schools assert, "When school leaders subscribe to conceptions of poverty that divorce individual instances from local and historical contexts, they risk employing prescriptive efforts that overlook individual and collective responses to poverty that can benefit learners" (p. 67). By contrast, when they understand the broader history of the community, school leaders and educators "are more likely to recognize community strategies that are used to cope with and counteract the conditions that maintain poverty" (p. 69).

Poverty looks different in every community. In a rural community where the formerly vibrant agriculture-based economy has struggled and the population is predominantly white, poverty will manifest itself in a specific way. It will look different in a suburban community that is, for the most part, working class but also serves as a refugee relocation site. And it will look different again in an urban setting with a racially diverse population and opportunities for employment that have been severely compromised for decades.

The educators in the HP/HP schools we studied were in tune with the neighborhoods and communities they served. Their leadership was informed by knowing the answers to questions such as these: What has happened in our community that has shaped collective experience? How have the demographics of the community changed over the years? What is the community's social and political response to poverty? What support is available? How are wealth and income distributed in the community—who are the "haves" and the "have-nots"? Is there a "wrong side of the tracks"? If so, who lives there? Where is the school located? Where do our families come from? How long have they been in the community? What are the traditional places of employment? What is the economic structure of the community? Who are the major employers? What are the hopes and dreams of our families for their children's futures? How are educators viewed? What does our community believe to be the purpose of school?

To be of benefit, research and the practical strategies it implies must be considered in light of unique factors found in the local context. Our intention is to present the lessons learned from HP/HP schools in a manner that supports what scholars refer to as *user generalizability* (Merriam, 1998). Although the schools we studied, and many others like them, had in common the foundational elements represented in the Framework for Collective Action, there was no single approach to success. These elements interact and play out differently in every school.

Improving student learning in high-poverty schools is one of the most daunting challenges confronting public education today. The work is highly complex and demanding. Yet public schools continue to demonstrate that the work can be accomplished and the successes can be sustained. In Chapter 2, we introduce the 12 public schools we recently studied. Their successes further confirm the viability of the Framework for Collective Action as a promising springboard and roadmap for any high-poverty school seeking to improve.

2 Learning from High-Performing, High-Poverty Schools

All over the country are educators who—quietly and without much fanfare—have figured out how to make schools better. Not just a little better. A lot better. They are ordinary educators in many respects, but they have found ways to marshal the power of schools to help students in a way that seems impossible elsewhere. They are transforming institutions into vibrant places of learning and growth— places where teachers want to teach and children want to learn—and in the process they are keeping the American Dream alive for the next generation.

—Karin Chenoweth (2017, p. 1)

Until early in the new millennium, little was known about how chronically underperforming schools with a high percentage of impoverished children could systematically improve. Efforts in the 1990s and early 2000s to improve schools yielded a growing body of recommendations, including correlates of effective schools, examples of successful schools, elements of comprehensive school reform, and a continuing array of curricular and instructional research on and analysis of effective classroom practices. But the specifics about how all the pieces fit together were, for the most part, just beginning to emerge in a comprehensive manner.

At that time, significant improvements in the technology used to keep and report state and district data began to sharply improve the availability of comparative data, making it easier to systematically identify schools whose achievement gains were showing steep trajectories. The Education Trust took one of the initial comparative looks at state-based achievement data on high-poverty schools (Jerald, 2007). By disaggregating factors of free and reduced-price meal eligibility, ethnicity, exceptionality, and achievement, Ed Trust researchers verified that in many schools, children

from low-income families and students of color were significantly outper-
forming their more advantaged peers.

What We've Learned

By now, we are fortunate to know much more about the inner workings of
HP/HP schools, thanks to Kati Haycock and Karin Chenoweth, who continued the pioneering work of the Education Trust. Between 2003 and 2014,
Chenoweth and her Ed Trust colleagues studied more than 40 of these
schools across the United States, honoring them as Dispelling the Myth
schools. She profiled these schools in two books, *It's Being Done* (2007) and
How It's Being Done (2009a), and she continues to study these and other
schools to the present.

Since our last study, the number of children and adolescents qualifying for free and reduced-price meals has surpassed 50 percent of the students enrolled in public schools (Suitts, 2015). More high-performing,
high-poverty schools likely exist today than before and are more easily
identified, thanks to advancements in data access. Such schools continue to be stark outliers from the mainstream, despite decades of studies
demonstrating what it takes for a high-poverty school to become a high-
performing school.

This book captures the results from our latest study; continues our mission to enhance what we have learned from HP/HP schools; and provides
new insight into the complex, persistent, and stubborn challenge of improving high-poverty public schools. Schools that have met the challenge of disrupting poverty's adverse influence on learning and sustained their success
over time can be found in every state. Moreover, we better understand the
pitfalls and challenges that beset schools that make significant gains in student outcomes, only to fall back again. In short, we know more today than
we ever have about how to successfully engage in this work.

Our Latest Study

We began our current study by identifying high-poverty schools that had
been recognized by national or state-level organizations for improvement
in student achievement. Multiple organizations, including the U.S. Department of Education, state education agencies and departments, and public
and private sector organizations and foundations, regularly award districts
and schools for excellence in serving high-poverty populations.

We identified the schools by analyzing various publicly available
databases. These included the following organizations and agencies: the

U.S. Department of Education (Blue Ribbon Schools and Distinguished Schools awards); the Education Trust (Dispelling the Myth awards); the National Association of Secondary School Principals (NASSP Breakthrough Schools awards); the National Center for Urban School Transformation (NCUST awards); and *U.S. News & World Report* (Best High School rankings). We also searched state departments of education websites and databases and those of entities such as Public School Review (www.public-schoolreview.com), School Digger (www.schooldigger.com), and NICHE (www.niche.com).

We constructed our own database from these sources and selected a sample of HP/HP schools for possible participation in the study. Schools selected had to first meet the following two criteria:

1. Secondary schools had to have a minimum of 60 percent of their students qualifying for the federal free and reduced-price meal program; elementary schools had to have a minimum of 65 percent qualifying.

2. All schools had to have demonstrated a pattern of performance at or above state averages for *all* public schools in their respective states in *all* areas of mandatory state achievement testing.

We selected an initial sample of 51 schools that met the criteria and represented various grade configurations, as well as demographic diversity (size of school, racial and ethnic composition) and geographic diversity (urban, suburban, and rural locations in various regions throughout the United States and Canada). We then ranked the schools by performance in grade-level groupings of elementary and secondary.

Next, we reviewed various state, district, and independent school databases, which enabled us to triangulate the data for the purpose of reconfirming that the schools we selected met our criteria. Although all 51 of the schools demonstrated impressive results, budget limitations required us to limit our travel, and thus we narrowed our sample to 12 schools that represented our grade configuration, demographic, and geographic priorities.

We contacted principals and superintendents to introduce the study, as well as to invite their participation. We explained our interest in interviewing leaders, staff, and other key individuals; observing classrooms and the operations of the school; and seeking assistance in gathering additional data regarding their journey to becoming a high-performing school. Every school and district leader we spoke with enthusiastically agreed to participate and welcomed us to their schools.

HP/HP schools often welcome visitors, are accustomed to frequent inquiry, and are pleased to share their successes. In every school we studied, we learned that educators from other schools were visiting as individuals or teams either before or after our visit. The word gets out about these schools. It was great to observe the flow of visitors and witness the receptiveness of the schools to these visits.

Meet 12 HP/HP Schools

The schools we studied demonstrated significant gains on multiple measures of student success beyond achievement tests, such as graduation rates, attendance, student behavior, parent engagement and satisfaction, and post-school success. They have sustained their high level of performance over time and have been recognized for their success by national, state, and provincial entities. Geographic, demographic, and organizational diversity characterize the 12 schools. Located in urban, rural, and suburban settings, some are large schools and others are quite small. They include six elementary schools, two middle schools, two high schools, one K–8 school, and one K–12 school. Ten are conventional public schools, and two are public charter schools. What follows are brief descriptions of each of the 12 schools, together with a snapshot of their achievement gains. This diverse array of high-poverty, high-performing schools pervasively and compellingly illustrates the viability of this work.

Concourse Village Elementary School (3K–5)

Concourse Village Elementary School (CVES), located in the Melrose section of the South Bronx, New York, leads the way in demonstrating that "your ZIP code doesn't determine your outcome," according to the school's founding and current principal, Alexa Sorden. The school's extraordinary success results from intensive dedication and focus on the part of the leadership, staff, and students. High expectations for every student and the adult support that students need to get there dominate the culture of the school.

CVES's results speak for themselves (see Figure 2.1). Significant, sustained success on the New York State Testing Program (NYSTP) in English language arts and math places CVES considerably above both district and state averages and has resulted in widespread national recognition. The U.S. Department of Education named CVES a National Blue Ribbon School (2018) and an Exemplary High-Performing School (2018), and the National Elementary and Secondary Education Act (ESEA) Distinguished Schools program honored them as a National Recognized Title I School (2018). Principal Sorden, a former reading specialist, literary coach, and director of student achievement, also received the prestigious 2017 Ryan Award,

Figure 2.1 Concourse Village Elementary School

New York Assessment Program (NYSTP)—Math NYC District
https://cves.connectwithkids.com/

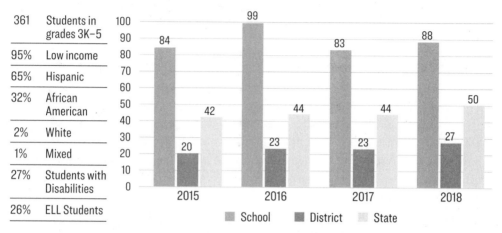

361	Students in grades 3K–5
95%	Low income
65%	Hispanic
32%	African American
2%	White
1%	Mixed
27%	Students with Disabilities
26%	ELL Students

Legend: ■ School ■ District ▨ State

2015: School 84, District 20, State 42
2016: School 99, District 23, State 44
2017: School 83, District 23, State 44
2018: School 88, District 27, State 50

Source: NYSED Data Site, https://data.nysed.gov/lists.

which honors transformational school principals, for exhibiting exceptional leadership in closing the achievement gap in urban K–12 schools.

In the six years since the school reopened in 2013 as part of the district's New School Model Initiative, replacing P.S. 385 of New York City's District No. 7, CVES has steadily climbed to high performance. The school has a preschool program for 3-year-olds, a full day for 4-year-olds, and a full-day kindergarten through 5th grade. The school's demographic portrait reflects a daunting challenge for any school: 95 percent of students are low income, 27 percent are students with disabilities, 26 percent are English language learners, and more than 15 percent are homeless. Nevertheless, Sorden and her school continue to outperform New York state averages by more than 50 points in English language arts and math. "It's not about how smart you are . . . [it's about] how hard you work," shares Sorden in a common refrain that applies to everybody at Concourse Village.

Tenets of CVES's success include close, trusting relationships with every student; a firm grounding in the school's core values of integrity, perseverance, optimism, willingness, empathy, and respect; and a palpable love for kids that emanates throughout the building. "We really know our students, their needs, strengths, and interests," explains Sorden.

Following this lead, instructional staff choreograph their lessons with a dramatic sense of urgency to effectively use every minute. Large timers are visible and used in every classroom by staff to manage a fast-paced blend of large- and small-group teaching, coupled with individual attention to the kids needing specific help.

The school deploys a number of instructional design innovations, such as the five-phase process developed by Sorden, which she refers to as the Collaborative Reading Approach, coupled with a blended literacy model, positive behavioral and intervention supports (PBIS), looping, thinking maps, close reading, tutoring, light music in every classroom, and a positive environment for all students and staff, all delivered through an uncanny level of collective teacher cooperation and efficacy.

Sorden voices passion to her staff about getting the kids what they need. "We need 180 amazing days with our kids because they can't afford any bad days," she says. The staff responds by working together to provide four intense hours of targeted instruction to meet the needs of every student. They know they have to be on the same page and work together as professionals to get there. CVES presents a system of consistent, shared successes for any school desiring rapid improvement. Sorden expects teamwork and collective efficacy: "I don't trust words. I don't trust actions. I pay attention to patterns."

And patterns—from high expectations; to authentic caring and relationships; to focused, carefully deployed instruction; to teamwork; to timely professional development that builds staff capacity—are all in place at CVES. Collectively, these patterns drive remarkable success for the students.

E.I. McCulley Elementary School (JK–8)

Every morning, just north of the Niagara River and Niagara Falls in the community of St. Catharines, Ontario, Canada, Derek Harley, self-described "proud" principal, reflects on how student performance has come so far. "The staff likes the kids, and the kids know it," he explains. "Our No. 1 rule: We don't complain about the kids. That may sound harsh, but it's a nonnegotiable here. Kids won't learn from people they don't like. So we fixed that right away."

In four years, E.I. McCulley climbed from being one of the lowest performing of the 79 schools in their district to becoming one of the highest, surpassing district and provincial averages in reading, writing, and mathematics (see Figure 2.2). More than 70 percent of the students' families qualify for public living assistance. Every morning, the school welcomes all the students to a breakfast club before classes begin; bagged lunches are also made available every day for students who do not have sufficient food. Nutritious snacks are available as a grab-and-go throughout the day for any student who wants them. "Our kids aren't hungry here," says Harley.

Figure 2.2   Data for E.I. McCulley Elementary School

District School Board of Niagara, St. Catharines, Canada
http://eimcculley.dsbn.org/

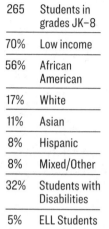

265	Students in grades JK–8
70%	Low income
56%	African American
17%	White
11%	Asian
8%	Hispanic
8%	Mixed/Other
32%	Students with Disabilities
5%	ELL Students

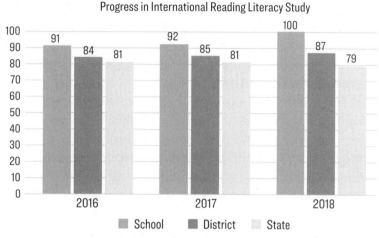

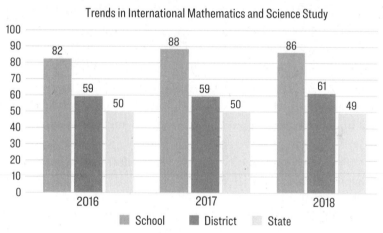

Source: Education Quality and Accountability Office. Available: http://www.eqao.com/en/assessments/results

When Harley came to the school initially, it was a different place. Student achievement was low, the facility was worn out, the front office was unwelcoming, and staff members were constantly complaining about students and their families. Notes Harley, "We knew we had to build trust and relationships all day with the kids, and as we did, it all began to change here."

The school also began a process of rebranding. They painted, they changed the school colors, and the kids voted in a new mascot. The Moose gave way to Jaguars. The front entry and office became a warm, welcoming environment. They started science, sports, and computer clubs for the kids. But most of all, they created and communicated a culture of caring and believing in their students.

The key attributes of E.I. McCulley's transition? "It all starts with the staff," explains Harley. "We have built an incredible group here that knows the kids so well, expects each one of them to succeed, and is made up of genuinely positive people. And we never could have done this without the total support of the district office."

Differentiation became the way teachers taught, all based on knowing what each student needs. Literacy and numeracy became the priority. Staff got comfortable with daily collaborating—learning together and helping one another. Instructional strengths were shared and matched with student needs. Teachers were willing to move around and be flexible, and they collectively kept their eyes on the prize of learning. They saw they could serve every student.

One-third of McCulley's kids receive special education services. The staff realized that if they used scribing or assistive scribing technology with those students, the students would do better on assessments, particularly if the scribe was someone the student knew and liked. "It really worked, and the students' performance soared," explains Harley.

E.I. McCulley has transformed into a school that the students, families, and community are proud to belong to. Known now as a high-performing school, a steady stream of visitors from across the province and border regularly visit to observe and learn. Harley gives all the credit to his staff: "It's such a team here, really the model of what a team can do. I'm so lucky and fortunate to work with them."

Evergreen Elementary School (K–5)

Following years of being the lowest-achieving elementary school in the Bethel School District in Washington State, Evergreen Elementary embarked on a journey to change its results. "We were on the verge of being closed . . . we needed to do something," voiced several of the school's original staff who continue to lead the school's improvement successes.

Led by a committed group of teachers and a supportive principal, the school slowly began to realize modest achievement gains that moved them up from last place. But the team wanted more and, with the district's support, attended the annual conference of No Excuses University (https://noexcusesu.com), which culminated in a group decision to apply for membership in the network and embrace its approach to school improvement. A sense of urgency among staff to do better galvanized into improved collaboration and classroom practice.

Five years later, in 2015, Evergreen, with an enrollment surpassing 67 percent low income, became the highest district performer of its 16 district elementary counterparts, and it continues to garner this distinction today. Evergreen's 2017–18 Smarter Balanced Assessment Consortium (SBAC) results illustrate the effectiveness of their approach (see Figure 2.3). The school earned a 74 percent in English language arts (as opposed to the district average of 57 percent and the state average of 53 percent) and a 72 percent in math (as opposed to the district average of 53 percent and the state average of 57 percent).

Figure 2.3   Data for Evergreen Elementary School

Bethel Independent School District, Spanaway, WA
https://www.bethelsd.org/ees

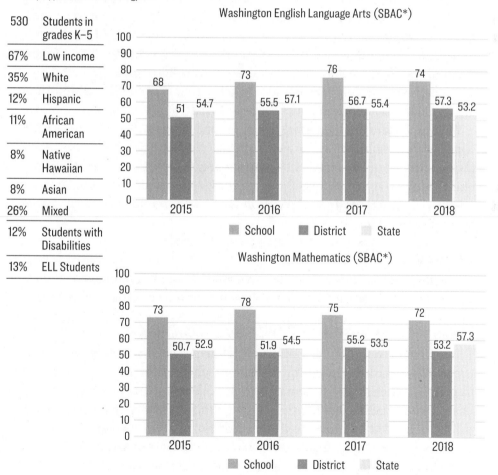

Source: Washington Department of Education. Available: http://washingtonstatereportcard.ospi.k12.wa.us
*Smarter Balanced Assessment Consortium

Evergreen has earned the Washington State Achievement Award (2012, 2014, 2015, 2016); the state's School Distinction Award (2011, 2012, 2013, 2014, 2016); the Title I National Award (2017–18); and the National Blue Ribbon Award (2017–18). In 2019, the school was selected as one of seven nationally for intensive review as a model for ESEA and its organization that supports Title I–eligible public schools, those enrolling 35 percent or more of students who qualify for free and reduced-price meals.

Principal Jamie Burnett fully credits the leadership and hard work of his "pillars," a group of veteran Evergreen teachers who were in place from the beginning, for leading the way. He further acknowledges the crucial structural importance of the school's partnership with No Excuses University, which helped them establish the Eight Exceptional Systems that drive their success: Culture of Universal Achievement, Collaboration, Standards Alignment, Assessment, Data Management, Interventions, Building-wide Discipline, and Character Counts. Blended together, these systems support growth in academic, social, and emotional learning throughout the school.

Burnett and his staff's daily standards-based instructional approach exemplifies how their systems adherence translates into increased academic success for Evergreen students. Classrooms reflect increased rigor and expectations for all students as staff turned to a consistent use of student data to guide instructional decisions and support. Teacher-led grade-level teams assume a "no excuses stance" as they collaborate to tackle challenges and improve practice, particularly for students who are underperforming. The instructional day increased to extend learning, and the supports of Response to Intervention (RTI) were deployed and shaped to better help individual students improve reading and math skills.

Burnett and his staff attribute their sustained success to a change of mindset regarding their expectations of their students, an established "code of collaboration" among staff that translates to growing collective efficacy across the school, and a sense of urgency to do better for their students.

Lillian Peterson Elementary School (K–5)

"Welcome to Lillian Peterson!" exclaims Tracy Ketchum, principal for the past two years, beaming as we enter the school. "We've got a great school that really cares about and loves our kids." The sentiment is as apparent in the front office as it is later on in the gathering of six core teachers and instructional coaches who have been at the school for a decade.

During this time span, Peterson Elementary, serving 358 students (74 percent low income), transformed from being one of the highest-poverty and lowest-performing schools in the district to performing in the top 5 percent of state achievement averages for all Montana public elementary schools (see Figure 2.4).

Peterson Elementary is located in the community of Kalispell, home to 23,938 inhabitants in northwest Montana. Principal Ketchum is quick to credit her staff for making and sustaining the school's gains: "We have a teaching staff that completely buys into our vision of 'committed to student learning'—and that means every student."

According to Stephanie Buzzell, veteran teacher and instructional coach, the previous principal established a culture of "keeping the main

Figure 2.4 Data for Lillian Peterson Elementary School

Kalispell ISD, MT
https://www.sd5.k12.mt.us/7/home

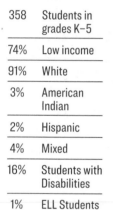

358	Students in grades K–5
74%	Low income
91%	White
3%	American Indian
2%	Hispanic
4%	Mixed
16%	Students with Disabilities
1%	ELL Students

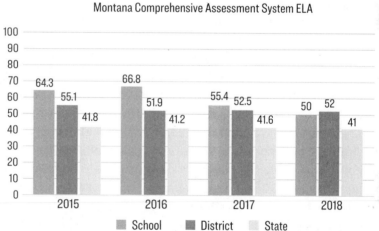

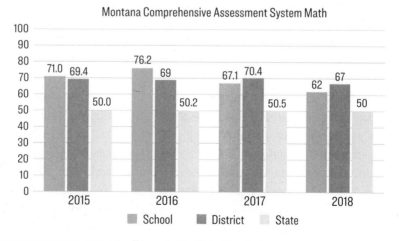

Source: Montana Department of Education. Available: https://gems.opi.mt.gov/Pages/HomePage.aspx

thing the main thing," which was reading and writing. He saw the power in collaborative cross-grade-level and vertical planning and empowered teachers to do what they do best—teach. He used to say, "No kid's going to fail. Kids at Peterson do hard things . . . *we* can do hard things." These words inspired Buzzell and a core group of teachers to build a focused, data-informed approach that thrives in their system of shared leadership and serves all kids to this day.

Through the early years of Peterson's journey to high performance, this core group of teachers collaborated; shared struggles, challenges, and wins; and grew together as a team. This collaboration paid off. Recently the district constructed a new elementary school and realigned elementary attendance boundaries. Peterson gained more than 180 new students, and their percentage of kids in poverty increased as well. The high level of collective teacher efficacy drives how the school sustains its successes (the Peterson Way, as it's known) and eased the transition of the new students into the high-functioning school.

The trademark of a high-poverty, high-performing school is the embedding of leadership capacity, which enables the school to pivot as needed to successfully address new challenges. Peterson Elementary had to act quickly to address the challenges this transition required, many of which were associated with the social-emotional needs of the entering students. They implemented the fully staffed "Panther Den," a quiet space where students can choose to check in for a few minutes or longer to get calmed down, self-regulate, or receive supportive help from an adult if they're having difficulties. They equipped all classes with oximeters to monitor student heart rates, which the teacher and staff periodically use to monitor an individual student's heart rate. And they make sure no student is hungry.

Peterson's staff members communicate frequently and support one another regarding the needs of all kids. "Kids love Peterson because they know they're loved" is a common sentiment of the staff.

That's the Peterson Way and it continues to work.

Parkway Elementary School (PK–5)

"Parkway Fever! Good things are happening at Parkway. I hear about it all the time. The parents are proud of it!" exclaims Krista Barton-Arnold, principal of Parkway Elementary. "We're no longer that school where nobody wanted to go. Our kids are coming back! We're fully accredited!"

Four years ago, Parkway was one of the lowest-performing schools in Virginia Beach, Virginia, a relatively high-performing district. The school was characterized by rampant misbehavior, fights, poor attendance, frequent retention of students, few positive connections with parents and the community, and little enthusiasm for the work. Of Parkway's 426 kids, 75 percent reside in Twin Canals, a nearby Section 8 public housing development of 300 apartments.

"I had been an elementary principal for 17 years and then was a director of elementary education for the district," explains Barton-Arnold. I loved the work, but I wanted to get back to kids and to those who needed the most help. I wanted to lead one of our most needy schools." Superintendent Aaron Spence agreed, and Barton-Arnold headed to Parkway.

First on her list was forming a highly functional leadership team of committed classroom teachers, instructional coaches, and building leaders with the goal of reaching full accreditation. "It's where the sausage is made. It's the key to success. You can't do it alone. You have to develop and grow as a team," explains Barton-Arnold.

The team engaged in a deep look at student data, created a process for intensive alignment to guide instruction and track formative assessment data, and focused on targeting interventions. They met weekly, setting and monitoring short-term expectations and benchmarks for growth.

To address the discipline, suspension, and attendance challenges, Barton-Arnold drew a firm line in the sand. "OK, I'll suspend those students tomorrow. But tell me what you're going to do the day *after* that when they come back and they're still doing this. Because I'm not going to suspend them again." Barton-Arnold and the leadership team then led the staff on a journey of learning and capacity building related to restorative and responsive classroom practices. "We learned and practiced together," explains Barton-Arnold. "We started morning meetings in every classroom; we supported each other in tackling challenges. Collectively, it made a huge difference with our discipline." The ineffective in-school suspension program was shuttered, retentions were all but eliminated, and discipline referrals plummeted.

Barton-Arnold and her team leaders incorporated frequent learning walks to support improvements in classroom instruction and assessments. They took advantage of staff openings to recruit and retain high-quality, committed adults to join their team. Retired master teachers were recruited to return part-time for targeted assignments in high-need areas, particularly math. High expectations for every student became the norm as the environment of the school improved (see Figure 2.5).

A new librarian transformed a seldom-used and badly outdated school library into a state-of-the-art Learning Commons. Through a process of "windows and mirrors," in which students were asked if they could see

Figure 2.5   Data for Parkway Elementary School

Virginia Beach ISD, VA
https://parkwayes.vbschools.com/

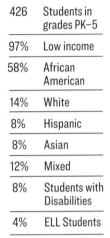

426	Students in grades PK–5
97%	Low income
58%	African American
14%	White
8%	Hispanic
8%	Asian
12%	Mixed
8%	Students with Disabilities
4%	ELL Students

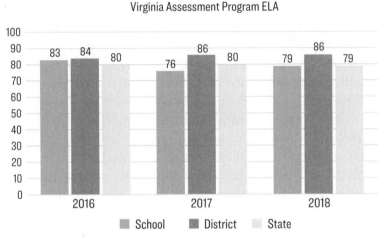

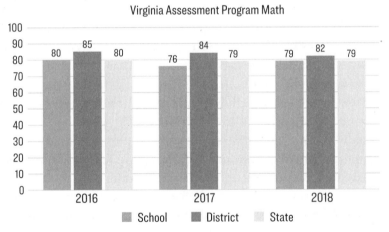

Source: Virginia Department of Education. Available: https://schoolquality.virginia.gov/

themselves in the collection and relate to the experiences in the nonfiction works, more than 6,000 books were replaced with more appropriate content materials. Other additions included a maker space and dream lab, which include creation, puzzle, robotics, and information centers. The school also initiated a full-day preschool, which Barton-Arnold calls a "game changer."

Finally, as Barton-Arnold explains, "It *is* a harder job. It's harder to teach kids who live in poverty, and it's harder to be a principal in a school where poverty is high. You have so much more social-emotional stuff to deal with."

Her best advice for high-poverty schools committed to breaking the cycle of underperformance? "Be brave. Develop a strong instructional team. Focus on small-group instruction, alignment, and relationships. It's the most rewarding job I've ever had. It's life-changing for the kids."

Pugliese West Elementary School PK–5

Pugliese West Elementary School, commonly referred to as "West," is one of only 68 schools across the United States that were named in 2019 an ESEA Distinguished School for exceptional student achievement. It stands as clear evidence that a high-poverty school—78 percent of students are eligible for free or reduced-priced meals—can not only succeed, but also sustain its gains. Awards for high achievement are not new to this Ohio School of Promise (2016, 2017) and Performing School of Honor (2016, 2017). The school has also been recognized as one of the top 5 percent of all Ohio public elementary schools.

Located on the west side of the Ohio River, Steubenville represents a community like so many others, where the economic downturns altered the town's once robust steel and manufacturing environment. "We've gone from six elementaries to three," explains Lynnett Gorman, West's principal for the past nine years. "With the mills closing, I think most of Steubenville's population would be considered low income, as the middle class has faded away."

Despite a shrinking tax base and economy, the school continues to thrive as a place where kids perform well in all tested subject areas. Principal Gorman credits the school's success to a firm adherence to their adopted model, Success for All, and to its comprehensive approach to school improvement, embedded in West for 18 years. The program's highly structured and leveled approach to reading and math, combined with staff-led, data-driven, highly collaborative efforts, has created and sustained a cooperative culture with parents and families, improved attendance and student behavior, and resulted in the implementation of successful interventions for students who require them. "It's our approved curriculum; it's in school board policy," Gorman explains. "It's how and why we're able to do all we do for our kids."

Effective reading and math instruction are the drivers of each instructional day. "We refer to our mornings as 'holy time,' which means a carefully designed 90 minutes of reading and 90 minutes of math for every student," she says. This approach, steeled by years of support from Success for All and by staff members who have honed their instructional practices, annually guides students to remarkable successes in their English language arts and math achievement (see Figure 2.6).

Figure 2.6   Data for Pugliese West Elementary School

Steubenville ISD, OH
http://www.steubenville.k12.oh.us/westelementary.html

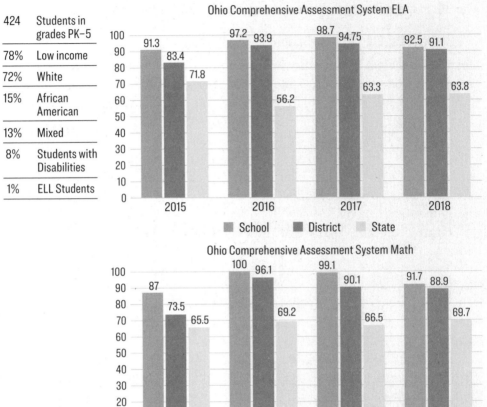

424	Students in grades PK–5
78%	Low income
72%	White
15%	African American
13%	Mixed
8%	Students with Disabilities
1%	ELL Students

Source: Ohio Department of Education. Available: https://reportcard.education.ohio.gov

The school's staff also volunteer to join teacher-led solutions teams that form each quarter to take on sticky schoolwide challenges, such as attendance, parent engagement, cooperative cultures, and interventions. Some teams focus on students who are dealing with specific issues. Says Gorman, "The teams usually have multiple grades represented so they really think about whole-school needs and solutions. They keep our instructional coach and me in the loop, and together we collaborate to get solutions in place." And those solutions work.

Pugliese West's culture of high expectations provides tangible evidence that despite 78 percent of their students qualifying as low income, their students can and do achieve, propelling West to its numerous recognitions and awards as a high-performing, high-poverty school.

"We build relationships with our kids," explains Gorman. "We show them compassion, we let them know we care, and we expect them all to succeed. This positive approach has really worked for all of us."

East Garfield Elementary School (PK–4)

East Garfield Elementary School, also known as "East," joins Pugliese West Elementary as one of two high-poverty, high-performing elementary schools in Steubenville, Ohio. Despite having 94 percent of their students receiving free or reduced-price meals, East Garfield continues to outperform state averages on both math and English language arts. Garnering a variety of recognitions for their sustained progress, the school received an Ohio State Board of Education Momentum Award in 2016 and a National Blue Ribbon School Award in 2017. In 2018, it earned state grades of *A* for Gap Closing, Progress, and Improving At-Risk K–3 readers, thus continuing their recognition as an *A*-graded Ohio Elementary.

Each morning Shawn Crosier, principal of East Garfield, greets the parents as they drop their kids off for the schoolwide hot breakfast in the gym, and he's there again at lunchtime greeting each student as he hands them their tray. "The kids know we care about them; being sure they're not hungry is just a small part," Crosier explains. "Most of our kids come from the federal housing project across the street. A lot of them count on us for breakfast and lunch. We take that issue off the table, and the result is they're ready to hit it hard in the classroom."

And hit it hard they do. The comprehensive structures of the Success for All program drive East's achievement success as they do at neighboring Pugliese West Elementary. East Garfield has the same 90-minute reading and math blocks, the same diversified intervention time, the same teacher willingness to help any child who is struggling, and similar positive outcomes (see Figure 2.7). The district's motto reads, "Children are our business—and our only business." And Steubenville's system is clearly working.

East Garfield has transformed from a low-performing, high-poverty school to a high-performing, high-poverty school. The district deserves thanks for its support of and sustained effective implementation of a consistent, collaborative, success for all improvement model. "The kids do great here; they buy into our system, and it really shows in their reading and math and how well they do in school," explains Crosier. "It's not easy, but we can do it for our kids."

Figure 2.7 Data for East Garfield Elementary School

Steubenville ISD, OH
http://www.steubenville.k12.oh.us/eastelementary.html

423	Students in grades PK–4
94%	Low income
41%	White
38%	African American
21%	Mixed
23%	Students with Disabilities
1%	ELL Students

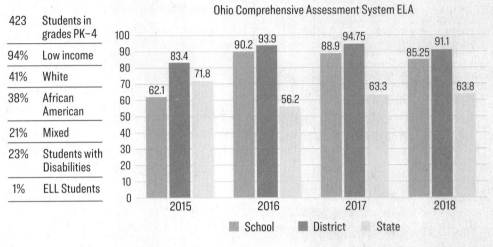

Ohio Comprehensive Assessment System ELA

School   District   State

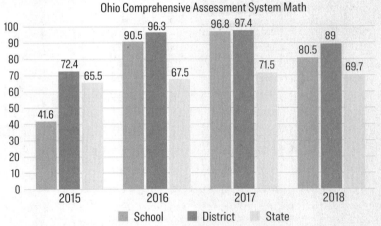

Ohio Comprehensive Assessment System Math

School   District   State

Source: Education Quality and Accountability Office. Available: http://www.eqao.com/en/assessments/results

Murtaugh School (PK–12)

"Ready, set, go!" Another group of four kids in red capes sprint down the middle of the school's 50-yard hallway between three-deep throngs of cheering, high-fiving kids on both sides. "You did it—yay!" In this monthly ritual, staff and kids celebrate the K–3 students who met their Idaho Student Indicator of Progress (IP) reading goals. The kids get to wear their red capes for the rest of the day as the normal business of school resumes following the celebration.

Located just above a steep canyon of the Snake River in the high desert plains of south central Idaho, the community of Murtaugh takes great pride in its nationally recognized, award-winning PK–12 school of 380 students. "Our community really values our school. There's really nothing to draw people here besides the school," explains Superintendent Michele Capps. "Almost half of all registered voters in Murtaugh cast ballots in our recent $2 million bond referendum. Other communities in the county average 10.5 percent voter turnout. And Murtaugh's passed by almost 80 percent."

Seventy-five percent of the Murtaugh kids qualify for free and reduced-price meals; the racial demographics are almost equally split at 49 percent Caucasian and 48 percent Hispanic. Most of the students ride the 30 miles of bus routes to get to school each day. The school has been steadily improving since its redesign as a PK–12 school in 2010, after having been identified as a persistently low-performing school by the U.S. Department of Education. That designation changed everything. Twelve-year superintendent and elementary principal Capps, along with the school and district, embarked on an aggressive improvement course to high performance.

"You can build culture and still have low achievement," notes Capps. "But to build culture and have high-achieving schools, the key is to have really great people." By 2018, Murtaugh PK–12 was named one of the two National Title I Distinguished Schools in the state for closing achievement gaps.

"We attract and keep the best teachers and staff—that's the story of our success," shares Capps. The school focused intensively on improving reading during those early years through implementing a blended reading curriculum, supportive professional development from the state education department, and Capps's hands-on instructional leadership. "We don't have an instructional coach, but we collaborate really well. Teachers coach one another, and they're really awesome at it," beams Capps. "If I walk into my two 2nd grades, maybe the teachers are teaching the same standard, but they're doing it differently. It's because of their 'tool belts'—their prior knowledge, experience, or something they know about their kids. We just have good teachers; we let them teach, and they get results."

Building collective efficacy, the highly capable staff have propelled their students to success, closing gaps along the way (see Figure 2.8). Their students outperform state averages for all schools, despite the fact that more than 75 percent of the students live in poverty.

Capps also attributes their success to having full-day kindergarten for the past 25 years—"way before it was the thing to do," she says with a smile—adding that the state only funds and requires one-half day. "We also have preschool for all 4-year-olds in the district. We cover the other half of

Figure 2.8   Data for Murtaugh School

Murtaugh SD, ID
http://www.murtaugh.k12.id.us/schools/mes

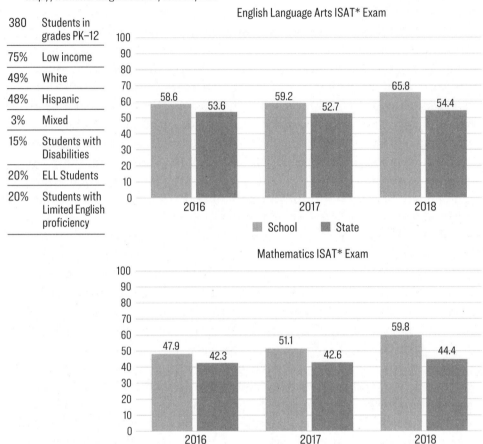

380	Students in grades PK–12
75%	Low income
49%	White
48%	Hispanic
3%	Mixed
15%	Students with Disabilities
20%	ELL Students
20%	Students with Limited English proficiency

*Idaho Standards Achievement Test
Source: Idaho State Department of Education. Available: https://idahoschools.org/state/ID/achievement

kindergarten with general funds and have a grant to cover preschool. I can tell you it works. I can show you it works."

Murtaugh School is small. One of the great opportunities of a small school, something that many large high-poverty, high-performing schools successfully emulate, is being able to deeply know the kids, and this can make any school feel smaller.

Murtaugh also excels in the next step of expecting every student to succeed. "This was the dream. It actually feels good to be on top of it," shares Capps. "As the school's success becomes more widely known, the enrollment increases. Growth brings different problems, just a different set of challenges, but we'll conquer those, too."

Stillman Middle School (6–8)

At Stillman Middle School in Brownsville, Texas, multiple study teams are monitoring glide angles, trajectory, and design efficiency as the students launch their rockets over the athletic field behind the school during their 6th grade science class. "The kids just love the hands-on engagement," exclaims Principal EJ Martinez. Coding for the 6th graders, robotics for the 7th graders, and engineering for the 8th graders will follow.

Stillman Middle School, one mile east of the Rio Grande River and Mexican border, is the largest middle school in its district. Each day, more than 1,000 students (98 percent of whom are Hispanic and 87 percent of whom qualify for free and reduced-priced meals) flood through the doors, to be greeted by a welcoming staff that expects every student to succeed.

Despite being a high-poverty school, Stillman continues to outperform both district and state averages on the annual State of Texas Assessments of Academic Readiness (STAAR) English language arts and math exams (see Figure 2.9). Martinez, in his seventh year of leading the school, explains, "When we're at 100 percent, then we're good. If we're not, then we have to keep on working to get to that 100 percent. We want all of our kids to be successful."

Along with being the highest-performing middle school of the 10 in its district, Stillman also gained national attention for its students' academic success, honored with the 2017 National Center for Urban School Transformation Award (NCUST) for National Excellence in Education. "We were the only middle school in Brownsville to get it, and we're really proud," shares Martinez. "The staff earned it by working so hard for the kids."

The Stillman staff attribute their success to working closely as a team to deliver a comprehensive approach to learning. Teacher-driven flexibility takes advantage of strengths and leads staff to continually look for best practices to help all kids succeed. Every student in grades 6–8 takes an English language arts and a reading class.

"We really push reading here; the kids have to read well in math, science, social studies, everything, to do well in school," says Martinez. An emphasis on vocabulary development contributes to student success in reading.

"Misanthrope," this week's schoolwide word, brought a chuckle from Martinez. "We're in the southernmost part of Texas, and a lot of the dominant language is Spanish. We don't pick small vocabulary words [in English]; we pick words that maybe the kids will never hear to expose them to vocabulary they'll need to move on to higher education."

Figure 2.9   Data for Stillman Middle School

Brownsville ISD, TX
https://stillmanbisd.weebly.com/

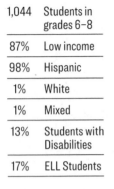

1,044	Students in grades 6–8
87%	Low income
98%	Hispanic
1%	White
1%	Mixed
13%	Students with Disabilities
17%	ELL Students

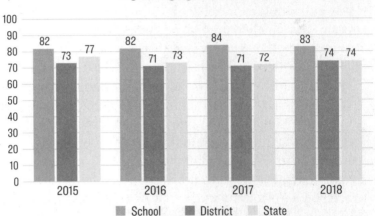

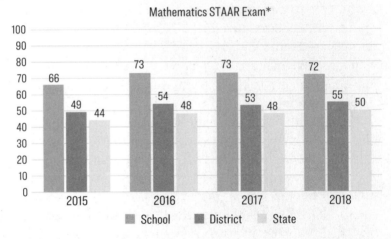

* State of Texas Assessments of Academic Readiness
Source: Texas Education Agency. Available: https://tea.texas.gov/perfreport/src/index.html

The school also highlights universities, a new one every week, to help students better understand that anybody can go to college. Flags, pennants, classroom mascots, field trips, and a steady refrain of "You can do it—you can go!" represent a constant message at school.

Creating a bond between students and school is a priority at Stillman. Students are expected to participate in extracurricular activities—choir, band, dance, sports, chess, and a host of other clubs. "It's what kids need, and the school regularly excels in district and state competitions in multiple areas," says Martinez. The school helps students through tough situations through kindness—by caring for them and wanting them to succeed.

"More than 160 of our kids come to tutoring and our Supper Club after school before they head home," explains Martinez. "You saw our sign out front, 'No One's Hungry Here.' It's all part of the picture here."

Stillman Middle School exemplifies how a large urban high-poverty school can succeed. "It's takes years to get to this point," says Martinez. "It's genuine teamwork. We all want the school to be the best that it can be."

Henderson Collegiate Middle School (4–8)

Henderson Collegiate Middle School (HCMS), in Henderson, North Carolina, opened its doors in 2010, serving only 100 at-risk 4th graders. The school's founding educators, led by Eric and Carice Sanchez, added a new grade level each academic year to become a fully functioning 4–8 middle school by 2014. A charter school, HCMS has grown to serve 555 mostly low-income students (94 percent), and it has experienced considerable success. It was honored as a Title I Reward School from 2013–16, and it was selected as one of two of North Carolina's National Distinguished Schools in 2015. Since then, HCMS has earned a School Performance Grade of *A* (2015–18), placing HCMS in the top 3.6 percent of all North Carolina public schools (see Figure 2.10).

The HCMS mission is for every one of its students to successfully enter and graduate from college. Students visit at least one college campus every year. They enroll at HCMS through an application process to the school's annual lottery, which is open to any student who resides in North Carolina. Student transportation is free and provided to all students, and nutrition services, available through the Community Eligibility Program, provide free meals. The school operates on an extended day (an additional 75 minutes); requires school uniforms; issues cell phones to teachers so they can be in regular contact with students and families; and asks that everyone—the principal, teachers, parents, and students—sign a Commitment to Excellence agreement on entering the school that outlines the promises each party must make to ensure student success.

The school has recently incorporated its extended day and mandatory summer program into a year-round approach of nine-week rotations. "After every nine weeks, we do two or three weeks off and have three or four work days to do professional development," explains Director Eric Sanchez. "We're always pushing ourselves to learn—that's driven our constant improvement." It's the same for the students. The extended day, week, and year, coupled with enhanced access to teachers and staff, correlate directly to HCMS students' academic, social, and emotional success.

As four-year veteran principal Frank Terranova, explains, "Each of our grades has a theme that connects our high expectations for character and academics." The 4th grade focuses on team and family, the 5th grade on

Figure 2.10   Data for Henderson Collegiate Middle School

Henderson Collegiate ISD, NC
www.hendersoncollegiate.org

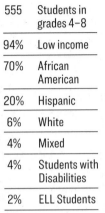

555	Students in grades 4–8
94%	Low income
70%	African American
20%	Hispanic
6%	White
4%	Mixed
4%	Students with Disabilities
2%	ELL Students

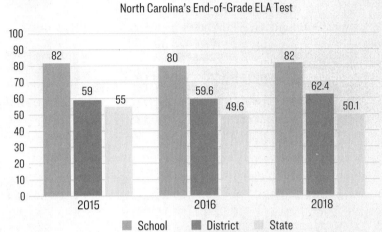

North Carolina's End-of-Grade ELA Test

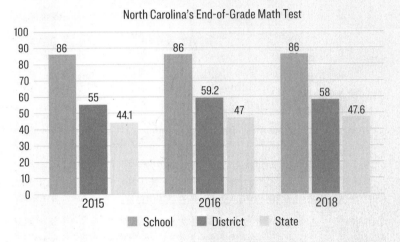

North Carolina's End-of-Grade Math Test

Source: North Carolina Department of Education https://ncreportcards.ondemand.sas.com/src/

kindness, the 6th grade on community and embracing diversity, the 7th grade on what it means to be a teenager, and the 8th grade on leadership. These themes permeate the daily expectations that HCMS staff hold for themselves and their kids.

Beginning with the core value of high expectations and a belief in the importance of authentic relationships, the founders of HCMS drew from the wisdom of organizations and models that have successfully served students in poverty, including the Knowledge Is Power Program (KIPP); Uncommon Schools; Teach For America (TFA); and Achievement First. They combined this with wisdom from practitioners and scholars to successfully craft their own "Henderson Collegiate Way." Director Sanchez explains, "We learn from studying successes and adapting them to our setting. We're not trying to follow somebody else's playbook. We're trying to follow our own playbook."

HCMS deploys a data-driven approach to instructional coaching and aggressively monitors all teaching and learning. "Others choose to spend a lot of money on other things, and frankly we don't have those things because we've decided to spend that on coaches," shares Sanchez. The school has developed a sophisticated instructional coaching model where staff members can partner with subject-matter experts daily and weekly. "Our teachers grow and improve, as do their students," says Sanchez.

The Henderson Collegiate Way finds Principal Terranova greeting every student as he or she enters the building every morning. He knows almost each of the 555 students by name, encouraging them to work hard and have a great day. "Our job is to help kids, first and foremost, become good people," he adds.

HCMS leaders and staff know their students can and will achieve at the level necessary to go on to succeed in college. The school clearly demonstrates that a poverty rate exceeding 90 percent is not a barrier to what kids can accomplish.

Pass Christian High School (9–12)

Located on the southwestern Gulf Coast of Mississippi, Pass Christian High School (PCHS) demonstrates that a high-poverty high school can indeed sustain high performance. Despite being virtually destroyed by Hurricane Katrina in 2005, the school and its district emerged from the destruction and reestablished their future vision as "Committed to Excellence"; they made it their mission "to empower *all* students to be college-career ready, critical thinkers, and contributing citizens." PCHS continues to embody these goals in all that it does. And its journey demonstrates remarkable success.

Explains Robyn Killebrew, who was the school's principal for five years and recently moved into the position of assistant superintendent, "We really know every one of our kids and care deeply about their experience here . . . and they respond." PCHS, a Title I school with more than 62 percent of its students qualifying for free or reduced-priced meals, now significantly outperforms state averages in English language arts and math (see Figure 2.11) and has established its own "Pass High Way."

Starting with a schoolwide belief that every student can and will succeed, the adults who staff the school attribute their success to the close relationships they maintain with students and families and to a vertically

Figure 2.11 Data for Pass Christian High School

Pass Christian Public SD, MS
pchs.pc.k12.ms.us

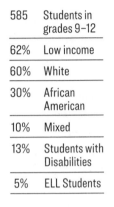

585	Students in grades 9–12
62%	Low income
60%	White
30%	African American
10%	Mixed
13%	Students with Disabilities
5%	ELL Students

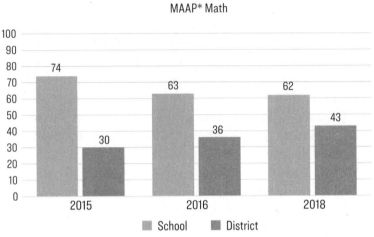

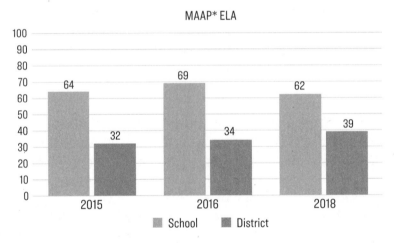

*Mississippi Academic Assessment Program

Source: Mississippi Accountability System. Available: http://www.mdek12.org/OPR/Reporting

aligned curriculum coupled with a standards-based instructional process that deploys 3-6-9–week common assessments. "Those assessments were all made in house, and it took about a full year to complete," says Killebrew. "We tweaked them over the first couple of years, but now we have them in good shape. They really help teachers identify how students are doing and who needs help."

The school places all entering 9th graders into a highly effective freshman academy that launches the students on a path to success. The students are surrounded by caring, highly competent teachers who mold them into a cooperative, confident group. All staff are committed to providing extra help to the students who need it. "We don't have a single teacher who won't stay after school any day to help a student who is struggling. And that makes a huge difference in a high school," Killebrew explains.

PCHS continues to be nationally recognized, receiving multiple awards over the years, including being named a U.S. Department of Education Blue Ribbon School of Excellence (2005) and receiving both a Lighthouse School Leader Award (2012) and an Education Trust Dispelling the Myth Award (2013). The school was ranked by *U.S. News & World Report* as the No. 1 high school in Mississippi for 2006–10. Principal Killebrew was also recognized with the state's Milken Educator Award (2018). During the 2017–18 academic year, the school's graduating class garnered more than $21 million in college scholarships to postsecondary institutions.

When Killebrew was asked to name the topmost factor in the high school's success, she responded, "The 3-6-9 assessments and freshman academy have been game changers, but it's really all about the relationships we have with our students and with one another. We're like a big family. That's what makes it happen here."

A student passed us a note during our visit to PCHS. It read,

> Our secret is, we as a school have a mission that we want and need to accomplish. And we all know what it takes to achieve the mission. We set goals as students, teachers, administrators, janitors, and even the lunch ladies. It was never easy, but with the support of our peers, teachers, and even our community, we built up a program that I am proud to be a part of and represent every day.

The Preuss School UC San Diego (6–12)

The Preuss School was created to enroll, serve, and graduate first-generation college-going low-income students. Chartered by the San Diego Unified School District, the school operates on the University of California San Diego campus in La Jolla. The Preuss School, now in its 20th year, continues to outperform both California and its local district in both math and English language arts on state test scores, despite having a student body that is 95 percent low-income (see Figure 2.12).

Throughout two decades, the school has garnered frequent national recognition, which includes earning a U.S. Department of Education National Blue Ribbon Award (2010) and being named a State of California Gold Ribbon School (2015) and a State of California Distinguished School (2019). *U.S. News & World Report* ranked it the Best High School in San Diego (2018), and *Newsweek* named it a Top Transformative U.S. High School (2015, 2016, 2017).

This high-performing middle and high school public charter school provides bussing for its 840 students, the majority of whom reside in the inner city of San Diego. To attend Preuss, a student's family must qualify as low income and the student must be the first generation in his or her family who could graduate from a four-year college. Students enter through an annual application process followed by a lottery.

"There are no silver bullets here," explains Scott Barton, Preuss's principal and one of the school's founding faculty members. The school focuses on four overarching goals: bridging the gap for underserved students, offering a rigorous curriculum, providing wraparound services for all students, and ensuring successful transitions into graduation and beyond, into college. "Our formula is actually pretty simple," notes Barton. "High expectations for every student and a commitment from all adults here to get them to graduation and into college, a high-quality staff who work incredibly hard, weekly professional development that pushes us to get better, and a school culture where academics are perceived as cool by the kids."

The school provides all students with a rigorous, detracked curriculum designed to meet and exceed the admission requirements of the University of California system. All students take several advanced placement (AP) classes during their high school years, complete portfolios, and participate in SAT prep to get ready for their exams. The school provides wraparound services—counseling, mentoring, tutoring, and advising supports—to meet the academic and social-emotional needs of each student.

Preuss extends the day and week to maximize learning. The school has an eight-block schedule and multiple after-school academic supports (e.g., tutoring and project/homework help), along with clubs and enrichments, such as the increasingly popular robotics team, sports programs, and a Saturday Enrichment Academy. A longer school year helps students prepare for graduation (which more than 95 percent of students accomplish on time) and get accepted to colleges, universities, and other four-year institutions of higher learning (almost all students do so).

"A major key to student success is our advisory program," explains Barton. Every Preuss student participates in an advisory class. A faculty member guides each class through their yearly load of coursework and assessments; promotes student awareness of current societal issues; encourages KBAR (kick back and read); and helps students with their social-emotional needs. Advisors focus the 90-minute sessions around the school's primary goals of having students graduate and get accepted into college. Advisories at Preuss connect students with a caring adult who forms a family-like bond with each 6th grade class and accompanies them through their seven years to graduation.

Figure 2.12   Data for The Preuss School

The Preuss School UC San Diego
http://preuss.ucsd.edu

840	Students in grades 6–12
95%	Low income
67%	Hispanic
18%	Asian
11%	African American
4%	Mixed
8%	Students with Disabilities
7%	ELL Students

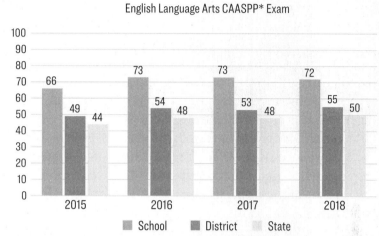

English Language Arts CAASPP* Exam

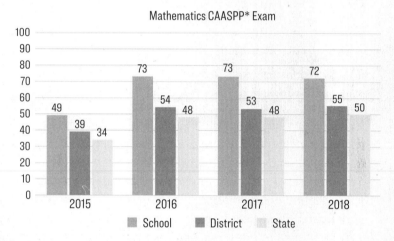

Mathematics CAASPP* Exam

*California Assessment of Student Performance and Progress
Source: California Department of Education. Available: http://www.cde.ca.gov/ta/ac/sa/

"Last year, 100 percent of our graduates were accepted to four-year colleges," shares Barton. "We surround our kids with support to help them rise to our expectations. And they do it every year. We're a pretty good school!"

Validating and Refining the Framework for Action

During visits to these schools, we listened as educators—administrators, teachers, professional and classified staff, and other key individuals—described the actions they believed had resulted in their school's improvements, and we looked for evidence that confirmed or refuted the leadership concepts represented in our framework. We reviewed data from school improvement plans, district and state report cards, state and district websites, school evaluations, and other sources.

Our exploration into the function of leadership in the 12 schools enabled us to again confirm our framework. The elements in the Action section of our framework—building leadership capacity and collective efficacy; fostering a healthy, safe, and supportive learning environment; and focusing on student, professional, and system learning—indeed appeared vital to success.

As a result of our visits to these schools, we added two characteristics to our framework that were clearly drivers of success. They are (1) a searing sense of urgency to improve and (2) the ubiquitous collective efficacy of adults, particularly teachers. Each characteristic was prominent in each school.

We considered not only leaders' and educators' explicit statements of actions taken and the apparent results, but also their perceptions of changes in the culture of the school (that is, in norms, beliefs, and values). In our initial conceptualization of the role of leadership in shaping the culture in HP/HP schools, we included the value that educators placed on relationships, their belief that students in poverty could be held to high expectations, and their courage and will to take action.

Schools like those we visited have unequivocally demonstrated that the barriers posed by poverty to learning and achievement can be overcome. Yet poverty presents a daunting set of circumstances that can overwhelm even the best-intentioned educators in their efforts to teach kids who live within its influence. High-performing, high-poverty schools begin their efforts by learning about the unique needs of their students who live in poverty and those of their families, something we will look at next, in Chapter 3.

3 Understanding Poverty and Our Moral Responsibility

The hardest part of my job is seeing families going through hardship. Sometimes they are displaced from their home, and they have to go to a shelter. I can't fix it, but we support them the best way we can. We provide them with coats, book-bags, school supplies so they feel like, "I can still go to school." And it's not just about those things. How is the child feeling? How can we get the child prepared to learn? We reach out to businesses and organizations. And I try to get as much as I can for the children when it comes to hygiene [products] because they're becoming aware of themselves.

—*Teacher, high-poverty elementary school, East Coast*

Many of us grew up hearing admonitions from parents that we should clean our plates "because there are children starving in India" (or China or Africa). It was not clear how eating everything on our plates would help hungry children, but what *was* clear was that hunger was a terrible thing that happened to other people in faraway places.

In the United States, we have been reluctant to acknowledge class distinctions, often viewing ourselves as a society composed of one big middle class. In one of the wealthiest countries in the world, the number of children forced to live in poverty is unconscionable. Before you continue reading, we urge you to complete the survey shown in Figure 3.1 to reflect on what you know and believe about poverty.

Understanding Poverty

Children who live in poverty are as worthy of attending good schools as their more affluent counterparts. Improving schools begins with educators who are unequivocally committed to equity—and that commitment starts

Figure 3.1   Assessing Your Knowledge and Beliefs About Poverty

	What do you know about poverty? Respond to the following statements by circling the best answer and reflecting on your thoughts.							
1	Childhood poverty rates are higher in the United States than in any other industrialized nation.			True		False		
2	Childhood poverty rates are rising in the United States.			True		False		
3	We are living in an era of increasing inequity between the wealthiest and the poorest.			True		False		
4	One in five school-age children lives in poverty.			True		False		
5	The formula for establishing the "poverty threshold" is based on the "thrifty food plan formula" established in the early 1960s.			True		False		
6	The U.S. Census Bureau has proposed 12 alternative methods for determining the poverty rate in the United States, all but one of which result in a greater rate of poverty than the current formula.			True		False		
	What do you believe about poverty? Respond by circling the best answer and reflecting on your thoughts.							
7	Poverty is caused by poor character and the poor choices an individual makes.	−3	−2	−1	0	1	2	3
8	People in poverty do not work, or they have a poor work ethic.	−3	−2	−1	0	1	2	3
9	Education, as a way out of poverty, is readily accessible to everyone.	−3	−2	−1	0	1	2	3
10	Parents of students who live in poverty are uninvolved in their children's education because they do not value it.	−3	−2	−1	0	1	2	3
11	The biases and assumptions we hold about poverty can pose barriers to effective problem solving and change.	−3	−2	−1	0	1	2	3
12	Schools can have only a limited effect on students who live in poverty.	−3	−2	−1	0	1	2	3
13	Schools are only part of the solution to the problem of poverty.	−3	−2	−1	0	1	2	3
14	Schools are holding up their end of the deal in eliminating poverty in the United States.	−3	−2	−1	0	1	2	3

with a better understanding of the meaning and influence of poverty in the lives of the students they serve.

Poverty in the United States is not easily defined, nor can its causes be simplistically explained. It can be experienced by anyone—male and female, as well as people of all ages, racial or ethnic groups, and immigration status. In this chapter, we focus on what we believe to be most important for educators and other professionals to understand in the context of their efforts to improve academic achievement and other measures of school-related success for children who live in poverty.

How Is Poverty Defined?

In the United States, the federal government defines poverty as a certain level of income relative to family size. For example, in 2016, the poverty threshold ranged from $16,543 for a family of two to $24,339 for a family of four (Koball & Jiang, 2018). Originally coined the "thrifty food plan," the formula used to establish the poverty line was created by federal statisticians who based it on what was determined to be three times the annual cost of food for a family of three in 1963. Although the basic formula for defining who lives in poverty is viewed as excessively conservative and controversial, it continues to be used as the official measure. In 2007, the U.S. Census Bureau released 12 alternatives to the current formula, all but one of which set the official poverty rate at a higher level (Neuman, 2008). The current income threshold is inadequate for even the bare necessities, and in some areas of the country it is grossly inadequate. For instance, a family of four living in McAllen, Texas, needs approximately $53,600 to meet its basic needs; in locations where the cost of living is higher, such as Boston, the same family requires $85,800 (Koball & Jiang, 2018).

How Do We Talk About Poverty in Schools?

It's important to be aware of the ways in which we, as educators, define and discuss poverty in schools. When we define poverty in schools, we primarily mean the percentage of students who are eligible for the free and reduced-price meal program. For the 2018–19 school year, income eligibility for reduced-price meals was 185 percent of the federal poverty line and 130 percent for free meals. In other words, a family of four with a gross income of $46,435 was eligible for reduced-price meals; if they earned less than $32,630, they could receive free meals (*Federal Register*, 2018).

In practice, educators use many terms or labels to discuss children and families who live in poverty. Gloria Rodriguez and James Fabionar (2010) assert that the many terms we use should serve "as a reminder of how often we are called on in education to talk about—but not necessarily to" (p. 64)—our students and their families who live in poverty. The authors claim these terms reveal varying understandings of poverty in the context of school that are largely influenced by thinking about children and families who live in poverty as a "deficit." They identify the following commonly used terms or labels, together with their purposes in schools:

- *Low income*—Typically describes a family-level measure indexed against a certain average or range. It can be assigned to students and their families by determining their eligibility for specially funded programs that rely on a particular income cutoff to select program participants.
- *Free or reduced-price lunch eligible*—Using the poverty threshold established by the U.S. government for low-income students, eligibility is determined for meal programs offered by the U.S. Department of Agriculture based on income.
- *Title I eligible*—Individual eligibility is based on a combined consideration of academic performance and income eligibility using similar guidelines as those used to determine eligibility for free or reduced-price meals.
- *Economically disadvantaged*—Lower economic status creates a disadvantage in securing full educational benefits that, in turn, might guarantee certain economic benefits. Accountability systems that require disaggregation of data by certain student subgroups typically include the category of "economically disadvantaged" students. Application of this label can vary, but it is often equated with eligibility for free or reduced-price meals.
- *Low socioeconomic status (low SES)*—The term identifies students who are low income and identified according to certain social background characteristics that are believed to operate in tandem with economic status to facilitate or impede social mobility. Within schools, "low SES" is often used as shorthand for many status definitions or social processes. (Rodriguez & Fabionar, 2010)

As children, we may have been taught that "sticks and stones can break our bones, but names can never hurt us." Unfortunately, that is simply not true. Jeff Sapp (2009) writes about the snide remarks children made about him in the halls and the putdowns they had learned from their parents that they flung at him in the playground. "The 3rd grade was a bad year," he wrote. "Third grade was the year I learned in school that I was poor."

Children who live in poverty, like all children, deserve to be treated with respect and in a manner that preserves their dignity. The words we use to describe and label children *do* matter. Educators must reflect on these labels and critique their own use of such terms to become attuned to the many ways that schools unwittingly limit students' self-determination.

Poverty shapes one's view of self and others. Living in poverty affects many of the basic necessities that people of middle- and upper-income levels tend to take for granted, such as personal appearance; condition and size of home (if one is not homeless); availability and quality of food; health and well-being; and even the value of one's work. In *See Poverty . . . Be the Difference!* (2006), Donna Beegle describes the shame that she and others felt growing up in poverty. All of the participants in Beegle's study (college graduates who had lived in poverty throughout their childhoods) reported that they and other members of their families felt a great deal of shame and humiliation. They related stories of smelling bad because they lived in their cars and had limited access to showers; of being embarrassed by the condition or style of their clothing; and of being humiliated by the snickering they heard about members of their family, the content of their lunches, or the nature of their parents' work.

In many cases, living conditions entailed a perpetual state of hunger and exposure to chronic health conditions. For most, not having money contributed to their sense of hopelessness. Their lives were "a series of reactionary battles for survival with little, if any, opportunity to shape or choose their futures. For too many, this comes with a strong feeling that something is personally wrong with them and that there is nothing they can do to change it" (Beegle, 2006, p. 53).

As educators, we must be sensitive to the effects of poverty on our students' states of mind and ensure we separate their developing sense of self from their living conditions. As a starting point, we must be extremely careful how we talk about children who live in poverty. For example, describing these students as living in homes *with* a low income or *with* low socioeconomic status (SES) is more accurate than calling them "low-income students," "low-SES students," or "high-poverty kids." This distinction may seem like splitting hairs, but it is important.

The Scope of the Problem

Childhood poverty rates are higher in the United States than in any other industrialized country, and this rate has decreased only slightly since 2010, the middle of the Great Recession. As of 2017, 19 percent of all people who live in poverty were children—more than 14 million, or 19 percent of all children in the United States. Another 22 percent reside in families with low incomes. Between 2010 and 2016, the number of children living in poverty decreased from nearly 17 million to 14 million. A staggering 6 percent of children live in deep poverty (less than 50 percent of the federal poverty threshold) (U.S. Bureau of Labor Statistics, 2019). Equally startling, between 60 and 75 percent of people who live in the United States will live below or near the poverty line for at least one year of their lives (Neuman, 2008).

Increasing Inequality

Whether or not one personally experiences poverty, if unabated, its effects are likely to touch everyone in the United States. Since 2013, income inequality has risen in nearly every state (Reinicke, 2018). In 2015, the top 1 percent of families in the United States made more than 25 times what families in the bottom 99 percent did, according to the Economic Policy Institute (Sommeiller & Price, 2018). Although wages have increased over the years, Pew Research found that today's real average wage (the wage accounting for inflation) holds the same buying power it did 40 years ago (Desilver, 2018).

From 1980 to 2016, the inflation-adjusted average income for the bottom half of American households went from $16,000 to $16,200. However, in the top 1 percent of American households in that same period, inflation-adjusted wages grew from $428,200 to $1.3 million (Reed, 2019). To be in that top 1 percent in 2015, a family's income was $421,926 (Sommeiller & Price 2018). The average hourly wage crawled from a little over $20 to $22.65. High school graduates who work full-time had an average of $718 for weekly earnings, whereas full-time workers with an advanced degree earned $1,451 weekly (U. S. Bureau of Labor Statistics, 2019).

Wealth inequality is different from income inequity. Income is cash wages and other cash sources of earning, whereas wealth refers to the total of one's assets—houses, real estate, cars, furniture, bank accounts, retirement funds, stocks, and so on—minus one's debt. The degree of wealth inequality in the United States is now the same as it was in the 1920s, a time in U.S. history when wealth inequality peaked (Hubmer, Krusell, & Smith, 2016). Such inequality weakens the fabric of a democracy.

Who Lives in Poverty?

In the United States, any discussion of poverty must acknowledge the inextricable link between poverty and race, gender, immigration status, and family structure. When student outcomes are considered, these intersecting factors are often at play.

Children of all races live in poverty. However, African American, Latinx, and Native American children, as well as children of two or more races, disproportionally live in poverty in the United States (see Figure 3.2). When the percentage of children living in poverty from a given group is greater than the percentage of the same group of children in the overall population, that group is considered to be disproportionally represented. Whites make up 76 percent of the general population, whereas 62 percent of all

Figure 3.2   Children in Poverty by Race, 2017

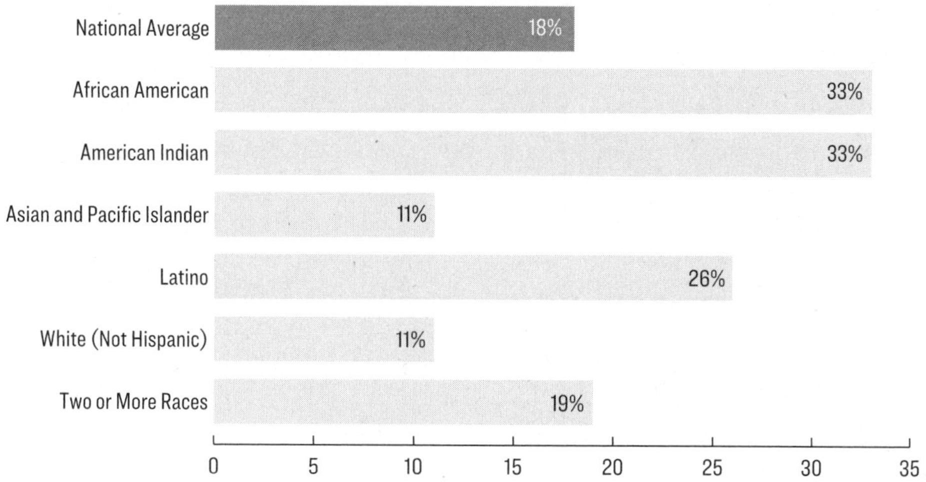

Source: U.S. Census Bureau, 2017, American Community Survey.

low-income people are white. On the other hand, although blacks and His-panics make up only 13 and 18 percent of the population respectively, each group makes up about 23 and 27 percent of the low-income population (U.S. Census Bureau, 2017).

In *Disrupting Poverty: Five Powerful Practices,* we described dispro-portionality by considering a hypothetical classroom with 24 students: "If all those students were American Indian, Hispanic, or African American, chances are more than one in three would be living in poverty. If that same class was composed of all white children, one in eight would be living in poverty (Koball & Jiang, 2017)" (in Budge & Parrett, 2018, p. 32).

Albeit an important factor, race is only one demographic characteristic that intersects with poverty. Other factors provide a glimpse into which children are more or less likely to live in poverty. For example, it is more probable that a child living with parents who are immigrants or refugees will live in poverty than a child whose family is native to the United States. Indeed, 51 percent of children whose parents are immigrants live in low-income families (National Center for Children in Poverty [NCCP], 2018).

Likewise, the prospect of a child living in poverty is less in a two-parent family than in a single-parent household. Forty-one percent of children who live with a single parent live in poverty in contrast to 13 percent when the family structure includes two parents (NCCP, 2018).

Children are more likely to live in poverty if their parents do not hold a high school diploma than if their parents have a high school degree or some level of college. Fifty percent of children whose parents have less than a high school degree live in poverty, as compared to 32 percent with a high school diploma and 11 percent with some college or more (NCCP, 2018).

Where Do They Live?

Childhood poverty is found in every geographical area of the United States. Although it presents challenges in inner cities and depressed rural areas, poverty has increased in suburban locales since 2000 (Sanburn, 2014). Figure 3.3 shows the percentage of children living in poverty by state. Combined, these data present a grim portrait of the bleak landscape of poverty that confronts so many U.S. children. Living in this condition, one in five of our children heads to school.

Figure 3.3   Child Poverty in United States

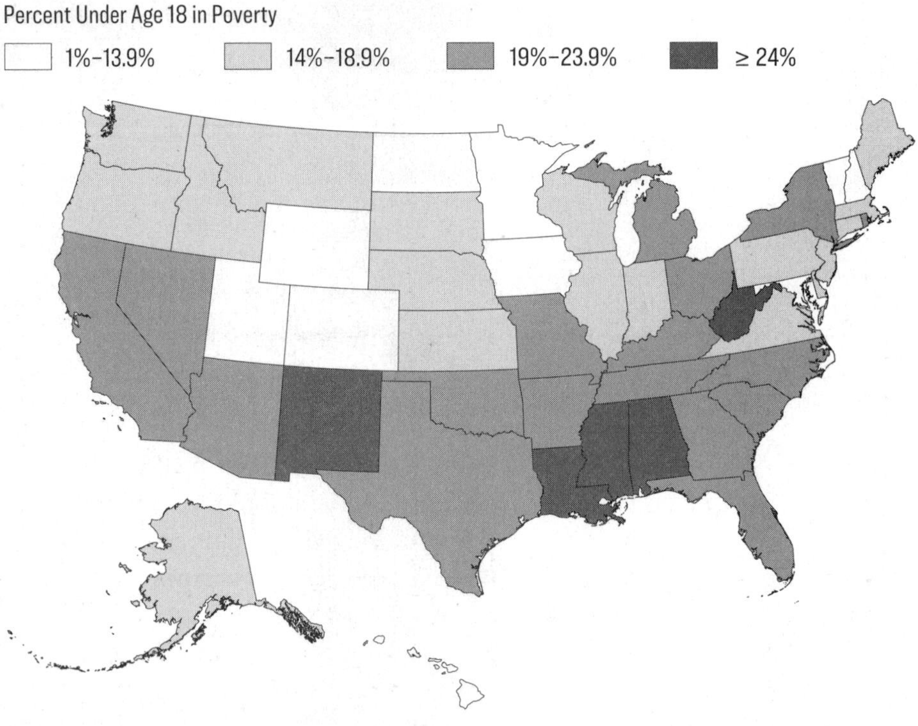

Percent Under Age 18 in Poverty

| 1%–13.9% | 14%–18.9% | 19%–23.9% | ≥ 24% |

Source: U.S. Census Bureau. (2019, September 26). American Community Survey Data. Retrieved from https://www.census.gov/programs-surveys/acs/data.html.

Why Does Poverty Exist?

There's a widespread lack of understanding about poverty and about the people whose lives are so severely circumscribed by it. Its causes have been explained from primarily three perspectives.

The Personal-Individual Perspective

In this perspective, poverty can be explained by the character of poor people and the choices they make. It's difficult to overstate the pervasiveness of this perspective (Bradshaw, 2006)—and we've found it prevalent among educators. Educators who ascribe to this theory might say, "Those parents just want a handout. They're lazy. They're *choosing* poverty." The personal-individual perspective is consistent with the belief that poverty is the result of a weak work ethic, poor choices, and lack of intelligence. It's thought to be the oldest justification for poverty, with ties to religious doctrine and eugenics—a theory of intelligence as primarily inherited (Bradshaw, 2006). Economic theories that claim that the welfare system creates dependency are consistent with the personal-individual perspective on the existence of poverty.

The Culture of Poverty Perspective

Closely linked to the personal-individual perspective, the culture of poverty theory alleges poverty exists and is sustained because people "create, sustain, and transmit" such a culture through their social, moral, behavioral, and intellectual deficiencies (Jordan, 2004, p. 190). Theorists have been debating this highly controversial theory for decades. Paul Gorski (2008) claims decades of studies have demonstrated "There is no such thing as a culture of poverty" (p. 33).

Educators who ascribe to this theory may say something like this: "These kids just want to do the same thing their parents did—live on welfare. They're lazy, they don't care about education, and they've learned from their parents how to use the system." It's not unusual for teachers to ask us questions that are consistent with this notion. They wonder why students choose to follow a similar life path or make similar choices as their parents, especially when those students have the opportunity to "break out." However, if breaking out of poverty means students have to leave their family, support system, social networks, community, and home, how many of us would want, or be able, to do so?

The Structural-Institutional Perspective

Scholars and policymakers have argued that our economic, political, and social systems provide unequal opportunity (Bradshaw, 2006). Low-wage jobs that rarely offer benefits; the limited number of full-time, living-wage jobs in the places where most people in poverty live; and the erosion of buying power due to wage stagnation, in addition to various forms of discrimination and oppression toward certain groups of people, are believed to contribute to the existence and perpetuation of poverty (Bradshaw, 2006; Jordan, 2004). Oppression, the power and privilege of one group over another—such as racism, genderism, ableism, and religious bias—has caused persistent disadvantage for specific groups of people. Social institutions, including schools, confer unequal relationships in terms of power and privilege based on income level, race, ethnicity, gender, and constructs of ability.

For example, education is often thought of as key to socioeconomic mobility. Consider the GI Bill, which went into effect after World War II. Technically *all* who had served were eligible to participate in the program, which provided college tuition payment. However, only 4 percent of African Americans were able to benefit because colleges and universities had quota policies that severely limited the number of black students accepted (Smith & Ternes, 2004).

Discriminatory housing and lending practices are another example of the way in which people of color have been systematically denied opportunity. Where one lives determines the degree to which one is able to access safe housing, quality schools, libraries, parks, and public services. In addition, purchasing a home is often the primary avenue through which the middle class increases its overall level of wealth, and lending practices often make home ownership an impossibility for people of color.

Testing Multiple Explanations for Poverty

Gregory Jordan (2004) sought to empirically establish the degree to which the competing paradigms were intertwined in their influence on poverty. Contrary to his hypothesis, Gregory was unable to demonstrate a relationship between the cultural aspects thought to contribute to poverty (divorce, crime, teenage pregnancies, and welfare) and the structural aspects (unemployment, income, race, income inequality, gross domestic product [GPD], and incarceration). Gregory also discovered that none of the cultural variables had a statistically significant influence on poverty, either independently or in conjunction with the structural-institutional variables. Jordan did, however, find that unemployment, income inequality, and the GDP demonstrated a statistically significant influence on poverty.

How Does Poverty Influence Lives and Learning?

Although some scholars and practitioners contend that educators can better understand the daily realities of poverty by focusing on "patterns or traits" ascribed to people who live in poverty, this stance can be a slippery slope that perpetuates damaging stereotypes. A better approach considers the constraints that poverty often places on people's lives, particularly children's, and how such conditions influence learning and academic achievement.

Three Types of Capital

By definition, people who live in poverty have limited economic capital (money). But it's not only lack of money that can compromise the ability to develop personal agency. Three other types of capital often affect personal agency: human, social, and cultural capital.

Limited opportunity to develop human capital. *Human capital* refers to the skills, abilities, and knowledge that an individual brings to the table, including the "capacity to deal with abstractions, to recognize and adhere to rules, and to use language for reasoning" (Putnam & Feldstein, 2003). Poor communities offer fewer opportunities to develop human capital than do wealthy communities because they often have inadequate schools, libraries, and medical facilities to promote healthy development.

Limited opportunity to develop social capital. *Social capital* is gained by forming relationships in formal and informal social networks, which typically benefit parents with middle and upper incomes as they negotiate the bureaucracy of schools and advocate for their children. People who live in poverty are often isolated from these networks and can be isolated from one another.

Limited opportunity to develop cultural capital. Students living in poverty often don't begin school with the same kind of *cultural capital* as their more affluent peers. These latter have a cultural advantage because they have typically been socialized to the cultural benefits of exposure to libraries, museums, books on Western civilization, theater, and travel. Such knowledge is rewarded in schools (Parker & Shapiro, 1993).

Poverty and Student Learning

Material resources. Poverty often places constraints on the family's ability to provide material resources for their children. They may have limited access to high-quality day care, limited access to before- or after-school care, and limited physical space in their homes to create private or quiet environments conducive to study. They may not own a computer or have the fiscal resources necessary to complete out-of-class projects.

Health and well-being. Substandard housing, inadequate medical care, and poor nutrition can affect the rate of childhood disease, premature births, and low birth weights, all of which influence a child's physical and cognitive development and, consequently, his or her ability to benefit from schooling. Living in daily economic hardship can also adversely affect students' mental health (Winter & Cowie, 2009); self-efficacy (Conrath, 1988, 2001); self-image (Ciaccio, 2000a, 2000b); and motivation to do well in school (Beegle, 2006).

Food insecurity. Inadequate daily nutrition impairs healthy growth and brain development, particularly in the earliest years of life. In the United States, 40 million people lived in food-insecure households in 2017, according to the U.S. Department of Agriculture (2018).

Neurocognitive and neurobehavioral development. "Poverty has cascading effects on neurocognitive development" writes researcher Sheeva Azma (2013, p. 40), and the longer a child lives in poverty or the deeper the poverty, the greater the adverse effect (Brooks-Gunn & Duncan, 1997). Poverty contributes to problems with executive functioning, which includes the ability to plan, self-regulate, attend to task, understand what information is relevant or irrelevant to a task, and retrieve and store information over time (working memory).

Housing instability. Poverty often means families have difficulty securing stable and safe housing. It can also mean no home at all. In 2016–17, more than 1.3 million students were homeless, and approximately 118,364 students were living on their own (National Center for Homeless Education, 2019). Many students live in families that are "doubled up" with others; others live temporarily in hotels or motels or spend at least some nights in cars, parks, campgrounds, or abandoned buildings. Homelessness is often a particularly shaming experience that children are reluctant to disclose to their teachers or other adults, and because of its effect on health and hygiene, it can also make homeless students a target for bullying (Dill, 2015).

Family stress and trauma. Poverty can trigger a "host of life-conditioning experiences that erode the protective capacity of the family in ways that traumatize both parents and their children" (Craig, 2015, pp. 23–24). Stress and trauma can adversely affect the ability to make decisions, solve problems, and set goals. It can cause people to lose hope and view their actions as futile. It can leave children with "little or no 'buffer zone' to safeguard their development" (Craig, 2015, p. 250).

Neighborhood risk factors. Neighborhoods with concentrated poverty are commonly characterized by unemployment, crime, and violence, as well as few resources for child development, such as parks, playgrounds, child care facilities, health clinics, libraries, or museums (Brooks-Gunn & Duncan, 1997). Neighborhood influence has also been linked with juvenile delinquency, drug use, conduct disorder in teenagers, and teenage out-of-wedlock births (Brooks-Gunn, Duncan, Klebanov, & Sealand, 1993).

Language and literacy development. Children who live in poverty often come to school behind their more affluent peers in terms of literacy and language development. In *Educating the Other America,* Susan Neuman (2008) states that more than 50 years of research indicate that children who are poor "hear a smaller number of words with more limited syntactic complexity and fewer conversation-eliciting questions, making it difficult for them to quickly acquire new words and to discriminate among words" (p. 5). A significant body of literature also points to differences in access to reading materials by students from low-income families in comparison to their more affluent peers (Allington & McGill-Franzen, 2008).

Interrupted schooling. Chronic absenteeism occurs at a higher rate in high-poverty schools (Balfanz & Byrnes, 2012). Students who experience long periods of interrupted schooling face some of the highest risks of failure (Walsh, 1999). When students come back into the school system after an extended absence, they tend to lack understanding of basic concepts, content knowledge, and critical thinking skills.

The Deficit Model of Thinking

How educators think about poverty is important because it influences how we respond to students and their families. One barrier that is likely to prevent educators from being as successful as they might otherwise be is the prevalence of "deficit model thinking" (Rodriguez & Fabionar, 2010). Deficit theory (Valencia, 1997) explains the cause of poverty as located within students and families, rather than viewing the problem of underachievement as lack of school responsiveness to the unique needs of these students. Deficit thinking reinforces the idea that there is a universal norm (usually white, middle class, male) against which all students should be assessed and to which all students should aspire. And it may rarely take into account the many factors that may influence and constrain children's ability to achieve.

Rodriguez and Fabionar (2010) suggest that some well-intentioned school practices seek to intervene in the lives of children living in poverty by asking them to replace the cultural norms, beliefs, and language of their families with school-defined notions of success—for example, not allowing students to speak in their native language in school, designating absences from school for cultural celebrations or traditions as "unexcused," or requiring students to use body language that is inconsistent with students' cultural norms.

To better understand poverty, it's helpful to understand what poverty *isn't.* We need to develop the "will and skill" to challenge common myths and stereotypes about people living in poverty, which means we must confront our own biases and blind spots.

Myths, Stereotypes, and Mental Maps

Confronting Myths

Myth: Poverty is an issue that solely affects people of color. Poverty cuts across all racial categories. Blacks and Hispanics are overrepresented among people living in poverty. However, over the past 40 years, poverty rates for black and Hispanic children have declined, whereas the poverty rate for white children has increased (Sommeiller & Price, 2018). When considering student outcomes, class and race are intersecting factors, and racism, as well as classism, is often at play.

Myth: With government assistance, people can get out of poverty. Donna Beegle's (2006) personal experience with government assistance provides insight into the complex nature of poverty-related policy and the barriers it can pose. Receiving a welfare check of $408 each month, with her rent at $395, Beegle had $13 left for basic necessities such as transportation, laundry, utilities, and other needs. When she didn't pay her rent and she and her children were evicted, her welfare counselor suggested that she needed to take money management classes. She describes how current welfare policies create barriers to getting out of poverty:

> When I was presented with the opportunity to go to school, I was notified that the state welfare policies dictated that to qualify for welfare I needed to be available for any minimum wage job. If I were in school, I would not be available. If I went to school, the government would sanction me and cut my welfare check from $408 to $258. . . . I began calculating how my kids and I could survive on $258 a month. . . . I was one of the lucky few who received help with housing costs. Only 14 percent of those who qualify for housing assistance receive it. Others are put on a wait list or turned away. (p. 29)

She continues, "The available assistance from government and social services barely helps people in poverty cope with their poverty conditions, let alone break loose from its grip" (p. 29).

Myth: Education, as a way out of poverty, is readily accessible to everyone. Many in the United States believe that people who live in poverty just need to "pull themselves up by their bootstraps" by working hard and availing themselves of a good education. Yet unequal opportunity for a good education begins early for children in poverty. In 2017, 86 percent of 5-year-olds, 68 percent of 4-year-olds, and 40 percent of 3-year-olds attended preschool (NCES, 2017). Children with parents who have a graduate degree were 20 percent more likely to attend preschool than children whose parents had less than a high school diploma (NCES, 2017). Despite the fact that children who attend Head Start are more likely to graduate from high school and go to college, only 31 percent of eligible children ages 3 to 5 have access to the program (National Head Start Association, 2018).

Problems related to equal opportunity for learning compound when students who live in poverty attend K–12 schools where a long history of inequitable treatment has been well documented (Banks, 1997; Brown, Benkovitz, Muttillo, & Urban, 2011; Delpit, 1995; Duncan & Murnane, 2014; Kozol, 1991; Ladson-Billings, 1994, 2009; Larson & Ovando, 2001; Milner, 2015; Neuman, 2008; Rist, 1979; Valenzuela, 1999). In the United States, children who live in poverty are more likely than their more affluent peers to have teachers who are less experienced and who are teaching outside their area of certification (Darling-Hammond, 2010; Goldhaber, Lavery, & Theobald, 2015), as well as substandard and unsafe school facilities (Kozol, 1991). Students of color and students in poverty are often overrepresented in special education and remedial programs; underrepresented in advanced course work, gifted and talented programs, and extracurricular activities; and disproportionally represented in disciplinary infractions. Rigid ability grouping/tracking and retention are common practices that too often create unequal access to opportunities for powerful learning (Barr & Parrett, 2007; Budge & Parrett, 2018).

Concerning educational opportunity beyond high school, Beegle (2006) suggests that "although some progress has been made in diminishing the educational barriers [to higher education] of race, gender, geography, and religion, poverty is the one barrier that has not been overcome" (p. 32). Drawing on Mortenson's (1993) research, she claims, "it is less likely today for a person born into poverty to go to college than it was in the 1940s" (p. 32).

Confronting Stereotypes

Stereotype: People in poverty abuse drugs and alcohol more than people who are wealthy. Drug and alcohol abuse affects all socioeconomic classes. In fact, studies have demonstrated that drug abuse is a problem equally distributed among classes and that alcohol abuse is more pervasive among wealthy people than among those who live in poverty (Gorski, 2008). Two recent studies suggest that individuals living in high-income neighborhoods have a higher use of alcohol and marijuana than individuals living in low-income neighborhoods. However, use of heroin and opioids is on the rise in all socioeconomic groups, the difference being who can afford treatment (Jones, 2015; Utti, 2016).

Stereotype: People in poverty do not work or have a poor work ethic. Socioeconomic mobility is thought to be possible for anyone with a strong work ethic. At some point in the workshops we conduct across the country, we always ask the question "What do people in the United States believe about people who live in poverty?" The first answer usually is "They're lazy." Yet working adults who live in poverty spend more hours working than do their wealthier counterparts and 4.4 million people work full time but fail to lift their families out of poverty (U.S. Bureau of Labor Statistics, 2014). It's not a matter of not working hard enough or not working enough hours, but rather it's about the shortage of living-wage jobs available for people with little education or training. Many low-wage workers involuntarily work part-time or are employed in a series of temporary jobs between which they may experience periods of unemployment. Some employers are careful to only offer a part-time schedule to avoid providing benefits they're required to give to full-time employees. Most people who live in poverty and who are eligible and able to work, do so. Thirty-five percent of the people who live in poverty are children, retired, disabled, or adult students. Of the remaining 65 percent eligible to work, 63 percent are working full- or part-time.

Stereotype: Parents of students who live in poverty are uninvolved in their children's education because they do not value it. Scholar Bernice Lott (2003) has studied low-income parental engagement in schooling and can point to numerous studies that demonstrate that low-income parents make a connection between success in school and their hopes and dreams for their children. Even when parents mistrust the school because of personal experience, they continue to report school success as a family priority (Harry, Allen, & McLaughlin, 1995; Webster-Stratton, 1997). A study conducted by Holloway and colleagues (1995) found that poor single mothers, although suspicious and fearful of public schools, viewed education as a key to social mobility for their students. Delgado and Ford (1998) interviewed Chicano parents, who reported that their child's education was the most important goal in their life.

Confronting Our Mental Maps

Mental maps underpin our professional practice as educators. They are the images, assumptions, and personal perspectives that we hold about people, institutions, and the world in general (Argyris & Schön, 1974), and they are formed by our lived experiences. Often tacitly held, they may not be something we are aware of; consequently, they are often left unexamined.

For example, one common mental map interprets low-income families' lack of "at school" involvement as lack of interest in their child's education. The fact is, low-income parents and families often have far less access to school involvement opportunities because they work multiple jobs, work evenings, do not have paid leave, are unable to afford child care, or do not have transportation (Gorski, 2008, 2012). Research also demonstrates that parents are dissuaded from "at school" involvement by the unwelcoming and judgmental environment many schools project (Keller & McDade, 2000; Lott, 2003). Aware of differences in educational attainment, income, and occupational status between them and educators, these parents are much more hesitant to advocate for their children than are middle-class parents (Lareau, 1987). Nonetheless, parents who live in the crisis of poverty support their children's education in ways that may be other than "at school" involvement. Studies show parental warmth and positive comments about the importance of schooling support learning in school (Hill & Taylor, 2004; Joseph, Vélez, & Antrop-González, 2017). Low-income parents report reading with their children, having discussions about school at home, monitoring their children's homework and progress in school, and attending after-school activities as ways they support their children's success in school.

People living in poverty also may appear not to value education because of reasons related to its relevancy in their lives. Beegle (2006) suggests that education lacked meaning for many of the people she studied. They attended school for such reasons as "it was the law" (p. 69). For all of the participants she studied, school was "a source of discomfort, unhappiness, and stress" (p. 69) and a place they felt they did not belong.

There's also a strong link between parental education level and parental expectations related to education. Many in Beegle's study stated that during their formative years, they had limited communication with their parents about educational expectations, issues related to success in school, or higher education. This situation was not attributed to the parents devaluing education, but rather to their limited frame of reference for discussing educational aspirations beyond their own experiences.

Why It Matters

Although our mental maps may be invisible to us, they are important because they are the foundation for our behavior—how we plan, implement, and evaluate our actions. In other words, they influence the theories that guide our choice of action. These theories can be espoused (e.g., the rationale we give for our action), or they can be tacitly held (e.g., the unspoken rationale for our action). These two kinds of theories are known as theories *of* action and theories *in* action. Effective leaders and educators have only a small gap between the two (Argyris & Schön, 1974). In other words, they are reflective and introspective enough to have challenged their own mental maps, and most of the time the rationale they give for a chosen action is congruent with their mental maps.

The myths and stereotypes presented in this chapter represent commonly held beliefs and biases about people who live in poverty. They are part of our mental maps as educators, and to the degree they are unexamined, they can limit our effectiveness. One story we're familiar with illustrates this crucial point. Eileen was a new assistant principal in a school in which 80 percent of the students were eligible for free and reduced-price meals, and she was trying to crack down on tardiness—specifically with one 7th grader, Sean, who was consistently 30 minutes late first period. He was passing all his courses, except for that first period course, pre-algebra. When asked to explain his tardiness, Sean was reluctant to respond, which greatly annoyed the assistant principal. The multiple attempts made by the 7th grade team to resolve the issue failed. Moreover, the school had great difficulty contacting the boy's parents. When at length they did locate them, the parents were asked to sign in Sean whenever he came in late. It's when Eileen finally met with the parents that she learned they were living out of a car and that Sean was often late because they chose to wait until the shower facilities opened in a public campground. With the mother in tears, the father explained, "We just didn't want kids to make fun of him because he looked bad or wasn't clean."

This story exemplifies how our mental maps can pose barriers to effective problem solving. Some of the governing variables in the mental maps were explicitly stated and known; others were likely unspoken and tacitly held. Eileen and her colleagues believed school attendance was important, as was getting to school on time. This commonly held value was made explicit through policy. She and the faculty had also made explicit their belief that parents should take responsibility for their child's tardiness, and thus they established a signing-in procedure. However, the educators' tacitly held assumptions about Sean and his parents—that they didn't care about education, were lazy, were absent, or were sleeping off a hangover—may have prevented them from rethinking the problem.

Although it can be difficult to surface our assumptions, a good place to begin is by asking the question "Are we sure we're solving the right problem?" If Eileen and the 7th grade team had brainstormed all the possible reasons Sean might be tardy, they may have surfaced some of their tacit assumptions, reframed the problem, and tried new strategies rather than continuing to solve the wrong problem. In fact, once Eileen and her team knew the problem was homelessness, they had an entirely new set of strategies at their disposal to help Sean succeed. For example, they connected Sean's family with community resources, allowed Sean to make up the seat time he missed in the mornings during lunch, and gave him access to a parent volunteer to help him with math.

What Schools Can Do

In the United States, intense public and policy debate related to poverty has occurred for decades. In the 1960s, the intent of welfare reform policy was to reduce poverty. But since the mid-1990s, policy has focused not on reducing poverty but on reducing dependency on welfare and increasing work among the poor. In fact, changes in welfare policy accompanied by the economic boom of the late 1990s resulted in a decline of 70 percent in welfare recipients (Danziger & Danziger, 2008). However, a decline in the welfare rolls differs from a decline in poverty.

Antipoverty measures take many forms. Some are intended to ease economic hardship by raising income (e.g., cash welfare, food stamps), and others aim to ease the constraints that poverty poses (e.g., subsidized housing and child care). Looking to successful policies in other industrialized countries, Danziger and Danziger (2008) point to the relatively modest increase in the level of income needed to turn the tide for families in poverty. They suggest that reasonable policy changes are possible and point to four specific strategies: (1) raising the minimum wage, (2) subsidizing health insurance, (3) reforming the unemployment insurance program, and (4) providing "transitional jobs of last resort" (p. 29) for those who are unable to find steady employment. Working to change structures that perpetuate poverty in the broader society is vital to its elimination; at the same time, much can be done to improve the way in which institutions serve those living in poverty. Foremost among those institutions is public education.

James Coleman's (1966) conclusion that schools could have only a limited effect on students who live in poverty began a debate that has continued for decades. In an article published in *Educational Leadership* in April 2008, Richard Rothstein, research associate at the Economic Policy Institute, asked the question "Whose problem is poverty?" He suggests that schools can have only a limited influence on closing the achievement gap between students who live in poverty and their more affluent peers—unless school improvement is combined with broader social and economic reforms. Without such a combined effort, he claims, the mandate for schools to "fully close achievement gaps not only will remain unfulfilled, but also will cause us to foolishly and unfairly condemn our schools and teachers" (p. 8).

Others assert that schools can and do make a significant difference in the lives and the academic outcomes of students who live in poverty (Barr &

Parrett, 2007; McGee, 2004). As Kati Haycock (2010) contended in her key-note address at the 2010 Education Trust conference, "Some say we can't fix education until we fix poverty. It's exactly the opposite; we can't fix poverty until we fix education." Although it's clear to Haycock that we need to work on improving the conditions of families in poverty, she points out that "we can in fact get even the poorest children to high standards of achievement if we really focus in our schools on that goal."

Successfully educating all students to high standards is crucial to eliminating poverty. If, as educators, we feel powerless to address bigger issues such as living-wage jobs and health care reform, Gorski (2008) proposes that we ask ourselves, "Are we willing, at the very least, to tackle the classism in our own schools and classrooms?" Gorski (2007) provides the following 10 suggestions as a starting point:

- Assign work requiring a computer and Internet access or other costly resources only when we can provide in-school time and materials for such work to be completed.
- Work with schools to make parent involvement affordable and convenient by providing transportation, on-site child care, and time flexibility.
- Give students from poverty access to the same high-level curricular and pedagogical opportunities and high expectations as their wealthy peers.
- Teach about classism, consumer culture, the dissolution of labor unions, environmental pollution, and other injustices disproportionately affecting the poor, preparing new generations of students to make a more equitable world.
- Keep stocks of school supplies, snacks, clothes, and other basic necessities handy for students who may need them, but find quiet ways to distribute these resources to avoid singling anyone out.
- Develop curricula that are relevant and meaningful to students' lives and draw on their experiences and surroundings.
- Fight to get students into gifted and talented programs and to give them other opportunities usually reserved for economically advantaged students and fight to keep them from being assigned unjustly to special education.
- Continue to reach out to parents even when they appear to be unresponsive; this is one way to establish trust.
- Challenge colleagues when they stigmatize poor students and their parents, reminding them of the inequitable conditions in our schools and classrooms.

- Challenge ourselves, our biases, and our prejudices by educating ourselves about the cycle of poverty and classism in and out of U.S. schools. (p. 35)

The need for broader social and economic changes in the United States is no excuse for maintaining the status quo in schools. Four decades of research have demonstrated that schools can improve academic outcomes and other measures of success for children who live in poverty (Ball, 2001; Barr & Gibson, 2013; Barr & Parrett, 2007; Brinson, Kowal, & Hassel, 2008; Chenoweth, 2007, 2009a, 2009b, 2017; Education Trust, 2002; Fullan, 2011; McGee, 2004; Parrett & Budge, 2012; Teddlie & Stringfield, 1993). As Horace Mann asserted, public education is the most universal of institutions, and it can shape young minds and hearts. It is still our best hope. Although improvements in public education alone will not eliminate poverty, such improvements are an important part of the solution. The question is not whether too much is being asked of public schools, but rather, have we held up our end of the bargain?

As Jacquelyn Jackson (Neuman, 2008) wrote in her foreword to *Educating the Other America*, "Solutions to poverty are like pieces of a puzzle. Those pieces include education, housing, health and nutrition, employment, child care, and community support services to name a few. . . . Education is the glue that can help keep the other pieces in place."

Education—A Civil Right

In the richest nation in the world, it's possible to eradicate poverty, and a vital step toward doing so is to provide a high-quality education for every child. We know there's a correlation between education and earning power. On average, a four-year college graduate earns two and a half times as much as someone without a high school diploma (San Antonio, 2008). Both affluent children and those living in poverty attend schools of varying quality. However, for the latter the quality of their school may be of greater consequence.

In high-performing, high-poverty schools, excellence and equity are compatible goals, and the effects of poverty are not offered as an excuse to maintain the status quo; rather, such effects serve as "design parameters" for understanding how best to serve students (Calkins, Guenther, Belfiore, & Lash, 2007, p. 85). Too often, schools have attempted to support students who live in poverty by attempting interventions that did not take into consideration their unique needs. By focusing on the constraints that poverty poses for students and their families, schools can more effectively develop multiple pathways for improving academic achievement and school success.

To understand HP/HP schools' commitment to excellence and equity, it's crucial to understand not only what they do *but also what they no longer do.* Leaders and educators in HP/HP schools are willing to examine data and ask questions in order to peel back the layers of the ways in which schools systemically perpetuate underachievement. Such critical inquiry provides the impetus for eliminating destructive policies and practices, such as inequitable funding, retaining and tracking students, and providing what Martin Haberman (1991) calls the "pedagogy of poverty."

This approach to working with students who live in poverty is different from other popular approaches. From educators in HP/HP schools we have learned that the solution to the problem of poverty is not about fixing students and families so they can "fit" into school; rather, it means fixing schools so that *all* students have a sense of belonging and the opportunity for success. A high-quality education has become increasingly important for all children. Without such an education, many are excluded from what is foundational to a democratic society—the opportunity to become responsible citizens, to contribute to one's economic well-being and to that of one's family and community, and to enjoy productive and satisfying lives. Indeed, a high-quality education has become so vital that it is viewed by many as the civil rights issue of our generation.

"We can reconfigure the world if we can reconfigure our way of thinking," noted Muhammad Yunus, 2006 recipient of the Nobel Peace Prize. High-performing, high-poverty schools are doing just that, using education to challenge conventional wisdom.

In the next chapter, we describe our Framework for Collective Action, including the changes we made and the insights we gained since the 2012 publication of this book.

4 Using a Framework for Collective Action

How many effective schools would you have to see to be persuaded of the educability of poor children? If your answer is more than one, then I submit that you have reasons of your own for preferring to believe that basic pupil performance derives from family background. . . . We can, whenever and wherever we choose, successfully teach all children whose schooling is of interest to us.

—*Ron Edmonds,* Educational Leadership, *1979, pp. 22–23*

In the first edition of this book, we asked the following question: "As educational leaders, do we have an extensive body of knowledge related to how low-performing, high-poverty schools become high performing, or are we primarily left to our own devices to figure it out?" (Parrett & Budge, 2012, p. 52). At the time, we argued that although there were three decades of research on how low-performing, high-poverty schools could improve, much of the research focused on elementary schools as opposed to high schools.

In the near decade that has passed since our last study, the factors that contribute to low-performing, high-poverty schools becoming high performing are more apparent. This second, more recent study, which is inclusive of more schools and has a higher bar for participation, provided us with a deeper understanding and revealed more specific actions and practices that drove and sustained the schools' improvement. The educators we interviewed seemed more convinced that significant improvement was not only possible (and could point to research-based approaches, models, and frameworks that informed their actions), but also highly likely when best practices were well implemented. Several educators described policy imperatives and various forms of "nudging" from district-level leaders or other entities that kickstarted their improvement efforts, for which they were usually grateful. The body of knowledge related to how high-poverty, low-performing schools improve indeed has grown and now provides even greater guidance for educators.

Our intention in developing the Framework for Collective Action remains the same—to contribute to this body of knowledge and provide guidance and support to educators from various vantage points in the system. The framework is neither a to-do list nor a cookbook. It's a source of research-based information about how improvement appears to happen in high-poverty schools; a collection of practical ideas offered by dedicated, hardworking educational leaders; and a set of tools that can be used to guide the work of others. Our desire is to begin crucial conversations, plant seeds of optimism and hope, and prompt action suited to a school's unique context. Using the information in this chapter, together with the rubrics in the action-oriented chapters that follow, educators across the board can access the existing knowledge base and learn from the success of others while they consider the unique needs of their school and community.

Representing this complex work in the two-dimensional world of printed text is challenging. This is a good time to refer to Figure 4.1, a visual representation of the Framework for Collective Action and the interactions among its crucial components. This will be a helpful visual support as we explain the relationship among the various interactive components that need to be in place for a high-poverty school to become a high-performing school.

Understanding the Framework's Gears

As you can see, the framework features the following gears: (1) All Students Learning, (2) Actions, (3) School Culture, and (4) Spheres of Influence. These four gears are placed within the largest gear, which represents the idea that school improvement process is propelled from within—by the smaller gears. The interior gear, All Students Learning to High Standards, reflects the central mission of high-performing, high-poverty schools. It is the "drive gear." In these high-performing schools, it is recognized that each student matters and each student's needs are known, supported, and met through the interaction of all components of the gears.

The Actions gear focuses on three arenas in which educators need to act: They must develop and build the *leadership capacity and collective efficacy* needed to foster the creation of *healthy, safe, and supportive learning environments* and support a relentless focus on *student, professional, and system learning.* Taking action is the necessary first step in making any kind

Figure 4.1   A Framework for Collective Action: Leading High-Poverty Schools to High Performance

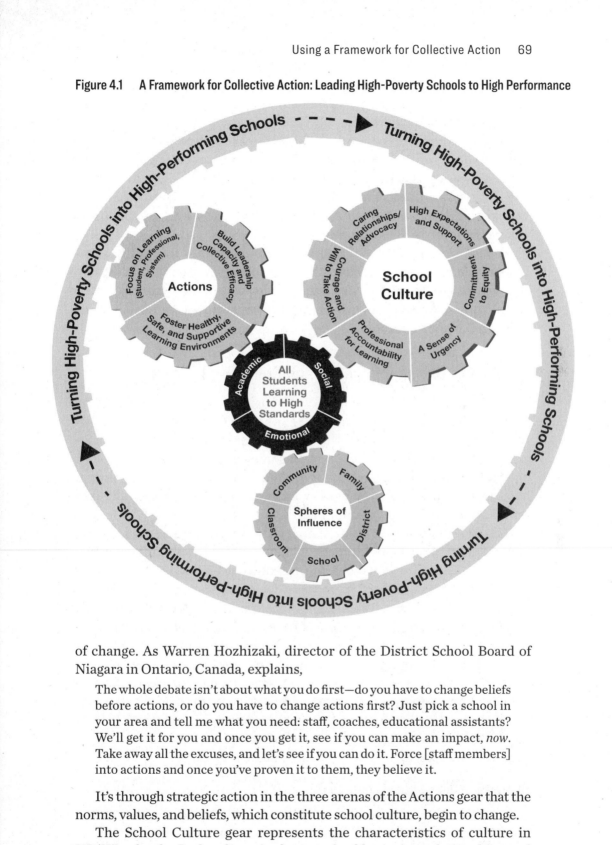

of change. As Warren Hozhizaki, director of the District School Board of Niagara in Ontario, Canada, explains,

> The whole debate isn't about what you do first—do you have to change beliefs before actions, or do you have to change actions first? Just pick a school in your area and tell me what you need: staff, coaches, educational assistants? We'll get it for you and once you get it, see if you can make an impact, *now*. Take away all the excuses, and let's see if you can do it. Force [staff members] into actions and once you've proven it to them, they believe it.

It's through strategic action in the three arenas of the Actions gear that the norms, values, and beliefs, which constitute school culture, begin to change.

The School Culture gear represents the characteristics of culture in HP/HP schools. Such culture is characterized by caring relationships and advocacy for students, high expectations and support, a commitment to equity, a sense of urgency, professional accountability for learning, and courage and will to take action.

Finally, educators' concerted efforts to take action and change the school's culture are targeted to affect the many Spheres of Influence on students' education, including their classroom, school, school district, family, and community. Leaders and the entire school community work in partnership and collaboration with stakeholders in these various spheres to ensure that every student succeeds.

Following is an overview of the three components of the Action gear—building leadership capacity and collective efficacy; fostering healthy, safe, and supportive learning environments; and focusing on student, professional, and system learning. We'll explore each of these arenas in more depth in Chapters 5 through 7.

Building Leadership Capacity and Collective Efficacy

Conducting this new study of HP/HP schools has prompted us to refine our thinking about leadership capacity. We continue to view it as both context for the other two arenas of action and the necessary infrastructure to make and sustain improvements. We remain confident that shared, distributed, and reciprocal leadership is necessary. And we maintain our view of principal leadership as vital to success. What has changed is a greater emphasis on the absolute necessity of building a *collective sense of efficacy*.

Leadership capacity acts as the context for improvements in learning and the learning environment. When such leadership infrastructure is present, HP/HP schools look much like what Linda Lambert (2005a) describes as "high leadership capacity" schools. She defines leadership capacity as "broad-based, skillful participation in the work of leadership" and further clarifies the term *work of leadership* as "reciprocal, purposeful learning together in community" (p. 38). According to Lambert (2005b), schools that develop high leadership capacity "take on a different character" than schools with less leadership capacity (p. 65). Figure 4.2 displays the characteristics of schools at three levels of leadership capacity.

As was found in Lambert's (2005b) high leadership capacity schools, three elements characterize leadership in HP/HP schools: (1) shared and distributed leadership, (2) a spirit of reciprocity, and (3) the principal as lead learner.

Shared and Distributed Leadership

A principal's position of formal authority affords that person a unique and vital role in the effort to turn around a low-performing school. In

Figure 4.2   Characteristics of Schools with Differing Levels of Leadership Capacity

High Leadership Capacity Schools...	Medium Leadership Capacity Schools...	Low Leadership Capacity Schools...
• Are learning communities that amplify leadership for all, learning for all, and success for all. • Develop a fabric of structures (e.g., teams, communities, study groups) and process (reflection, inquiry, dialogue) that form a more lasting and buoyant web of interrelated actions. • Feature a shared vision for where the school is going and how it's getting there. *In such schools,* • The principal is only one of the leaders in the school community, and he/she models collaboration, listening, and engagement. • Individuals understand how they contribute to attaining the shared vision. • The quality of the school is a function of the quality of conversations within the school. • Student success is revealed by multiple measures, including the presence of student voice in the direction of the school.	• Lack a compelling purpose and focus. • Are governed by norms of individualism. • Hold few conversations among the whole community. • Are fragmented and polarized. • Feature small groups of more skilled educators who are concerned that others are not "buying in" and may form an isolated inner core of decision makers. *In such schools,* • Disaggregating student scores inevitably reveals a lack of success for the most vulnerable or challenged students.	• Are principal-dependent. • Have a lack of professional culture. • Are significantly unsuccessful with children. • Are characterized by an absence of internal accountability. • Are subject to the whims, demands, and pressures of parents, districts, and states. *In such schools,* • Only the principal as "top-down manager" is referred to as the leader. • Educators deflect responsibility while preferring blame. • Educators avoid focusing on teaching and learning while holding fast to archaic practices. • Professional relationships are congenial, but not collegial. • Test scores may be considered the only valid measure of success.

Source: From "What Does Leadership Capacity Really Mean?" by Linda Lambert, *JSD,* Spring 2005. Adapted with permission of Learning Forward, www.learningforward.org. All rights reserved.

HP/HP schools, principals frequently acknowledge that they cannot go it alone; leadership functions must be shared and distributed among many stakeholders. Recognizing the crucially important opportunities others have to lead from various vantage points throughout the system (e.g., other administrators, teachers, support personnel, school trustees, parents, families, and community members), HP/HP principals seek to share decision-making authority and governance of the school.

EJ Martinez, principal at Stillman Middle School in Brownsville, Texas, told us, "When I got here, it was a good school. We just wanted to be better.

My expectation was that all kids do well. The teachers wanted to be the very best and [wanted] their kids to perform really well." A teacher at Stillman reinforced the idea that leadership and responsibility are shared, explaining why he loves to teach at the school and why he loves to teach 6th grade: "It's because it's up to us 6th grade teachers to build the foundation that gets the students smoothly through 7th and 8th grade. We [teachers] really work well together. . . . We like being No. 1, so we work hard every year to maintain that."

A Spirit of Reciprocity

Shared and distributed leadership depends on a spirit of reciprocity. Autocratic leadership encourages a dependent relationship between leader and follower. Dependent relationships between principals and teachers can lead to blaming and abdicating responsibility for improvement (Lambert, 2005b).

On the other hand, principals who embrace the approach of holding others accountable while holding themselves equally accountable present a dramatically different type of leadership. Harvard University professor Richard Elmore (2000) describes a relationship of reciprocal accountability between principal and teacher, saying, "If the formal authority of my role [as principal] requires that I hold you accountable for some action or outcome, then I have an equal and complementary responsibility to ensure that you have the capacity to do what I am asking you to do" (p. 21).

Reciprocal leadership was unequivocally key to the success of a network of high-poverty, high-performing schools in Niagara, Ontario, as Marian Reimer Friesen, area superintendent, asserts.

> It is so tempting to mandate. It is so tempting to push things out that you think are going to do the right things for kids, but if you stop to get to know the people you're working with, you will find that they have the answers that will make a difference. They need to be given the opportunity to articulate them and then supported to enact them. So to really engage with them at that level, we can't come down from on high and offer them slap and dash advice or strategies. But we can say, "Well, let's puzzle through this together. I don't know, what do you think? Where could we get more information? Let's talk to the grade six teacher and see what he says."

The Principal as Lead Learner

Interdependent relationships and reciprocal accountability characterize the concept of the principal as lead learner among a community of learners. This was true of all the principals we studied. As one principal in an HP/HP urban elementary school admits,

> It's scary for me to think about everything I need to do and then to know that I am supposed to be an instructional leader too. Instead of being an instructional leader, I am a *learning leader*. I like that because it's about me bringing everything I can to the table and about empowering this community of learners to do the best job possible. It's about offering opportunities for collaboration and really honest, deep conversations about our practice.

Principals most often begin the conversation about what is truly possible in a high-poverty school. They facilitate the development of a common vision of high levels of learning for all—students and adults—and become the chief stewards in keeping that vision alive and in the forefront for the school staff, parents, and community. They act out of a commitment to equity, which often begins with an analysis of data. As a teacher in one of the schools we studied explains,

> We're a data-driven school. We're lucky to have a principal who helps us target the students with the highest needs and helps us set goals for those students. We get a lot of training on how to use data. We use it to make curriculum decisions and to individualize instruction. Our principal is an amazing leader and is learning with us. We haven't always had the best track record with our kids, but I like how things are done here now.

Sharing and distributing leadership functions, fostering a spirit of reciprocity, and viewing the principal as lead learner among a community of learners constitute the leadership capacity or "leadership infrastructure" necessary to maintain the continual focus on learning and the learning environment found in HP/HP schools. Leadership capacity also influences the level of collective efficacy from which the school is able to focus on such improvements. As improvements in these areas are made and sustained, the level of collective efficacy increases.

Collective Efficacy

High-performing, high-poverty schools are exemplars of collective efficacy. Collective efficacy is the shared or "collective" perception of teachers that the faculty as a whole can and will have a positive effect on student learning (Eells, 2011; Jerald, 2007). Such collective efficacy is sometimes referred to as "collective teacher efficacy" or CTE. Studies have demonstrated that collective efficacy can prevail over the negative influence of poverty on student learning (Bandura, 1993; Donohoo, Hattie, & Eells, 2018; Goddard, Hoy, & Hoy, 2000). It also enhances relationships, strengthens teacher commitment to the school, and improves student achievement (Brinson & Steiner, 2007; Hattie, 2018).

Here's how Eric Sanchez, executive director of Henderson Collegiate, explained what collective efficacy looks like in his school:

> We have three core virtues that we believe our school should have; we want everybody to be humble, hungry, and smart—and really work together. We . . . support [our teachers], help them get better, and make them feel confident and strong in what they're doing. We listen to that talent and what they want to pursue and draw them a pathway to get there. You want to be somebody who lifts up our science program, then we'll send you to the best science school—go learn from it. This place is not about evaluation; it's about development.

John Hattie (2018) found that of all the factors analyzed, collective efficacy had the greatest potential positive influence on student achievement (effect size 1.57). He maintains that anything with an effect size greater than .40 has a likelihood of positively affecting student achievement. In a brief video, Hattie (2018) explains that collective teacher efficacy is more than "rah-rah thinking" and a collective perspective that a group of teachers "can make the difference." It also requires that belief be "fed by the evidence" that indeed student learning is improving.

Donohoo, Hattie, and Eells (2018) explain that the best way educators can influence student beliefs about learning is by developing a culture of collective efficacy. They assert its power lies in the fact that it can be cultivated and that the principal can indeed control the narrative of improvement:

> If the narrative is about bus timetables, tweaks in the curriculum, and test schedules, this percolates through the school as the purpose of schooling—compliance to procedures. In such schools, students think learning is coming to school on time, sitting up straight, keeping quiet, and watching the teacher work. But if, instead, the narrative is about high expectations, growth in relation to inputs, what it means to be a "good learner" in various subjects, and what impact means, then teachers and students will think about learning in a different way. They will believe that learning is about challenge, about understanding and realizing high expectations, and that setbacks are an opportunity to learn. Students will also believe that coming to school means investing energy in deliberate practice. (p. 44)

Leaders in HP/HP schools control the narratives in their schools. They take action to establish cultures of high expectations and expected growth for students, staff, and themselves. Alexa Sorden, principal of Concourse Village Elementary in the Bronx, asserts, "Principals need to be the designers of what's happening in their building, and then they can have co-designers."

Jenni Donohoo (2017) has identified six conditions that cultivate collective teacher efficacy: (1) teacher influence in decision making, (2) faculty consensus on goals, (3) teachers' knowledge of one another's work, (4) cohesive beliefs about fundamental educational issues, (5) responsive leadership, and (6) effective intervention systems. Educators in the schools we studied spoke of these same conditions as key to their success.

Although the Framework for Collective Action encompasses each of Donohoo's six conditions, we organize them differently. In Chapters 5–7, as we discuss the three arenas of action, we include strategies and wisdom shared by the educators we interviewed for enabling each of the six conditions. Moreover, we identify three practices that we consider "meta-practices" because they are interwoven throughout each arena of action and because they greatly contributed to the development of collective efficacy in the schools we studied: (1) assuming an inquiry stance and embedding reflection into professional practice, (2) engaging in data-informed problem solving, and (3) developing relational trust (Bryk & Schneider, 2002).

Fostering Healthy, Safe, and Supportive Learning Environments

More than four decades of research have demonstrated that schools can influence the outcomes for children who live in poverty and the concomitant situations that put them at risk behaviorally, emotionally, cognitively, and academically. High-performing, high-poverty schools provide *protective factors* that help build a bond between students and school. These factors include fostering caring relationships between adults and children, as well as among peers; setting high expectations and providing the support needed to meet those expectations; ensuring academic success; providing opportunity for meaningful involvement in school; and providing a safe and orderly environment in which the rules are clear (Benard, 1991).

One principal we interviewed told us about a scene in the cafeteria early on in her career. She explained,

> We had rules, but no expectations that they would be followed. . . . I met with every teacher, and we began to talk about the Correlates of Effective Schools. The first correlate is safety and order. Creating a safe environment had to be addressed before we were going to be able to address anything else.

Creating the kind of environment in which students living in poverty can flourish becomes possible when leaders, teachers, and other staff work collaboratively to meet each student's learning needs. But such collaboration is not always the norm; indeed, in many schools it is the antithesis of the way they do business. In far too many schools, teachers and other staff continue to work as independent contractors who share a building. This is not true of HP/HP schools. In these schools, learning is the focus and collaboration is the means.

Focusing on Student, Professional, and System Learning

Despite the challenges that their students face and the odds against them, leaders and educators in HP/HP schools maintain high expectations for their students as well as for themselves. A teacher we interviewed from a rural elementary school pointed to some of the challenges they face:

> We have a lot of kids who move in and out of the school, or they miss a lot of school. More of our kids are coming to school impacted by metham-phetamines in the home. When we assessed our kindergartners at the end of last year, we had 20 kids start at the zero point. They didn't know even five sounds or letters. You might be wondering what's going to happen to those 20 kids this year. I'll tell you what's going to happen—they're going to learn to read.

Educators in HP/HP schools demonstrate a tenacious focus on learning—in fact, on three kinds of learning. In high-performing schools, *student learning* is purposefully and intentionally linked to two other learning agendas—professional learning and system-level learning (Knapp, Copland, & Talbert, 2003). We are using the term *professional learning* to refer to the adult learning that occurs in schools. The term *system-level learning* describes how the school as a whole "learns" to be more effective in accomplishing its mission and goals. In other words, as individuals learn, the school (or system) learns to do business differently and better.

The three types of learning—student, professional, and system—interact and influence one another. One of the greatest challenges that educators face is to grasp the opportunity for learning that each agenda gives rise to, to see the connections among the various kinds of learning and the manner in which they mutually influence one another. Meeting this challenge is the "essential first step" for educators to begin to improve learning (Knapp, Copland, & Talbert, 2003).

How does this look in practice? One of the schools we visited provides a good example.

Imagine a team of 4th grade teachers, along with the school's literacy coach, examining the results of a recent classroom-based assessment and discussing the instruction that occurred before administering the assessment. The teachers conclude that they need to learn more about how to help students make inferences when reading fictional text. This information becomes "data" or "inputs," which, in this case, informed the system. School leaders, teachers, and staff subsequently engaged in professional development on the topic of making inferences from fictional text and received embedded coaching to reinforce what they had learned in a workshop format (evidence of system learning). Teaching improved (evidence of professional learning), as did student assessment results (evidence of student learning).

Implementing the Arenas of Action: 10 Key Strategies

Think of this overview of the Framework for Collective Action as the 30,000-foot view of what high-performing, high-poverty schools do. We know that no school's approach to high performance is exactly the same as another's, so as we begin to take a closer look, we discovered 10 key strategies that were present to some degree in each school (see Figure 4.3).

1. Ensure safety. Physical and emotional safety are essential for learning. HP/HP schools take multiple approaches to ensuring the safety of children and adults (see pages 109–111).

Figure 4.3   10 Actions for Commitment to High Performance

2. Gain an accurate understanding of poverty. Understanding one's mental map of poverty and people in poverty is necessary to disrupt poverty's adverse influence on learning. This often includes challenging one's blind spots and implicit biases, understanding deficit thinking, and confronting stereotypes. Developing an accurate understanding of poverty also entails coming to deeply know the children, families/caregivers, and communities the school serves (see Chapter 3).

3. Use a common instructional framework. High-poverty schools become high performing by improving the core instruction occurring in each classroom or teaching space. Teachers develop a *common* understanding of good (or even excellent) teaching and a *common* vocabulary to describe such teaching. They mutually agree to implement evidence-based instructional and classroom management strategies consistently (see pages 140–141).

4. Focus on literacy. Exercising a host of approaches, HP/HP schools work to ensure *all* students become proficient readers (see pages 150–152).

5. Promote engagement and ownership. HP/HP schools employ pedagogies that engage students and promote ownership of their own learning (see pages 141–142).

6. Level the playing field. An unwavering commitment to equity is the lifeblood of HP/HP schools. Based on this commitment, educators in these schools assess and continuously reassess the processes, structures, policies, and practices they use to ensure all students have equal opportunity to learn at deep levels (see pages 164–166).

7. Provide additional quality targeted instructional time. After educators in HP/HP schools have ensured safety, improved classroom instruction, and engaged students in their learning, some students will inevitably need additional quality instructional time to succeed (see pages 153–155).

8. Engage parents/caregivers/families. Educators in HP/HP schools understand that parent/family/caregiver engagement enhances student learning. Because they strive to understand the barriers poverty poses for the families they serve, the partnerships they establish effectively respond to those families' circumstances, needs, and interests (see pages 119–124).

9. Use formative assessment to guide instructional decisions. Teachers in HP/HP schools use formative assessments (often *common* formative assessments) to guide their instructional moves (see pages 142–147).

10. Provide job-embedded opportunity for professional learning. High-poverty schools become high performing by transforming the school into a learning organization for students and adults. Intentional and explicit steps taken not only increase educators' skills and knowledge in their area of expertise, but also enhance individual and collective efficacy and develop leadership capacity (see pages 155–156).

In subsequent chapters, we will actually land the plane and provide examples of the varied ways in which schools implement these strategies. Before we do so, we turn to another component of the Framework for Collective Action—the School Culture.

Leading Change in School Culture

In high-poverty, low-performing schools, changes in policies, practices, and structures are necessary but insufficient to gain and sustain improvement in student achievement and other measures of student success. Leaders and educators in high-performing, high-poverty schools take action, which sparks change in the ethos and culture of the school. In an HP/HP school, it's the culture or ethos we notice first. In *Disrupting Poverty: Five Powerful Classroom Practices*, we describe how the culture of a school makes itself felt within the first few minutes. You can sense the feeling of belonging, how everyone seems to have a purpose. And when we talked to the educators in those schools, they would point out the importance of "forming caring relationships with students, holding high expectations, ensuring equity, assuming professional responsibility for learning, and challenging both themselves and the status quo. . . . What they were making explicit . . . was their school's significantly improved culture" (pp. 12–13).

When we asked Michele Capps, superintendent and elementary principal of Murtaugh PK–12 School District in Murtaugh, Idaho, if hiring front office bilingual staff was "by accident," she remarked,

> Oh, heavens no. Nothing is by accident here! They are not only bilingual, they are fantastic, bilingual, and critical to the communication with our Hispanic population, which is half of our students and families. I don't just mean the families who only speak Spanish, I mean all of them.

Capps had this to say about one particular bilingual front office staff member: "Parents will call, and they don't want to talk to me; they want to talk to her. She's the glue. She's so effective with our families and just so caring, and they love her."

Educators in HP/HP schools know that relationships with students and families begin at the school's front door and that the ethos of the front office reflects the broader culture of the school. Many shared stories of how in the early days of their journeys to high performance, they had to make immediate changes "out front" for the school to be warm, welcoming, and responsive to students and their families.

School Culture: Beliefs, Values, and Norms

A school's culture is defined by three elements: beliefs or assumptions, values, and norms. These aspects of school culture exist on a hierarchy of abstraction. Norms are more easily observed and are more concrete than values are. In turn, values are less abstract than beliefs and assumptions are, which are often tacitly held (Hoy & Miskel, 2008). Low-performing, high-poverty schools are often distinguished by a toxic culture of low expectations, excuse making, blame, and resignation. Differing dramatically from such cultures, the culture of HP/HP schools suggests a confluence of six crucial attributes: (1) caring relationships and advocacy, (2) high expectations and support, (3) an unwavering commitment to equity, (4) a sense of professional accountability for learning, (5) a sense of urgency, and (6) the courage and will to take action. These attributes represent what is collectively valued in HP/HP schools and form the basis for a set of beliefs that serves as the foundation for school norms (see Figure 4.4).

Figure 4.4   School and Classroom Cultures in High-Poverty, High-Performing Schools

Values	Examples of Beliefs	Examples of Norms
Caring Relationships	Caring relationships are necessary if significant learning is going to occur.	Teachers are intentional about fostering relationships with their students in all aspects of their daily work.
High Expectations and Support	All students are capable of meeting high standards when appropriately supported.	Teachers have empathy for students and an understanding of the challenges they face. They hold students to high standards, give them the appropriate supports to succeed, and value the importance of effort.
Commitment to Equity	An *equal* opportunity to learn requires equitable conditions for learning.	Teachers differentiate their support based on the needs of individual students and do all they can to "level the playing field" in their classrooms for every student.
Professional Accountability for Learning	Teachers are responsible for student learning.	When students fail to learn, teachers go "back to the drawing board." They view themselves as "being on the same team" with their students.
Sense of Urgency	For many children living in poverty, success in school is a matter of life and death, and there is no time to waste.	All adults in the building are professionals who understand they are contributing to a collective moral purpose. They bring their best selves to the task, knowing they have a finite amount of time to influence student learning.
Courage and Will to Take Action	Barriers to learning are difficult, but not impossible, to eliminate.	Teachers confront their own biases and blind spots, as well as work to eliminate conditions that perpetuate underachievement in their classrooms, schools, and districts.

School Culture: The Power of Mental Maps

In low-performing, high-poverty schools, the degree of change needed to foster a culture conducive to deep levels of learning for all—students, professionals, and the system—often presents a formidable challenge. In our research and that of others, the seeming intractability of a negative school culture appears to result from focusing on changing people's beliefs without supporting them to change their behavior or failing to recognize the magnitude of the needed change and, in doing so, underestimating the intensity of the leadership needed (Marzano, Waters, & McNulty, 2005).

Educators who hope to lead cultural change in low-performing, high-poverty schools must understand the power of mental maps, those myths and stereotypes that people cling to about those who live in poverty. Educators who are successful in courageously encouraging the examination of mental maps don't do so by challenging peoples' beliefs; rather, they encourage changes in behaviors and norms first. *Changes in behavior most often come before changes in beliefs.*

Educators in the schools we studied did not use the term *mental maps*; they used the term *mindset*. No matter the word, they took action that prompted themselves and others to reflect on their existing perspectives and assumptions about poverty. They used data, and they shared information to challenge long-held assumptions about students living in poverty to build a shared vision of equity and excellence and create a sense of urgency. These educators seemed to understand that they wouldn't be able to just infuse their own values and beliefs in others. Rather, they engendered changes in beliefs and values by providing others with new experiences in a relatively nonthreatening environment.

Educators in these schools encouraged others to join in what became a collective effort to improve the learning of their students in poverty by taking risks and trying new things. These changes in behaviors challenged the tacit assumptions underlying educators' mental maps and, in turn, prompted changes in beliefs and values. For instance, in some schools, carefully planned home visits promoted a better understanding of low-income families and the challenges they face. These home visits became opportunities to explore stereotypes about students who live in poverty. They challenged the deficit perspective held by many and made teachers and staff more responsive to poverty's intervening factors that threaten students' well-being and readiness to learn.

As a result of better understanding the impact of poverty, one school provided supplies for every student and abandoned extracurricular pay-to-participate fees. Connecting with families helped change expectations in another school, where the notion that all children can and will learn to high standards became the norm. In this school, when student achievement lagged, teachers held themselves accountable and addressed the issue head-on, rather than blaming children and families.

Working in Many Spheres of Influence

At one school we worked with, there had been a lot of complaining before the new principal, Derek, came on board. "You would often hear, 'Somebody should, somebody should . . . ,'" one educator shared with us. "And then Derek came, and it was like, 'Oh, *we* can be that somebody. Let's better connect with our community.'"

Leaders and educators in HP/HP schools don't work in isolation. These schools often develop positive relationships with district office leaders, students' families, and the broader neighborhood and community. For instance, many schools serve as community centers, which affords them greater opportunity to build relationships with families and other members of the community while providing needed resources. Many high-performing, high-poverty schools also establish community-based learning programs, which have demonstrated particular effectiveness for students living in low-income homes and for those with other risk factors (Barr & Parrett, 2007). In practice, effective partnerships enable schools to garner resources from sources external to the school. One of the most important partnerships that schools can establish is with district office personnel to leverage needed support.

Addressing the High-Leverage Questions

David Cooperrider, professor at Case Western Reserve University and developer of Appreciative Inquiry, says, "Organizations gravitate toward the questions they ask" (Berger, 2014, p. 19). When we speak of schools assuming an inquiry stance, we mean they ask questions of themselves. HP/HP schools become curious places where it's not only safe to ask questions but also expected. Statements such as "That's the way we've always done things" become questions such as, "*Why* is that the way we've always done things? How might we do it differently?" Again, Cooperrider explains, "We all live in the world our questions create" (Berger, 2014, p. 19). So it's not only important that we ask ourselves questions, but also that we ask questions that will produce the world we want to live in.

In the three chapters that follow, we will look at the three focal points of leading HP/HP schools—building leadership capacity and collective efficacy; fostering a healthy, safe, and supportive learning environment; and focusing on student, professional, and system learning—both in terms of what to *initiate or improve* and in terms of what to *confront and eliminate.* Based on our study of HP/HP schools, and with Cooperrider's insights in mind, we have developed a series of high-leverage questions that not only structure each of these three chapters but also can serve as a starting place for your school.

5 Building Leadership Capacity and Collective Efficacy

As principal, you're pushing that elephant up the hill, keeping everybody going. You're asking, What do we need to change? How do we tighten up? So it takes energy. It's harder to teach kids who live in poverty, and it's harder to be a principal in a school where poverty is high. . . . That's just what is. And it's the most rewarding job I've ever had.

—*Krista Barton-Arnold, principal, Parkway Elementary School, Virginia Beach, VA*

When Krista Barton-Arnold went to Parkway, it was her third principalship. One of the first things she did was assemble a strong instructional leadership team. "I knew there were strong coaches in the building, and I knew I had teacher leaders, too," she explains. "So organizing them and enabling them to do what they needed to do was something I did right away, because you can't do it on your own, right?" Meeting weekly, the leadership team set and monitored short-term expectations and benchmarks for growth. They engaged in a deep look at student data, created a process for intensive alignment to guide instruction, tracked formative assessment data, and focused on targeted interventions.

A second team, the Shared Inquiry/Transformational Learning Team—consisting of the librarian, the staff member who worked in the school's Dream Lab, the technology specialist, and the gifted resource specialist—focused on supporting teachers with problem-based learning and problem-based assessments. "Problem-based learning encourages student engagement in shared inquiry and sparks students' curiosity, and teachers are happier because they're not doing just drill and kill," Barton-Arnold adds.

In addition to sharing and distributing leadership, she made staffing changes. "I hired people who wanted to be part of a movement," she notes. "They wanted to be part of making change, and they [believed] that with high-quality instruction, these kids would learn to the level of [the students in] whatever previous, more affluent schools those teachers had been in." She also made changes in the school schedule and some tough decisions on the reallocation of resources.

Fast-forward four years. After being on the verge of losing accreditation, Parkway is fully accredited. The school was actually fully accredited after the second year, but according to Barton-Arnold, "we had some warnings in our subgroups—special education being one of them and African American males the other. But last year we had no yellow lights—all green lights in all our subgroup categories."

There's a strong sense of community at Parkway. "There's nobody at Parkway who's like, 'That's not my kid,'" she explains. "If they see someone in the hallway who's upset, they stop and talk to the kid. They figure out what the problem is and try to help the kid solve it." Barton-Arnold's experience and expertise are respected in her district and the region. When she works with other principals, she tells them, "You need credibility, integrity, and trust. And you can't lose any of those or they'll all fall apart."

Building leadership capacity also requires the principal to assume the role of lead learner. The notion of the principal as lead learner is crucial to understanding that in HP/HP schools the work of leadership *is* learning—learning as individuals, as a community, and as a system. Developing a sense of efficacy requires both individual and collective learning.

By building leadership capacity and developing collective efficacy, educators construct the infrastructure needed to improve academic, social, and emotional learning and the learning environment. Use the self-assessment rubric in Figure 5.1 to focus your learning and reflect on your school's current situation.

Finding the Leverage Points

Because HP/HP schools are places of reflection and inquiry, educators' work in these schools is better characterized in the form of questions than formulaic lists of strategies. Six guiding questions can serve as leverage points for building leadership capacity and collective efficacy:

1. How are we developing an inquiry stance and embedding reflection into professional practice?
2. How does our data system support data-informed problem solving?
3. How are we developing relational trust?
4. How are we deploying resources effectively?
5. How are we optimizing time?
6. How are we ensuring equity?

Figure 5.1   Building Leadership Capacity and Collective Efficacy: Assessing Your School's Progress

Progress Indicators/Evidence	No Action Yet	Getting Started	Gaining Momentum	Sustaining Gains, Refining
		• Urgency is apparent. • School status is understood. • A vision for improvement is shared. • Implementation strategies are selected. • Staff is prepared to begin.	• People are empowered. • Barriers are being removed. • Implementation is becoming routine. • Commitment is increasing. • Progress is monitored. • Initial gains are being made and celebrated. • Support for improvement continues.	• Improvements are embedded in daily practice. • Collaboration continues. • Refinements are made. • Gains continue to be made and sustained.
What is my school's progress?	0	1	2	3
Developing an inquiry stance and embedding reflection into professional practice (p. 87)				
Using a data system to inform problem solving (pp. 87–89)				
Developing relational trust (pp. 89–90)				
Recruiting, hiring, and retaining personnel who can disrupt poverty (pp. 90–95)				
Optimizing time (pp. 96–98)				
Ensuring equity in capacity building (pp. 98–99)				

Let's now look at each of these questions in depth.

How Are We Developing an Inquiry Stance and Embedding Reflection into Professional Practice?

All HP/HP schools we studied engage in some form of data-based inquiry. This process typically involves identifying a problem, gathering and analyzing data, setting goals, selecting and implementing strategies, and conducting an evaluation. Although this form of planning is likely used in many schools, what distinguishes HP/HP schools from others is the manner in which such a cycle of inquiry becomes the norm. In these schools, people tend to be curious about their practice and eager to innovate. They continually seek or create solutions to the challenges posed by poverty and are encouraged to take risks. Principals, school leaders, and educators in these schools play a key role in facilitating this work.

As part of the Success for All model at Garfield East and Pugliese West, four "solution teams," known as Leading for Success Teams, engage in an inquiry-based process to address challenges and solve problems. Each team consists of representatives from the school at large. Lynnett Gorman, principal at Pugliese West, says she began with one team focused on attendance. Teams set goals, gather data, study the barriers to meeting the goal, and determine the course of action to take. Although Gorman facilitates the process, teachers are empowered in each team to tackle problems of practice. Gorman elaborates:

> We were giving incentives for perfect attendance, gathering data, and monitoring. The team found the same kids had perfect attendance every quarter, and we were still not getting to the kids who were chronically absent. Teachers determined that we needed to start targeting the kids who are constantly missing. For example, we had a kid who was tardy every day. His mom said his older sister goes to middle school and after she drops her off, she goes home because it's too early to drop him off here. We told her, drop him off. We won't charge for Latch Key (day care); we'll have him reading to our other kids or listening to other kids read. She brings him every single day. He comes early, and she doesn't pay for Latch Key. It's a win-win situation.

How Does Our Data System Support Data-Informed Problem Solving?

All schools in our study implemented data systems to guide their decision making. In fact, using data-based decision making was one of the two most common explanations offered for the schools' success (the other was fostering caring relationships). Constructing and implementing a data system are essential components that move a school toward addressing the underachievement of students living in poverty. HP/HP schools facilitate an ongoing, courageous look in the mirror. These schools have access to accurate, timely data that enable educators to set goals and benchmarks; monitor progress; make midcourse corrections; as well as design and successfully employ effective instruction and targeted interventions.

SCHOOL CULTURE ALERT HP/HP schools use their data to create urgency for the work. "This is the chance for us to say 'Hey, we need to do something!' We can't sit and wait for this to fix itself," explains Marian Reimer Friesen from the Niagara District School Board. "The scores are going to drop again if we don't change something. When you label the need for immediate action, it changes conversations and creates a focus. Sometimes underperforming can give us that little shot in the arm that makes us say, 'Let's go; let's do this!'" ●

North Carolina's Henderson Collegiate trains all teachers to use data using concepts from *Driven by Data 2.0* (Bambrick-Santoyo, 2019). Teachers learn how to collect and use data to make instructional decisions. To inform daily lesson planning and unit design as well as monitor student progress, teachers regularly use exit tickets, quizzes, and unit assessments. Benchmark assessments are administered quarterly. Data from these assessments are analyzed during Data Days, when teachers determine adjustments that need to be made in instruction.

Victoria Bernhardt (2005), a nationally respected authority on data use in schools, suggests four types of data should be accessible: (1) data related to student learning (e.g., classroom-based assessments, standardized test data, teacher observations); (2) data related to perceptions held by stakeholders about the learning environment, as well as about values, beliefs, and attitudes (e.g., surveys and interviews); (3) data related to school and student demographics (e.g., attendance, graduation rates, race/ethnicity, class, gender, level of teaching experience, level of education of teachers); and (4) data related to structures, processes, programs, and policies (e.g., after-school tutoring programs, RTI Tier 2 intervention programs, summer schools).

UNCOMMON SENSE At Evergreen Elementary, as part of the No Excuses University model, common assessment results for all students are aggregated and displayed in the hallway. Principal Jamie Burnett shares their rationale, saying, "Student assessment data are put out in the hallway not by student name, but it shows the level where students are. The idea is being transparent with our data."

Burnett says the conversations changed at that point; people started talking about the test scores and about what they could do for one another. "If somebody wasn't quite getting students to where we expect here at Evergreen," Burnett adds, "something changed. We help one another. We move teachers to a different grade level if that needs to happen, finding the best fit for our teachers." ●

A comprehensive data system uses three types of data tools: student information systems, data warehouses, and instructional management systems. *Student information systems* provide information about such factors as student attendance, discipline referrals, student demographics, student course assignments, and specialized school programs. *Data warehouses* connect multiple databases and allow for longitudinal and comprehensive data analysis. *Instructional management systems* collect data related to ongoing assessment of students in relationship to standards in both individual classrooms and among and between grade levels. Of course, as Bernhardt (2005) notes, "[T]he hard part in selecting data tools is figuring out what you want the tools to do, which tools do what you want, and which tools you need first" (p. 66).

Gaining access to high-quality data tools can be expensive, requiring significant district support. Bernhardt (2005) provides six suggestions that can guide the selection of effective data tools:

- Be clear about what type of tool you're looking for. Are you hoping to find one company that can provide all three types of tools? Do you want to buy them all at once or one at a time?
- Be sure the tools can talk with one another.
- Involve a team with broad membership in the [decision-making] process.
- Research the history and financial stability of possible vendors, and invite them to show the data tools in your environment.
- Stay aware of what you need a data tool to do, and don't automatically go to the lowest bidder.
- Talk with current users. (pp. 68–69)

How Are We Developing Relational Trust?

Anthony Bryk, president of the Carnegie Foundation for the Advancement of Teaching, and colleagues (Bryk, Bender Sebring, Allensworth, Luppescu, & Easton, 2010) contend that "relationships are the lifeblood of activity in a school community" (p. 137). They target trust as the essential building block in the positive relationships that in turn foster authentic school improvement and conclude,

In short, relational trust is forged in day-to-day social exchanges. Through their actions, school participants articulate their sense of obligation toward others, and others in turn begin to reciprocate. Trust grows over time through exchanges in which the expectations held by others are validated by actions. (p. 139)

In an earlier study, Bryk and his colleague Barbara Schneider (2002) defined relational trust as mutual respect, personal regard, competence to do one's job, and integrity. Their longitudinal research measured the degree to which relational trust existed among teachers; among teachers and students; among teachers and families; and among administrators and all three groups (teachers, students, and families). They concluded that schools have a 50 percent chance of improving student achievement if relational trust is high. If that sounds like bad news, it's not. When the level of relational trust is low, schools have a 1 in 7 chance of making any significant gains in student achievement.

Educators in many of the schools we studied spoke of trusting relationships, an extended family-like environment, trust between themselves and students and families, and a sense of community. They pointed to examples of mutual respect between educators and students, integrity in their own and their colleagues' work, and the fact that they felt cared for and they cared for others. Principals described instances where they had to address incompetence to maintain the trust of the faculty and students, such as when they place teachers on improvement plans or when they must work through due process to remove teachers from their assignments.

An educator at Concourse Village says, "We talk to [students] as we would our own kids. It builds trust, and they are able to come to us and say, 'I'm not having a good day, or I made a mistake, or I made a wrong choice and I apologize.'" The school engages in a lot of trust building, both with students and families. That same educator adds, "I love the children. I love the staff. I love the community, the family."

How Are We Deploying Resources Effectively?

Principals in high-performing, high-poverty schools ensure that the necessary financial, material, and human resources are available for students and adults to succeed (Ball, 2001; Leader, 2010). Several leaders in the schools we have studied began their remarkable turnarounds by making tough calls—and many of those decisions were about how to use resources. For example, one school deferred a planned textbook adoption in order to redirect monies to provide literacy coaching and targeted assistance for students. In another instance, a school resisted the all-too-common raid on the monies used for professional learning during a time of "budget tightening." Finally, schools committed to equity figure out how to eliminate enough expenditures from their budgets to provide all students with such things as field trips, band instruments, pay-to-play fees, and school supplies. They not only use the school's existing resources innovatively but also often secure additional funding from the district office and capitalized on relationships with external stakeholders to garner support for the school.

SCHOOL CULTURE ALERT As a matter of practice, leaders in HP/HP schools guide the use of resources by holding fast to the school's vision and goals. The budget in an HP/HP school becomes a moral document, reflective of the school's commitment to equity, as well as its values and beliefs about the conditions necessary to sustain success for all students and the adults who serve them. ●

Finding and Building a Talented Staff

Approximately 70 to 80 percent of a typical school's budget is dedicated to personnel, so it stands to reason that recruitment and retention of talented staff are a top resource management priority. Too often, principals have limited influence over personnel decisions. Teacher assignments are often made by district personnel offices and guided by factors that are not necessarily related to the needs of a school. These factors can include school closings and openings, boundary changes that influence school size and consequently staff size, collective bargaining agreements that favor seniority over teacher and staff qualifications, and the transferring of ineffective teachers from school to school.

When decision making about resources, chiefly personnel, is decentralized to the school level, the principal and other site-based leaders can further their improvement efforts by hiring teachers and staff with qualifications that match the school's needs. Three phases of the personnel process are crucial to consider: recruitment, selection, and retention.

Teacher recruitment. In this phase, principals should consider factors that attract excellent teachers to high-needs schools. Using strategies such as hiring bonuses and housing supplements may be beyond the purview of most principals; however, principals often do have some degree of control over other factors that may lure excellent faculty and staff to their schools. According to a study of 1,700 National Board–certified teachers (Berry,

2008), ensuring that teachers have updated technology, lower class sizes, and opportunities to work with colleagues as a regular part of the school day may entice highly qualified teachers to schools with greater challenges. Teachers who participated in Berry's study maintained, "Supportive principals, freedom to use professional judgment, and a guarantee to work with like-minded and similarly skilled colleagues mean more to good teachers than extra pay" (p. 769).

Teacher selection. When hiring teachers to work with students living in poverty, Howard, Dresser, and Dunklee (2009), authors of *Poverty Is* Not *a Learning Disability*, suggest school leaders (1) begin by identifying the characteristics they are seeking in a candidate, (2) conduct an analysis of their current faculty and staff strengths and weaknesses to clarify what the school needs, (3) seek support from district-level human resource personnel by clearly communicating the school's needs and interests, (4) structure the interview questions to elicit responses that will reveal the candidate's attitudes and values, and (5) take candidates on a short tour of the school to observe how they interact with others and relate to the environment.

Using behavior-based interviewing (BBI) may also be helpful. Mary Clement (2009) claims that BBI provides a "clearer sense of the candidate's suitability for the position, based on the premise that past behavior is the best predictor of future performance. BBI questions begin with the phrases 'tell me about a time when,' 'how have you,' or 'describe your experience with'" (p. 23). Ascertaining candidates' attitudes and values, as well as understanding how their past experiences might shape their future performance, could be especially valuable in determining who would likely be most successful working with students who live in poverty.

Alexa Sorden, principal of Concourse Village, uses a 14-point rubric she developed that outlines the characteristics she looks for when she hires. She requires candidates to teach three demonstration lessons, followed by an interview by a panel of teachers and students. She explains,

> We ask students, "Would you feel comfortable with the person being your teacher? Why? Why not?" The kids will give really good feedback. Then, if the demo lessons are good and teachers and students both agree that this person should move on to the final round, the [candidate] meets with me.

Teacher retention. Once excellent teachers and staff are hired, the challenge then becomes retaining them. Again, principals may have greater control over this dynamic than they believe. Schools with a high percentage of students who live in poverty can be tough places to work. Retaining faculty and staff begins with providing a healthy, safe, and supportive environment in which to work and learn. The challenges are greater than in more affluent schools, but the rewards also can be greater. The work becomes deeply personal for those who stay in such schools—both an asset and a liability for educators.

UNCOMMON SENSE   Recruiting, hiring, and retaining teachers in rural schools and communities can be a challenge. Yet Michele Capps, superintendent and elementary principal in Murtaugh School District, knows hiring excellent teachers has been the key to the PK–12 school's success. She jokes that she has no friends left among area superintendents because of her successful recruiting efforts. Still, not every teacher she hires is from outside the district. She explains, "I raise a lot of teachers. We grow our own. We have paraprofessionals who [we encourage to] get their education, and then we hire them." But most of the teachers she hires come with teaching experience. Indeed, under her leadership, Murtaugh has become a wonderful school not only for students and families, but also for the educators who serve them. Capps is a superintendent who has never forgotten she is also a teacher. ●

Although salaries and benefits are competitive with area school districts, the real secret of Capps's success in hiring and retaining teachers is the professionalism they are afforded. Collaboration is the norm among teachers, and although the district has adopted curricular materials, teachers have a high degree of autonomy with their use. They must teach to the standard, but teachers are not expected to be "on the same page on the same day." Capps has been extremely successful in securing additional resources through grants and partnerships, many of which have been used for professional development. She describes it as adding tools to teachers' tool belts. "We don't expect every teacher to use the same tools," she notes. "I expect them to have really good training. I expect them to be very effective with what they are teaching, and I may even question it at times. If I force them into one mold," she adds, "it's not going to be productive. I found that out. Those aren't the kind of teachers I hire."

Investing in Approaches to Avoid Burnout

Nathan Eklund (2009) studies teachers' job satisfaction and maintains that teachers' sense of calling to the profession both compels them to persist under stressful conditions and places them at risk for burnout. For this reason, high-poverty schools must make a positive staff climate a high priority if they hope to retain the high-quality personnel necessary to develop and sustain leadership capacity. Eklund stresses the need to create an environment in which teachers can regularly tap into the reason they became teachers in the first place. He argues that for most educators, teaching is a calling. He writes, "Teachers come to this work laden with strong beliefs about the work and deeply held convictions about their own self-image" (p. 26). He maintains, "Dedication is admirable, but martyrdom is unsustainable" (p. 27).

To avoid burnout and maintain a balance between home and work, educators who teach in high-poverty schools must attend to their own health and well-being. Pete Selleck, assistant principal at the Preuss School, shares this thought:

> I always preach to the folks about taking care of yourselves and your family first—and *then* we can take care of our children, the students here. I think there's a real balance needed. You've got to find people who care. But if they care too much and they can't find the balance and they can't separate themselves, then when they go home, they take it home with them. They don't last long.

Eklund (2009) provides suggestions for how schools can improve the climate of the workplace for teachers and staff, as well as how individuals can better maintain a balance between their work and their life outside school. He encourages teachers and school staff to work together to set norms of behavior, learn how to resolve conflict, celebrate their work, and use collegial hiring processes.

SCHOOL CULTURE ALERT   HP/HP schools manage to retain high-quality faculty and staff using multiple and varied approaches, but they make all relationships a priority and establish norms of personal regard and mutual respect. ●

Warren Hoshizaki is the director of education for the District School Board of Niagara, Ontario, Canada, where E.I. McCulley Public School is located. Hoshizaki has a rule that helps the passionate area superintendents he leads set boundaries. "We stop communication on Friday night at 6 p.m. until Sunday at 6 p.m. It really helps not only with balance, but also with what you're going to do the next week." Superintendents are not to send texts or e-mail messages to their principals unless there is a crisis. Marian Reimer Friesen, one of those superintendents, tells all the principals she supervises, "Just stop. Leave everybody alone unless it's an emergency. Help create a system of wellness." Her rule is intended for weekdays as well as weekends—no communication after 6 p.m. unless it's absolutely necessary.

Another way to attend to educators' emotional well-being is to make certain everyone has the knowledge and skills needed to be successful.

People do not want to work in a school where they cannot be successful. In a high-poverty school, this means everyone is given an opportunity to develop an accurate understanding of poverty so they're prepared for the complex challenges that poverty poses. It also means opportunities for learning are job embedded, focused on student work, and conducted in collaboration with peers.

After Marian Reimer Friesen selected four schools to be part of the School Board of Niagara's Focus School Initiative, she met with each principal and let them know that she would be coming to their schools every two weeks to spend a half day with each one of them. The principals were ambivalent about this, concerned at first that she was questioning their ability to lead. As Reimer Friesen explains,

> A lot of things started to bubble up, so I just kept talking with them and told them, "We'll figure it out as we go; we will build it together into something that works for you and for your staff." As soon as they realized that my role was to take away what comes after the word "but," they began to believe I viewed this as support. So if they said, "I'd really love to be able to support these kids, *but* we need more time for small-group instruction," I would reply, "I can provide that. I'll provide the money so you can bring in teachers so you can make those small groups."

Principals in HP/HP schools model reciprocal accountability, and so do district leaders who effectively support them. With the leadership of Reimer Friesen, all of the schools that took part in the initiative have made significant improvement, particularly E.I. McCulley. Educators at the schools noted, "When the culture is right, you love coming to work. These are not easy environments to teach in, and it's difficult some days to not take that home with you. But when the culture is right, we're all pulling together."

Rarely does a principal take the helm of a high-poverty school with the opportunity to wipe the slate clean and hire an entirely new faculty and staff of like-minded individuals. In *Good to Great*, a study of leadership in successful private and public organizations, author Jim Collins (2001) says "getting the right people on the bus" is vital to an organization's success. This goal can require leaders to move some of the current occupants off the bus. (See Chapter 8 for a discussion of how leaders have addressed ineffective teaching.)

SCHOOL CULTURE ALERT Although they use different approaches, principals in HP/HP schools challenge teachers who do not hold high expectations for their students or themselves and suggest that they need to get on board, find another school, or pursue another line of work if they can't improve. •

How Are We Optimizing Time?

The manner in which time is used is closely linked to retention of high-quality staff. In *The Principal as Curriculum Leader*, Allan Glatthorn and Jerry Jailall (2010) assert, "[T]hey who control the schedule control the school's resources" (p. 87). All students are likely to benefit from improving the quality of academic learning time, and those who live in poverty may require more instructional time to catch up to their higher-achieving peers. Teachers also need time to learn, especially in collaboration with others. The manner in which time is used can influence teachers' working conditions and their sense of efficacy. Teacher learning and student learning are two sides of the same coin. When teachers are afforded time to learn collaboratively, they can, in turn, optimize academic learning time within the school day and best plan for student learning outside the school day.

Extending academic learning time can occur in at least two ways—literally extending the available time for students to learn or better using the time within the traditional school day. High-performing, high-poverty schools do both. First of all, they find a way to extend learning time for students who need it. The schools offer a blend of before- and after-school tutoring, weekend and vacation catch-up sessions, summer school, full-day kindergarten, preschool, and sheltered classroom support. All the schools we studied find a way to extend learning time before or after school, and both Henderson Collegiate and Preuss use Saturday morning to address the needs of students and families. Summer instruction in particular may be as important as any extended-time intervention because it serves to maintain continuous learning, counters the loss of achievement gains caused by long gaps in schooling, and provides needed nutrition and other auxiliary supports (Borman & Dowling, 2006).

In addition to extending learning time, educators in HP/HP schools are vigilant about protecting time for learning during the school day. In schools in general, time for academic learning is lost to holiday celebrations, assemblies, announcements, testing, and too much review of old information. In a study of teachers' classroom practices conducted by Richard Elmore (2006) and his colleagues from Harvard, teaching new content occupied between 0 and 40 percent of the scheduled instructional time. Elmore claims that teachers spend a great deal of time on tasks other than instruction of new material, such as overseeing student seatwork, fulfilling administrative tasks, and listening to announcements on the intercom. He argues,

> [T]he use of time in classrooms is a measure of the respect adults have for the role of learning in the lives of students. It would be an enormous step forward if adults in the schools treated the time that children and their families give to schools as a precious gift rather than an entitlement. (p.7)

Academic learning time also is lost to the "end-of-year letdown" common in many schools, when instruction of new content ceases two to four weeks before the end of the school year (Elmore, 2006). All these practices considered, Elmore estimated that during a school year, between 245 and 450 hours (50 to 90 days) of academic learning time are lost.

UNCOMMON SENSE   Alexa Sorden, principal of Concourse Village, subtracted the time teachers were not with students (lunch, recess, preparation time) from their contracted day of 6 hours and 20 minutes—and found that the teachers really spent only about 4 hours of their day with students. She frames the discussion this way: "If you're a person who becomes overwhelmed by whatever is happening in your life and you can't give me four hours for 180 amazing days— because it's really four hours—then you're in the wrong business." •

As is true of a school's budget, the schedule is a reflection of what the school values and how it prioritizes competing objectives. Educators attempting to create the conditions necessary to raise the achievement of all students—particularly those living in poverty—might begin by developing a learning-centered schedule that encompasses a commitment to protect academic learning time. The following list reflects strategies educators have told us they use:

- Initiate bell-to-bell teaching (planned transitions and no downtime).
- Reduce scheduled and unscheduled interruptions.
- Be strategic about scheduling testing.
- Minimize the use of pull-out intervention.
- Do not schedule activities that require students to be released early.

Some schools and districts raise their consciousness about how time is used by taking a blank calendar and blacking out all the days that have traditionally been used for activities other than academic learning, such as weekends, holidays, summer vacations, parent-teacher conferences, holiday celebrations, school assemblies, testing, and other events. Schools may also want to conduct their own study of the use of classroom time by observing classrooms bell-to-bell on a sampling of days throughout the school year. Gathering such data might develop the sense of urgency needed to stimulate action. In addition, the National Center on Time and Learning provides rubrics, guidebooks, and time analysis tools that educators may find helpful for optimizing time.

Developing a learning-centered schedule is important not only to support higher-quality academic learning time for students, but also to provide time for professional learning. Time for collaborative professional learning, while important in any school, is especially important in HP/HP schools. Karin Chenoweth (2009b) from the Education Trust explains:

> The traditional organization of schools, which relies on isolated teachers doing their jobs with little interference and less support, means individual students are totally reliant on the knowledge and skills of their individual teachers. . . . Because middle-class students bring more social capital than students of poverty, this tradition of isolation, on average, hurts them less. . . . For the most part, parents living in poverty leave education to the schools—not because they don't care about their children's education but because they often don't feel competent to challenge the knowledge of teachers and because they're more likely to be overwhelmed with the daily logistics of life. This means low-income children are often completely reliant on their schools for their education. When schools understand that and step up to the challenge . . . and set up the structures and systems that allow teachers to work together, even students burdened by poverty and discrimination can achieve remarkable success. (pp. 42–43)

Schools must find ways to reorganize time to support the development of communities of practice (Wenger, 1998) that are consistent with the circumstances of their context. They can repurpose time that is traditionally set aside for faculty meetings, reorganize the schedule to accommodate common planning time, bank time for professional development, or locate funds for ongoing released time. Principal leadership in this area is crucial. Improving student learning requires more than competent individuals. To build leadership capacity throughout the school, principals need to focus their energy on creating the conditions necessary for teachers to work collaboratively.

District-level leaders can support site-based educators' better use of time by collaborating with them in the development of a learning-centered schedule. Scenario planning can be useful here. Scenario planning is a process by which policy-level leaders work with those who will implement the policy to lay out multiple possibilities—in this case, multiple master schedules with their accompanying policy options and budget implications. Scenario planning gives practitioners a voice in the process and policymakers an opportunity to better understand the implications of various policies.

How Are We Ensuring Equity?

To transform a low-performing, high-poverty school into a high-performing school, leadership must be shared, distributed, reciprocal—and equity focused. Such leadership begins with educators who have answered the question, as Parker Palmer (2007) puts it, "Who is the self that leads?" Understanding one's self means understanding one's mental maps, which entails facing personal biases and blind spots. Then such leaders ask a second vital question: "Why am I engaged in this work?" The embodiment of leadership cannot be separated from the leader's purpose, for good or for bad. Equity-focused educators build leadership capacity and collective efficacy for moral purposes.

For example, when we consider how leaders in HP/HP schools deployed human resources, we noted they were consciously making the choice to tackle the all-too-often entrenched practice of assigning teachers on the basis of seniority or on some perceived sense of having earned the right to only teach students who are not underachieving or those in advanced classes where students living in poverty are often underrepresented. They challenged the status quo and assigned the most effective teachers to the most vulnerable students, all while building the collective capacity of the entire faculty.

Moreover, questions such as "How are we fostering relational trust?" should compel us to ask, "Is there mutual respect among everyone in the school community?" Or, more to the point, "Is there mutual respect between educators and families who live in poverty?" Too often our prejudices and biases get in the way of developing such mutual respect.

Conducting an equity audit might result in useful data for high-poverty schools aiming to address inequities. An equity audit provides a "systematic way for school leaders—principals, superintendents, curriculum directors, and teacher leaders—to assess the degree of equity or inequity present in three key areas of their schools or districts: programs, teacher quality, and achievement" (Skrla, McKenzie, & Scheurich, 2009, p. 3). Equity audits can also provide useful data for answering equity-focused questions by confronting and eliminating policies, practices, and programs that are likely to perpetuate underachievement for students living in poverty. This often provides clear focus and a starting point for any school concerned with addressing inequity.

The Principal's Role

Although developing leadership capacity requires that educators from various vantage points within the school work together (such distributed and shared leadership is inherent to leadership capacity), the principal's role is vital. Principals, by virtue of the authority typically granted them, are in a unique position to be the catalyst for improvement through the creation of conditions that make it possible to develop further capacity in leadership.

Figure 5.2   The Principal's Role in Building Leadership Capacity in HP/HP Schools

The principal—
- Begins the conversation about what is possible in a high-poverty school.
- Guides the development of a shared vision of high levels of learning for all.
- Is the chief steward of the vision for the school, keeping it alive and in the forefront of any rationale for action.
- Acknowledges that he or she cannot "go it alone," recognizing the important opportunity others have to influence/lead from various vantage points throughout the system.
- Shares decision-making authority and governance of the school.
- Acts out of a commitment to equity.
- Fosters interdependent relationships of reciprocal accountability with other stakeholders.
- Uses his or her formal authority to ensure school structures and processes are in place to build capacity in individuals and in the system, including the following:
  » Management of the school's budget in a manner that reflects collectively identified priorities, values, beliefs, and goals;
  » Personnel practices that recruit and retain high-quality teachers, not the least of which is an emphasis on trust building through relationships of mutual respect;
  » Construction of school schedules and calendars that are learning focused—for students and adults;
  » Use of data that allows for informed, shared decision making in the classroom and schoolwide; and
  » Use of data to prompt essential conversations about equity and the elimination of counterproductive practices.
- Uses data to provide evidence of the impact of collective teacher action on student learning.
- Engages in conversations with teachers about the use of dependable evidence and the difference between achievement, goals, and progress (Donohoo, Hattie, & Eells, 2018).

Figure 5.2 describes the actions that principals in HP/HP schools take to ensure resources are effectively managed, time is well used, and data-based decision making becomes the norm.

 Taking Action

- *Consider your school's budget.* Do you consider your budget a moral document? Does it reflect your values, goals, and priorities as a school?
- *Create and act with a sense of urgency.* Are the needs of your students who underperform known and being addressed?
- *Evaluate your hiring practices.* Do they result in hiring personnel who match the needs of the school?
- *Take action to retain talented personnel.* Have you taken stock of the ways your school encourages talented people to stay?
- *Hold high expectations.* Have you evaluated current practices that ensure all teachers hold high expectations for their students and themselves?

- *Provide extended learning time.* Have you explored ways to extend learning time for students who need that extra time?
- *Analyze your school calendar.* Is it learning centered and focused on the needs of students who underachieve?
- *Provide time for professional learning.* Have you reorganized the schedule and calendar to provide job-embedded professional learning opportunities?
- *Analyze the way decisions are made.* Are multiple forms of data used to make instructional decisions in the classroom and systemic decisions schoolwide?
- *Conduct an equity audit.* Have you assessed how equitably your school is meeting all students' needs?

6 Fostering a Healthy, Safe, and Supportive Learning Environment

We need faculty and staff who can talk to the kids and bring them out. They don't get here with a backpack of books. They come with a backpack of issues from home. We need to know how to work with those students.

—EJ Martinez, principal, Stillman Middle School, Brownsville, TX

To learn, children and adolescents need to feel safe and supported. Without these conditions, the mind reverts to a focus on survival. Educators in high-performing, high-poverty schools have always recognized the need for providing a healthy, safe, and supportive environment for academic as well as for social and emotional learning (SEL). Figure 6.1 provides a crosswalk between the Framework for Collective Action and the Indicators of Schoolwide SEL integration as recommended by the Collaborative for Academic, Social, and Emotional Learning (CASEL). CASEL defines SEL as

> the process through which children and adults acquire and effectively apply the knowledge, attitudes, and skills necessary to understand and manage emotions, set and achieve positive goals, feel and show empathy for others, establish and maintain positive relationships, and make responsible decisions. (2019)

The purpose of the crosswalk is to demonstrate the way in which HP/HP schools integrate SEL schoolwide. The HP/HP schools we studied are examplars of creating the conditions for academic, social, and emotional learning to flourish.

Recognizing the Importance of Social-Emotional Learning

Fueling the recognition of the importance of SEL was the passage by the U.S. Congress of the Every Student Succeeds Act. This 2015 reauthorization

Figure 6.1   Crosswalk: Schoolwide SEL and HP/HP Schools

HP/HP Sphere of Influence	CASEL Indicator of Schoolwide SEL	HP/HP Arena of Action	Examples in *Turning High-Poverty Schools into High-Performing Schools* for Integrating SEL Schoolwide
Classroom	Explicit SEL instruction—Students have consistent opportunities to cultivate, practice, and reflect on social and emotional competencies in ways that are developmentally and culturally responsive.	Learning Environment	Recognizing the importance of social and emotional learning (pp. 102–106 with examples of SEL program use in a West Coast school on p. 105 and Parkway Elementary on p. 106)
	SEL integration with academic instruction—SEL objectives are integrated into instructional content and teaching strategies for academics as well as music, art, and physical education.	Learning	• Using a "pedagogy of possibility" (pp. 135–150) (see also the example from Concourse Village on pp. 135–136) • Developing a common understanding of excellence in teaching (pp. 140–141) • Engaging and empowering students (pp. 141–142)
	Youth voice and engagement—Staff honor and elevate a broad range of student perspectives and experiences by engaging students as leaders, problem solvers, and decision makers.	Learning & Learning Environment	• Engaging students in schoolwide improvement of behavior (example from an East Coast school on p. 109) • Involving students in the hiring process (example from Concourse Village p. 92) • Increasing participation in extracurricular activities (p. 116; see Stillman MS p. 116) • Engaging students in the community (pp. 124–126) • Elevating student voice (see "mirrors [see themselves] and windows [see a future]" example from Parkway on pp. 27–28)
School	Supportive school and classroom climates—Schoolwide and classroom learning environments are supportive, culturally responsive, and focused on building relationships and community.	Leadership Capacity & Learning Environment	• Developing relational trust (pp. 89–90) • Finding and building a talented staff (pp. 91–93 with examples Concourse Village Elementary and Murtaugh School District on pp. 92–93) • Strengthening the bond between students and schools (pp. 111–112) • Fostering caring relationships (pp. 113–114) • Creating safe and supportive school cultures (see E.I. McCulley Elementary, pp. 116–117; and Murtaugh School, pp. 32–35)
	Focus on adult SEL—Staff have regular opportunities to cultivate their own social, emotional, and cultural competence; collaborate with one another, building trusting relationships; and maintain a strong community.	Leadership Capacity & Learning	• Investing in approaches to avoid burnout (pp. 93–94); example of District School Board of Niagara, p. 94) • Using learning-centered schedules (pp. 97–98; see also Henderson Collegiate MS, pp. 42–44) • Ensuring safety (see reference to a study on teachers' working conditions on pp. 110–111) • Collaboration, trust, and community building (example from Concourse Village on pp. 132–133) • Communities of practice (p. 148) • The importance of the teacher (pp. 148–150) • Providing job-embedded opportunity for professional learning (pp. 155–156), includes an example from Concourse Village (p. 156)

(continued)

Figure 6.1 (*continued*)

HP/HP Sphere of Influence	CASEL Indicator of Schoolwide SEL	HP/HP Arena of Action	Examples in *Turning High-Poverty Schools into High-Performing Schools* for Integrating SEL Schoolwide
School (*cont.*)	Supportive discipline—Discipline policies and practices are instructive, restorative, developmentally appropriate, and equitably applied.	Leadership Capacity & Learning Environment	• Recognizing the importance of social and emotional learning (pp. 102–108) • Ensuring safety (pp. 109–111)
	A continuum of integrated supports—SEL is seamlessly integrated into a continuum of academic and behavioral supports, which are available to ensure that all student needs are met.	Leadership Capacity & Learning Environment & Learning	• Ensuring safety (pp. 109–111) • Starting student advisories (pp. 114–115) • Creating smaller learning environments (pp. 115–116) • Becoming a trauma-informed school (pp. 112–113, with an example from Lillian Peterson Elementary) • Providing targeted interventions for students who need them (pp. 153–155) • Using systems (see Evergreen Elementary, pp. 22–24)
Family & Community	Authentic family partnerships—Families and school staff have regular and meaningful opportunities to build relationships and collaborate to support students' social, emotional, and academic development.	Leadership Capacity & Learning Environment	• Engaging parents, families, and caregivers (pp. 116–118 with an example on addressing family mobility (p. 117); and another example reconnecting with family needs with school resources from East Garfield Elementary (pp. 31–32) • Creating links between school and home (pp. 119–122) using technology at Parkway Elementary (p. 119) Saturday parent meetings at The Preuss School (p. 120), and conducting home visits on pp. 122–124
	Aligned Community Partnerships—School staff and community partners align on common language, strategies, and communication around all SEL-related efforts and initiatives, including out-of-school time.	Leadership Capacity & Learning Environment & Learning	• Creating full-service schools and safety nets (pp. 118–119) • Offering students multiple experiences for connecting with community (pp. 124–126) with an example from The Preuss School (pp. 124–126); Pass Christian HS (p. 126)
	Systems for Continuous Improvement—Implementation and outcome data are collected and used to continuously improve all SEL-related systems, practices, and policies with a focus on equity.	Leadership Capacity	• Using "solution teams" with examples from Pugliese West Elementary and East Garfield Elementary (p. 87) • Developing leadership teams with an example from Parkway Elementary leadership (pp. 84–85) • Developing an inquiry stance and embedding reflection into professional practice (pp. 82–83) • Using data-informed problem solving (pp. 87–89) • Ensuring equity (pp. 98–99; 126–128; 156–157)

of the Elementary and Secondary Schools Act energized the likelihood that more states and schools will expand their definitions of student success to include core competencies in social and emotional learning and foster the environment and climate necessary to develop such competencies.

Recommendations of the National Commission on Social, Emotional, and Academic Development (Berman, Chaffee, & Sarmiento, 2018) read as though they were inspired by the HP/HP schools we have studied. The commission suggests the following:

1. Social, emotional, and academic development is for all students;
2. Social, emotional, and academic development for students starts with adults;
3. Strong leadership is central;
4. Explicit and embedded instruction and a caring classroom and school climate develop social, emotional, and academic competencies; and
5. Home-school-community partnerships matter.

One HP/HP elementary school in a West Coast state uses the acronym CARES to express how they support social, emotional, and academic learning. CARES stands for Cooperation, Assertion, Responsibility, Empathy, and Self-Control. CARES provides the entire school community with a common language and common norms. Students, families, and educators alike live their "CARES."

HP/HP schools focus on the importance of developing supportive, positive relationships with their students. Educators in these schools know that "being there" for the kids is perhaps the most important action they can take. In the decade since our initial study, educators in HP/HP schools, together with the students and families they serve, are facing new challenges, such as the opioid crisis, gun violence and school shootings, and the effects of the political context surrounding immigration. As Pete Selleck, assistant principal of Preuss, explains,

> Over 100 of our kids are in therapy now. We have our own therapist, and we partner with local agencies and the university for the rest, but we still need more. We have three counselors, two ed-specialists, and a family support specialist; none of that was here in our early years. I've always talked about the 4 Ds—Debt, Disease, Divorce, and Drugs and Alcohol—that affect every family. And so now there's a fifth D—Deportation and the fear associated with losing your parents, being alone, being constantly afraid. Most of our kids are Hispanic, and 95 percent live in poverty. It's hard. We've really changed our mindset about trauma and kids who are suffering with depression and anxiety, and we're wrapping our services around them, trying to support them.

Educators maintain their resiliency by attending to their own health and well-being, as challenging as that can be in the context of a high-poverty school. They understand that for many children and adolescents, school is the safest, most friendly, and most comforting place in their lives. And the degree to which students feel safe and supported is directly proportional to their learning.

Each of the 12 HP/HP schools we studied places a high priority on attending to all aspects of safety and security. They ensure the physical safety of students and staff through the maintenance of secure facilities, positive behavior supports, restorative justice practices, character education, trauma-informed approaches, anti-bullying programs, as well as explicit and integrated systems to support the development of social and emotional competencies. As a part of the Responsive Classroom model, teachers at Parkway Elementary engaged in a book study of *The Power of Our Words* (Denton, 2013). At the conclusion of the book study, they committed to using "teacher language" that prompts students to self-regulate and empowers them to "own" their learning and behavior. The teachers also committed to holding Morning Meetings, which provide students with an opportunity to develop social and emotional awareness as well as practice emerging skills.

Ensuring a healthy, safe, and supportive environment also often includes providing food, clean clothes, medical attention, counseling and other family services, and, most of all, caring adults who create an atmosphere of sincere support. In turn, these wraparound services not only foster well-being but also support academic success.

SCHOOL CULTURE ALERT   Educators in HP/HP schools operate with a fierce sense of urgency and expect the same from their colleagues. As Alexa Sorden from Concourse Village shares, "We all have a sense of urgency for the work that needs to be done. There should be a sense of respect and seriousness for the children who are in front of us—and the urgency to teach them." ●

Comprehensive support derives from a "whatever it takes" mindset. Educators in HP/HP schools adhere to the key principle of continuous improvement—acknowledging that the work is never completely done—and ask five key questions to guide their actions:

1. How are we ensuring safety?
2. How are we developing an accurate understanding of poverty? (See Chapter 3.)
3. How are we strengthening the bond between students and school?
4. How are we engaging parents, families, and caregivers?
5. How are we engaging the broader community?
6. How are we ensuring equity?

A healthy, safe, and supportive learning environment enables students, adults, and the school as a whole to learn in powerful ways. Such an environment promotes innovation, inquiry, and risk taking. Moreover, such an environment enhances the leadership capacity in the school because competent, excellent, and dedicated educators want to work under such conditions.

Is your school fostering a healthy, safe, and supportive learning environment? Use the self-assessment rubric shown in Figure 6.2 to reflect on your school's current situation.

Let's now look at each of the five key questions in more depth.

Figure 6.2   Fostering a Healthy, Safe, and Supportive Learning Environment: Assessing Your School's Progress

Progress Indicators or Evidence	No Action Yet	Getting Started	Gaining Momentum	Sustaining Gains, Refining
		• Urgency is apparent. • School status is understood. • A vision for improvement is shared. • Implementation strategies are selected. • Staff is prepared to begin.	• People are empowered. • Barriers are being removed. • Implementation is becoming routine. • Commitment is increasing. • Progress is monitored. • Initial gains are being made and celebrated. • Support for improvement continues.	• Improvements are embedded in daily practice. • Collaboration continues. • Refinements are made. • Gains continue to be made and sustained.
What is my school's progress?	**0**	**1**	**2**	**3**
Integrating SEL schoolwide (pp. 102–108)				
Ensuring physical, emotional, and psychological safety (p. 109–111)				
Developing an understanding of the adverse effects of poverty on learning (Chapter 3)				

(continued)

Figure 6.2 (*continued*)

Progress Indicators or Evidence	No Action Yet	Getting Started	Gaining Momentum	Sustaining Gains, Refining
		• Urgency is apparent. • School status is understood. • A vision for improvement is shared. • Implementation strategies are selected. • Staff is prepared to begin.	• People are empowered. • Barriers are being removed. • Implementation is becoming routine. • Commitment is increasing. • Progress is monitored. • Initial gains are being made and celebrated. • Support for improvement continues.	• Improvements are embedded in daily practice. • Collaboration continues. • Refinements are made. • Gains continue to be made and sustained.
Using trauma-informed practices (pp. 112–113)				
Providing student advisories (pp. 114–115)				
Creating smaller learning environments (pp. 115–116)				
Increasing participation in extracurricular activities (p. 116)				
Creating a full-service school (pp. 118–119)				
Creating links between school and home (pp. 119–122)				
Conducting home visits (pp. 122–124)				
Engaging the community (pp. 124–125)				
Offering adult mentoring for students (pp. 125–126)				
Using the school as a community center (p. 126)				
Ensuring equity in creating a healthy, safe, and supportive learning environment (pp. 126–128)				

How Are We Ensuring Safety?

Safety, which we once assumed as a given in the vast majority of U.S. schools, can no longer be taken for granted. With all the school shootings in the news and the resultant deaths of so many students and educators, schools are confronted with the harrowing reality that they must now place the safety of their students and staff above all else. This requires thoughtful and constant attention to the security and safety of the facilities; creation of clear policies and procedures for student and staff conduct; frequent and effective communication with parents, families, and the school community; and attention to classroom management along with the requisite professional development. Without these conditions in place, learning cannot become a school's focus.

In the HP/HP schools we studied, the educators emphasized safety for students and staff as a prerequisite for learning. As one high school principal of a West Coast school shared with us,

> I was scared at times when I first arrived here. The gangs seemingly had control of the place. Teachers were afraid to discipline kids because their cars would get keyed. Neighboring schools had to hire security folks to escort their teams here for athletic events, and the worst was that a lot of our kids did not have a safe place to learn.

A principal from a middle school on the East Coast expressed similar concerns, explaining, "In the beginning, kids would hold their bladders all day out of fear of what might happen to them in the bathrooms." To help students become accountable for their actions, that school established structures, such as the frequent presence of school staff in bathrooms and hallways. By clearly setting expectations and modeling appropriate behavior and good citizenship, staff encouraged students to help promote school safety, which contributed to changing students' perspectives. Instead of "ratting out" their friends, they were part of promoting good behavior schoolwide; they engaged in civic responsibility to their school.

To ensure a safe learning environment, the educators attend to all aspects of daily life in schools. They ensure safety at bus stops and on playgrounds, as well as in lunchrooms, bathrooms, hallways, and classrooms. Matthew Mayer and Dewey Cornell (2010) refer to teasing, hateful language, and social exclusion as factors of "low-level incivility that impact a student's adjustment and psychological well-being" (p. 8). Through daily vigilance, consistent consequences, and continual monitoring of progress with frequent midcourse corrections by the adults, HP/HP schools wage war on such low-level incivility.

Still, the schools report that they did not become truly safe until the students came to believe that destructive behaviors would not be tolerated. Only then did students feel comfortable enough to trust one another and join the adults in collectively working against inappropriate behavior. As a principal of an HP/HP school on the West Coast explains, "Once the kids let the other kids (particularly new kids) know that we don't do that stuff in our school, it all began to change. They were taking responsibility for their school and liked the way that felt."

SCHOOL CULTURE ALERT Although staff must be aware of early warning signs of harassment and bullying and act swiftly to intervene if warranted, this awareness, action, and timely intervention will only happen when trust has developed and relationships of mutual respect have been formed between students and adults. Establishing daily contact and demonstrating concern for each child provide a comfort zone for communication between teacher and student. •

The educators in the HP/HP schools we visited and those in other studies report that their concerted mission to eliminate aberrant behavior required daily attention in the early weeks and months. Their tenacity in successfully addressing students' negative behaviors paid off. Discipline referrals dropped, overall behavior improved, and relationships of mutual respect became the norm in the school culture.

They also explain that as instruction became more focused and relevant, student engagement in learning improved, which, in turn, had a positive effect on behavior. When children and adolescents willingly engage in productive learning experiences in their classrooms, such as solving a challenging math problem, writing a compelling introduction to an essay, or grasping how a consonant blend works, they begin to see value in learning and experience success. At that point, their need to act out or disengage diminishes. The negative behavior is replaced by a newfound confidence that success in a classroom or course is something the student can actually attain. This phenomenon accounts for why, even in a highly dysfunctional school characterized by rampant misbehavior, some teachers are still able to maintain respectful, productive classrooms. These environments become islands of safety for the kids fortunate enough to be in them. High-performing, high-poverty schools strive to create a similar atmosphere of safety and security schoolwide.

Ensuring school safety goes hand in hand with developing optimal working conditions for teachers and staff. In 2006, Eric Hirsch and Scott Emerick examined working conditions for teachers in North Carolina and produced a report titled *Teacher Working Conditions Are Student Learning Conditions.* Not surprisingly, they found that student learning increases when schools create safe, supportive, and trusting school climates. They also found that teachers and staff viewed such a climate as directly related to their working conditions; when the school felt safe and trusting, they felt compelled to do all they could to enhance student learning. Educators in HP/HP schools optimize the link between professional learning and student learning; ensuring safety for all learners—students and adults— becomes a priority.

Once the establishment of a safe learning environment is underway, the challenging work of improving instruction can happen. As an HP/HP middle school principal in the East explains, "Once we reestablished law and order, we were poised to take off. It's our foundation . . . we had to get it fixed, and we did."

How Are We Strengthening the Bond Between Students and School?

It's 6 a.m., and three kids are waiting at the door for their math teacher to arrive. They each received a call on their cell phones the night before reminding them that their work was late and that they needed to get in early to finish it. Reminders like these are not unusual from their math teacher. The kids know he keeps close track of their progress, and although they may not always appreciate those reminders, they show up. As one principal noted, "If my kids don't get through this class, they won't graduate, and that means losing their dreams. We have to help them keep those dreams. It's the most important work we do."

UNCOMMON SENSE   Concerned with the growth of school cliques and their negative influence, students at a West Coast high school approached school leaders for support. Their plan was to launch several student clubs that would foster a more inclusive environment and develop a sense of belonging for students, particularly those who were feeling excluded. They created four clubs: a leadership club, a sports club, a club led by Latinx students, and a Gay/Straight Alliance club. These provided opportunities for students to become more engaged in their school, and the clubs' success is a reflection of the school's celebration of equity, diversity, and unity. ●

HP/HP schools are trauma-informed schools that foster caring relationships, start student advisories, create smaller learning environments, and increase the likelihood of student participation in extracurricular opportunities. Each of these components strengthens the bond between students and school.

Becoming a Trauma-Informed School

We now have unprecedented awareness of and concern for the millions of students who have experienced various forms of trauma in their childhood and adolescent years. The effects of trauma accompany the child to school. Although many public schools have for decades focused on trauma and the social and emotional needs of their kids, it's only recently that becoming a trauma-informed school has gained traction in mainstream public education.

According to the National Child Traumatic Stress Network (2008b), "One out of every four children attending school has been exposed to a traumatic event that can affect learning and/or behavior." The organization promotes "trauma-informed school systems that provide prevention and early intervention strategies to create supportive and nurturing school environments." Their Child Trauma Toolkit for Educators (2008a) includes information on a wide range of traumatic events, including physical or sexual abuse, abandonment, life-threatening violence in a caregiver, bullying, witnessing or experiencing community violence, and living in chronically chaotic environments, to name a few.

The National Child Traumatic Stress Network cautions that following exposure to traumatic experiences, students may demonstrate behaviors of reexperiencing the event, avoiding engagement, developing negative attitudes toward pleasurable activities, or being in a state of heightened alert or arousal. Each of these behaviors can render participating in classroom learning a distant reality for the child.

Adverse childhood experiences (ACEs) reflect multiple types of traumatic experience in people under the age of 18. In 2018, approximately one in seven children had an adverse childhood experience. Although children in poverty are five times more likely to experience adverse childhood experiences than their more affluent peers (National Centers for Disease Control, 2019), not all children or adolescents living in poverty experience trauma. ACEs can be assessed through the ACEs Quiz, which is frequently used in schools and districts.

The HP/HP schools we studied have actively worked to increase educator and staff awareness of and sensitivity to trauma in their students and to intervene appropriately. One teacher we spoke with told us about how hard she worked "to develop a community of safety in my classroom where kids can come in and cry about something, and their classmates hover around them and try to help [them] be more successful." It's not surprising to observe a heightened level of capacity in these schools to address the impacts of trauma on their students; the elevated value they place on building and maintaining relationships with their students; the supports they have constructed to foster enhanced relationships; and the frequent, targeted professional learning they engage in to enhance their instructional effectiveness in supporting academic, social, and emotional learning.

A teacher at Peterson Elementary points to the difficulties that some of her students have to deal with. "We could cry all day with them. It's that horrible," she says. "But we help them see themselves on the other side of the crisis, [that] they're going to be successful and have a great life ahead of them. Being able to see for them and believe it for them and help bring them along, it's huge."

UNCOMMON SENSE   "I remember a student who would crawl in my lap and cry because of stuff going on, yet he was able to grow so much that year because of the support and the relationships that we foster in our school," shares a Lillian Peterson teacher. "If students can't do their work in their class, they have an option to go to other 'buddy classes.' My student would go to his previous classroom where he felt comfortable and really calm down and get back to being productive. Or he could go to the Panther Den."

Peterson Elementary teachers allow their students, when having a bad day, to get to a place where they can find peace. The school's Panther Den is a dedicated, fully staffed room where kids can go any time to find calm. It's outfitted with bean bags, comfortable seating, and calming music and lighting—and a welcoming staff member is there to help. Peterson teachers also use oximeters to check their students' heart rates. "We teach zones of regulation here," the teacher explains. "If students' heart rates are between 60 and 100, they can learn; it's within their zone of regulation. If they're above 100, they need to get calmed, and that's why we have the buddy classes and Panther Den." ●

Fostering Caring Relationships

"They didn't know my name; they didn't care if I slept in class or even if I came to class," is a too common refrain voiced by students in public secondary schools in the United States. Yet, this refrain isn't heard in HP/HP schools, where a premium is placed on relationships. Eric Sanchez, director of Henderson Collegiate, explains how important student culture is "when it comes to the foundation of the school because if you're ahead in that, instruction will catch up. If you're ahead in instruction but your student culture stinks, you can't go the reverse route."

So relationships are your first best strategy. Building caring, trusting relationships between you and your students reflects the most powerful strategy for teaching any student, but especially those who live in poverty. A healthy, authentic relationship between teacher and student can result in increased effort and motivation, increased resilience and risk taking, and improved academic achievement (Budge & Parrett, 2018).

SCHOOL CULTURE ALERT   The HP/HP schools that we studied considered "protective factors" as paramount to their successes. Central among these factors is the promotion of caring relationships between adults and students as well as among peers. Far too many children, particularly at the secondary level, attend school in large impersonal settings where students can too easily become lost. ●

SCHOOL CULTURE ALERT   When children and adolescents know their teachers care about them and are trying their best to relate to the realities of their lives, they become far more inclined to trust and actively engage in learning. ●

Starting Student Advisories

Positive, productive, and caring relationships are indeed possible in secondary schools, but they don't just happen. At The Preuss School, the educators were committed to making the school more personal and helping students meet high expectations. So they created a highly effective advisory program as one of the required foundational blocks of the school's detracked curriculum and instructional day. Teachers, as well as the principal, convene their advisories of 25 students two to three times each week, guiding students on their path to success in school, graduation, and beyond.

UNCOMMON SENSE   At The Preuss School (6–12), each incoming 6th grader joins classmates in their grade-based advisory class, one of the eight 90-minute classes they take each week on their flexible block schedule. The same faculty member stays with the advisory class until graduation. The advisories provide individual tutoring; a 30-minute reading segment called KBAR (kick back and read);

additional time for math support in KBAC (kick back and calculate); a SEL-based counseling curriculum; and time to discuss current events. High school advisories include SAT prep and college application counseling; they also work with students to complete their FAFSA and prepare for graduation. Over the seven-year journey, advisors develop close relationships with their advisees and become both guides and fierce advocates.

Advisories at Preuss are a crucial component of the school's wraparound services that support their 840 students, 95 percent of whom come from low-income homes and 100 percent of whom were accepted to four-year colleges in 2018. "It's a wonderful program," shares Principal Scott Barton, "without question a key part of Preuss's success with all of our kids." Advisory teachers at Preuss and other HP/HP schools regularly review each student's progress, holding students accountable for staying on track. Advisors identify any student who falls behind and works with the student's teachers to intervene. ●

Properly implemented, advisories work. The most effective advisories are treated like classes. Meeting regularly, they provide support to their students in content subjects, homework, career guidance, and whatever individual needs the student shares. They exist in many HP/HP secondary schools and serve to connect adults to students in positive relationships, providing welcomed support for learning and life.

Creating Smaller Learning Environments

Many HP/HP schools provide additional protective factors, such as restructuring into small learning communities. These schools create focused learning environments that help keep smaller groups of students connected with one another, as well as to a smaller group of core teachers throughout the day.

In large or moderately sized high schools, this approach may be in the form of 9th grade academies. In effect, these academies "protect" 9th graders from the impersonal nature of the large, comprehensive high school experience in which it is too easy to get lost. Academies are a strategy for easing the transitions from middle school to high school. Creating smaller learning environments has the potential to authentically connect students with adults every hour of every day.

Robyn Killebrew, past principal of Pass Christian High School, describes how their 9th grade academy, started by their highest-performing teachers who volunteered for the job, has been a game changer. "Each group of incoming 9th graders is surrounded by caring teachers with high expectations for them. Together they transition the kids wonderfully from 8th grade to our high school. I don't know how we existed without it."

Increasing Participation in Extracurricular Activities

High-performing, high-poverty schools provide a protective factor when they find ways to ensure that their students living in poverty will be able to participate in extracurricular activities. Whereas middle-class children have opportunities to develop their skills and talents through private lessons and participation in community-based activities in their elementary years, kids who live in poverty generally do not. Poverty poses a variety of barriers to participation for many students, such as the cost of fees, equipment or instruments, uniforms, and transportation home after participation.

Stillman Middle School, where 87 percent of its students live in poverty, in Brownsville, Texas, considers extracurricular activities and clubs such as dance, sports, chess, robotics, coding, and engineering (and a host of others) as basics for every student. "Our goal is to get everyone engaged in something," shares Principal EJ Martinez. Beyond weekly participation, the school's performing arts, visual arts, chess, and robotics clubs and athletic teams provide students at all grade levels with opportunities to compete in competitions throughout Texas, the Southwest, and nation, regularly bringing home awards and honors to their school. "We're a team here, the Longhorn Team," proudly shares Principal EJ Martinez, "and we all really want all of our students to be well rounded. It makes a huge difference in their success at school. And when they get to travel, it even further enhances their learning."

In addition, students who live in poverty often face responsibilities that prevent participation, such as holding down a job or caring for younger siblings. Highly competitive cut policies, which dramatically reduce the number of kids allowed to make a team, pose another barrier. Waiving fees, supplying equipment or instruments, covering the cost of uniforms, providing transportation, partnering with community-based entities to offer scholarships for specialized skill and talent development, and eliminating cut policies are a few of the ways in which HP/HP schools work diligently to ensure that all kids have access to the benefits of extracurricular participation.

How Are We Engaging Parents, Families, and Caregivers?

Waanders, Mendez, and Downer (2007) indicated that parent involvement is a key protective factor that fosters cognitive and emotional resilience for low-income children. At E.I. McCulley school, the personal warmth and welcome from the school staff elicits smiles from almost every visitor. Once a place that parents and the community did not feel "invited," the entire environment has changed. "When I first visited here years ago, I was greeted with 'welcome to the hood,' shares principal Derek Harley. "Well, we changed all of that in a hurry." With 80 percent of the families receiving some form of public assistance, the school was once a stereotype of low performance. Now, the teachers and certified staff lead the way in creating welcoming classrooms and truly expect every student to learn, succeed, and thrive. "But it starts in the front office," explains Harley. "They provide that first impression whether you are a student, family, community member, or other visitor. When you walk through the doors into the reception area, you know you're welcome, respected, and appreciated."

UNCOMMON SENSE   An HP/HP elementary school in the Midwest, where more than 40 percent of the student body was annually mobile, took an aggressive approach to counter the ill effects of mobility. The school *planned* for mobility as opposed to reacting to it when it occurred, lessening its adverse effects. Staff considered student mobility as a daily expected occurrence and intervened as they did with any other immediate student need. A staff member was ready with intake materials, and the principal reserved daily time for meeting every new student and family the day they appeared to provide tours, explain available resources, and introduce the student to his or her new teacher. Skill and placement diagnostics began on arrival, but most important, the new student and family were met in a friendly, welcoming manner. The goal was for everyone to positively embrace the move, develop good relationships with the student and parents, and position the incoming learner for success. •

SCHOOL CULTURE ALERT   High-performing, high-poverty schools don't go it alone. Instead, they build positive and trusting relationships with students, their families, and the broader neighborhood and community. They know the success of their efforts often hinges on the relationships they can foster with and among these groups. •

The success of HP/HP schools in addressing the learning needs of their students who live in poverty doesn't always solely focus on academics. Instead, helping students' families meet their basic needs, which include housing, food, medical attention, and, in some cases, safety, can be part of teachers' or administrators' jobs. Educators in HP/HP schools are not naïve about their inability to solve the myriad problems their kids face, but they often can help families connect with the community resources available. They don't concern themselves with whether or not such a task is in their job description. If it helps kids learn, they do it.

Families living in poverty often work multiple jobs, may have limited English language skills, and, in some cases, may have had few positive experiences with their children's teachers or schools. These factors frequently work against a school's attempts to form relationships with families who live in poverty and engage them in their children's education. Even in high-performing schools, this problem is an ongoing concern. Educators in HP/HP schools continually look for ways to provide opportunities for involvement and to gain back their trust.

SCHOOL CULTURE ALERT   Educators in HP/HP schools endeavor to establish and, at times, to rebuild trust between the school and the families they serve. As trust develops, the learning environment of the school improves. Parents, families, and community members feel welcomed and listened to, and they begin to connect in meaningful ways with the learning and success of their and others' children. ●

In one HP/HP elementary school, a teacher remarked, "Without a trusting environment in our classroom and with the families of my kids, it's all uphill. We could never make the progress we could . . . we could never 'click.' Trust is what makes it all happen for us." Developing trusting relationships lies at the heart of successfully engaging parents, families, and the community. To do this, HP/HP schools employ a variety of strategies. They operate full-service schools, hire school/family/community liaisons, offer adult mentoring, connect the school and community through service learning, conduct home visits, ensure effective two-way communication between the school and the family, and use the school as a community center.

Creating Full-Service Schools and Safety Nets

Many HP/HP schools connect their students with needed social and medical services. These "full-service schools" typically provide social workers, physicians, dentists, vision and hearing specialists, and mental health and family counselors on site. Some schools offer a child care center and a family resource center. Joy Dryfoos, noted scholar and longtime advocate of full-service schools, studied these models for decades and concluded that when a full-service school works well, student achievement increases, attendance rates go up, suspensions drop, and special education placements decrease (Dryfoos, 1994; Dryfoos & Maguire, 2002; U.S. Department of Education, n.d.).

Another crucial purpose of a full-service school is to provide needed safety nets to catch kids in crisis and keep them from falling through the proverbial cracks of life. Homelessness, hunger, medical issues, social and emotional distress, imminent physical danger, and coping with illness and death can interfere with learning. High-performing, high-poverty schools often establish communication networks within their school community to stay on top of these issues on behalf of their students. Once challenges are identified, teachers and staff move quickly into intervention mode, using all the resources available to them.

Creating Links Between School and Home

Strengthening the family's ability to support their children's academic achievement and other forms of success in school is a priority in HP/HP schools. Sadowski (2004) identifies six activities a school might consider to establish linkages between students' homes and school: (1) dual-language classes for students; (2) English as a second language, General Education Diploma (GED), and parenting classes; (3) home-school liaisons (who are fluent in the home language); (4) preschool and early literacy programs; (5) early assessment; and (6) community and school activities and events.

All the HP/HP schools we visited made concerted efforts to connect with their students' homes and families. Parkway Elementary reaches out to parents by going to them, convening meetings and events in the Section 8 housing community where most of the students reside. To stay connected with parents and families, the school also uses SEESAW (https://web .seesaw.me), a platform that enables students to show what they know using photos, videos, drawings, text, PDFs, and links. Families can use this tool to see their child's work and leave comments and encouragement. According to Principal Barton-Arnold, the platform really gets parents engaged in their child's schooling. HP/HP schools also employ school-family liaisons, counselors, social workers, and family support specialists who work to connect families with the school and to multiple forms of agency and social supports the family may need.

One middle school teacher in an HP/HP school told us about the difficulties the school had experienced trying to connect with a family. "The telephone was disconnected, translated letters mailed home yielded no response, and notes sent through the student didn't work either," she said. "Finally, we reached them through a neighborhood connection one of our paraprofessionals had with the family. We had our conference in the community building at their apartment complex. It went great!"

UNCOMMON SENSE   The Preuss school convenes a monthly parent meeting on Saturday mornings to better connect families with the school. These sessions, which draw in excess of 250 parents, may feature a principal's update on the school; presentations from various clubs; and activities involving robotics, ecology, and choir. Parents then break into small groups with their student's advisory teacher. The PTA makes tamales and sells school uniforms as the parents mingle with staff and others during breaks. Translation devices for English are available to parents, as is translation in Spanish and Vietnamese. The school also provides additional grade-level Saturday sessions for each high school class and separate FAFSA workshops in English, Spanish, and various Dreamer languages during the college application season. "We've built great relationships with our families; they trust us," reflects Principal Scott Barton. "When I would get home on Saturdays, I was always charged up by how these parent sessions worked so well!" ●

HP/HP schools always seem to go the extra mile to support their students to reach success. Educators in these schools do not make excuses or settle for less than authentic connections with students' parents and families. The goal of fostering two-way communication between school and home requires educators in HP/HP schools to be relentless in their insistence that communications be respectful, honest, and timely.

In his article titled "Involvement or Engagement?" Larry Ferlazzo (2011) writes that authentic parent engagement requires us to examine the ways in which many schools involve parents. He argues that there's a difference between involving parents and engaging them. To "involve" is to "enfold or envelop," he asserts. In contrast, to engage is "to come together." This is the difference between "doing to" parents and "doing with" parents. He explains,

> A school striving for family involvement often leads with its mouth—identifying projects, needs, and goals and then telling parents how they can contribute. A school striving for parent engagement, on the other hand, tends to lead with its ears—listening to what parents think, dream, and worry about. The goal of family engagement is not to serve clients but to gain partners. (p. 12)

Despite their extensive efforts to engage parents, many schools, including HP/HP schools, find it challenging to engage parents in their child's learning. We have long advocated for schools to adopt student-led conferencing. As part of a focus on developing assessment literacy, student-led conferencing provides a forum for teachers, students, and parents to meet and discuss academic, social, and emotional learning progression. Students become more metacognitive as they develop a portfolio of artifacts reflective of their learning, which they present to their parents or caregivers as they lead the conference. In the highly practical, teacher-friendly book, *Powerful Partnerships: A Teacher's Guide to Engaging Families for Student Success*, authors Mapp, Carver, and Lander (2017) provide a how-to guide for implementing effective family partnerships, beginning in the same place we do in this book—with the need to examine core beliefs while designing yearlong family engagement opportunities and events.

One of the most powerful barriers to authentically engaging parents in the schooling experience of their child is our own mental maps. We tend to think of parent engagement as solely what happens *inside* the school, such as family nights, parent-teacher conferences, or volunteer work. We've discussed the many reasons that parents who live in poverty might not be involved on-site in schools. Studies (Lott, 2001; McWayne et al., 2004) have demonstrated that parents who live in poverty *are* involved in their children's education in a variety of ways. McWayne and others (2004) showed that parent reports of educational involvement at home, defined as providing a supportive home learning environment, were positively associated with teachers' ratings of children's reading and mathematics achievement. Other researchers have found that parents' attitudes (e.g., their educational expectations and aspirations for their children) are associated with academic achievement (Hill & Taylor, 2004). Lastly, a study comparing two low-income families found significant differences between the home life of one high-achieving and one low-achieving student (Gutman & McLoyd, 2000). Their findings suggest that parents of high achievers engaged their children in deliberate educational activities within the home, such as monitoring their homework and engaging them in pedagogical discussions and problem-solving tasks.

Hill and Taylor (2004) suggest specific ways to build social capital and social control for parents in poverty. Through increased social capital, children receive messages about the importance of schooling, which can increase their competence, motivation to learn, and engagement in school. Finding ways for parents in poverty to develop relationships with teachers and other parents increases their social capital and, in turn, can improve student achievement. If parents are able to view themselves as a collective group nested in a community bounded by similar interests and goals, this can create a foundation for parents to act collectively with teachers to benefit all students (Warren, Hong, Rubin, & Uy, 2009).

Conducting Home Visits

One of Kathleen's most profound experiences as a teacher was conducting home visits. At the time, she was working in the Aberdeen School District in Washington State as a preschool teacher. Classes were held Monday through Thursday, and on Fridays, teachers conducted home visits. Kathleen distinctly remembers one particular visit to student Michael's home.

Once Michael's mother invited her in, they all sat on a mattress on the floor next to a TV, which were the only two pieces of furniture in the room. Two large black trash bags in the corner appeared to contain clothing and toys. Michael's mom said she didn't like coming to the school. She apologized for not having another place to sit, but she appeared pleased that Kathleen had come to her home.

From Kathleen's school observations, she knew Michael had a life-threatening condition that required tube feeding. And she knew that he was a gregarious little boy and was full of energy at school despite his medical condition. That day at home, Michael was unusually subdued and shy. It was obvious his mother loved him and was genuinely concerned about his progress in school. They had a good talk about Michael's learning and about his enormously positive contribution to the class. Kathleen learned that Michael's father didn't live with them and that his mother had not finished high school. Walking down the stairs of the weather-worn apartment building, Kathleen realized how much more she knew about Michael and his mom. She knew that when she looked at him the next day that she would see him differently, and that with this stronger relationship with his mom, Kathleen would be a better teacher for Michael.

UNCOMMON SENSE   Some HP/HP schools encourage and conduct home visits as a core element of establishing and maintaining trusted relationships with students and their families. An elementary teacher in a HP/HP school recounted stopping by the home of one of her 2nd graders to let the parents know that their son, Luis, was coming to the after-school tutoring program in English and was doing well. When she was invited in, the father asked her to come into the kitchen and see what Luis had been doing since he started the tutoring program. "On the cupboards were taped a mishmash of cereal boxes, pasta containers, dairy product holders, and simple drawings," she said. "All were in English. The dad smiled and explained, 'He's teaching all of us to read English! We learn 5, maybe 10 words every day!'"

This story is a good example of the benefits of engaging parents and families. A simple home visit revealed how a young ESL student was connecting his tutoring and schoolwork with his family. In turn, his family was most appreciative of their son's progress in school and welcomed his newly gained English skills that were also helping them learn. His family was surprised and pleased that the teacher had come to their home. ●

Sometimes these visits have a truly transformational effect on both teachers and parents. Also, author and teacher Stephanie Smith (2013) brings up a salient point. "Why do teachers judge parents for not setting foot on our campus," she asks, "when we make no attempt to set foot on their front porch?"(p. 76). Sharing her experience of learning to embrace home visits, she provides a wealth of ideas, tips, and lessons that she learned from visiting her students' homes. She points out that educators need to take the first step. By doing so, they learn what their students' lives are like, an essential for educators who teach students who live in poverty.

The Sacramento Unified School District has led efforts across the state and nation to support home visits, in part by using Title I funds. They joined in a collaborative effort with the local teachers union and community partners in 1998 to enhance relationships between schools and their communities and families. This evolved into the Parent-Teacher Home Visit Project (PTHV), a nonprofit organization that trains and supports teachers in learning how to conduct home visits. This grassroots project has spread to 24 states and established PTHV hubs as regional training centers in California, Colorado, Maine, and Minnesota. PTHV supports its members with research-based evidence of effectiveness, training and outreach tools, and a toolbox of best practices, as well as distributing a newsletter and convening an annual summer conference. Their model (www. PTHV.org) includes five nonnegotiable core practices:

1. Visits are voluntary for all.
2. Educators are trained and compensated.
3. We share hopes, dreams, and goals.
4. We don't target students.
5. Educators go in pairs and reflect.

As was evident in the HP/HP schools we studied, relational trust among the school, students, and families was a crucial component for realizing high expectations and success and supporting students' academic, social, and emotional learning. Effective home visits can play an important role in reaching this goal. As one elementary teacher explains, "I now view [home visits] as part of my work, part of my job."

UNCOMMON SENSE   Every August, all 1,500 Newport Independent School District (NISD) students and their families participate in the District's Home Visit program, which is now in its fourth year. The Newport, Kentucky, teachers and administrators, wearing their district T-shirts, traverse the city, visiting all of their students' homes to meet the families, better understand their students' needs, and develop relationships with the parents and guardians.

More than 90 percent of Newport students qualify for free and reduced-price meals in a community that is also confronted with transience and homelessness. The program was awarded a 2019 National School Boards Association MAGNA award, one of five national awards for districts of under 5,000 students. Aside from the obvious strengthening of relational trust among all participants and the immediate expressions of appreciation from families and staff, NISD has observed significant increases in school year engagement of families, community involvement with the district, and student understanding of expectations—and a decrease in discipline referrals. ●

How Are We Engaging the Broader Community?

At the secondary HP/HP schools we studied, students are expected to participate in community service. Noted for connecting academic learning to real-world problems beyond school, community-based learning, particularly service learning, has become common in these schools. Many benefits accrue from service learning, including enhanced academic achievement, increased school attendance, improved student motivation to learn, decreased risky behaviors, increased interpersonal development and student ability to relate to culturally diverse groups, and improved school image and public perception (Billig, 2000a, 2000b). Community-based learning also provides an excellent means to initiate career exploration, internships, shadowing, and, in some cases, jobs.

Offering Students Multiple Experiences for Connecting with the Community

The Preuss School presents a model for engaging the broader community. Located on the campus of the University of California San Diego (UCSD), the school connects with the university and surrounding community through myriad structured experiences that take advantage of individuals who volunteer their time to tutor, mentor, or advise students at the school. Other examples leverage the school's mission and desire to contribute to the community. All these experiences enrich Preuss students' experiences by authentically connecting them to the real world through service learning projects, internships, research projects, and community-based service.

Each year Preuss School welcomes a number of mostly retired adults to serve as classroom tutors for the students. Mr. Andy, as he's known, is a retired electrical engineer who has been tutoring precalculus since 1991.

He comes every day and teams with the chair of the math department to provide additional help to the kids who most need support. During finals, he's there every day after school to offer additional help. Mr. Andy shared his approach:

> I really try to develop rapport with the student. When a student can't do a problem and asks me to help, I will almost always ask the student a question about something he or she has already learned that relates to the problem they're struggling with, and I continue with that approach until they get it. Since so many of the kids here don't have English as a first language, I also try to say "hello" to them in their language. I started studying Spanish when I was 58 and can say a few words in Mandarin, Vietnamese, and Amharic, which is spoken in Ethiopia.

Beyond the school's regular adult tutors, Preuss welcomes 120 UCSD students each year to also serve as tutors. Another 40–50 adults volunteer at the school as mentors to students and as advisors to clubs, such as robotics and ecology. Finally, all 12th graders participate in a senior Wheel Course, which focuses on out-of-school learning. Students are expected to complete three aspects of the Wheel: research, a service project, and an internship. A student might focus on neighborhood reading challenges. He or she might complete research on the topic, volunteer at a local elementary school with struggling readers, and decide to construct a Little Lending Library (like those found in many affluent neighborhoods) and introduce it to the neighbors who live nearby. The Wheel experience culminates with the student presenting his or her work to an adult committee from the school and community that has been connected to the student's project.

Mentoring Students

The National Dropout Prevention Center (2019) identifies mentoring as one of the most effective strategies to keep kids engaged and in school. The Western Regional Center for Drug-Free Schools and Communities (Jackson, 2002) identifies five positive outcomes of mentoring programs: (1) personalized attention and care, (2) access to resources, (3) high expectations for staff and students, (4) reciprocity and active youth participation, and (5) commitment. Many HP/HP schools draw from this knowledge to create and operate their own programs with local staff and volunteers; others access the help of Big Brother/Big Sister programs, local YMCA/YWCA services, and a host of other community-affiliated programs that offer adult mentoring.

Adult mentors are a common fixture in HP/HP schools. Not only do they provide an invaluable opportunity to connect students who don't have a stable adult in their lives with a caring, supportive advocate, but they also serve as a fruitful connection to the greater community of adults who often have much to offer and want to help, but don't know how. Many of the schools have also created a mentor coordinator role for a staff member to recruit, connect, and support community volunteer mentors in their willingness to regularly meet with and help kids.

Following an application process and vetting by the school, the volunteers at Preuss school are assigned to students. "We have about 50 adult mentors who come and meet with kids at lunchtime to just chitchat about how life's going. 'Have you ever been to a play? Maybe we should go to the opera, or a baseball game.' Just good conversations for the kids to have with an adult," shares principal Barton. Mentors can also make arrangements with the student and parents to engage in some activity outside school. Mentors might spend their time tutoring students in their classes, coaching the basketball team, leading the robotics or ecology club, or working with kids in the gardening club or in other activities.

UNCOMMON SENSE   Close to $20,000—that's how much money Pass Christian High School students and staff raise in their annual Pirate Palooza. The community comes out in a big way on a spring evening to support their kids. All monies raised go to the students, funding incentives, academic block parties, pep rallies, or T-shirts, along with other student activities, needs, and projects. It all happens on one evening when the students present a talent show and help organize a chili cook-off and silent auction. This annual tradition represents a great way to engage the community with the school and students, and it enables the students to become more unified as a student body. ●

Using the School as a Community Center

Many HP/HP schools engage parents, families, and other community members by opening their doors and expanding their schedules to offer clubs, parent support and education, early childhood activities, GED programs, advisory groups, community education classes, and a host of other events and activities of interest to the community. These HP/HP schools partner with community or city organizations, local foundations, state and municipal agencies, service clubs, universities, and businesses to host these valued activities in their buildings, as well as to offer services at times that better fit families' work schedules.

How Are We Ensuring Equity?

One of the first objectives of equity-focused approaches in this arena is leveling the playing field. These approaches typically begin with meeting students' most basic needs. Specific strategies include providing breakfast and lunch (and sometimes dinner); hosting a food pantry; sending food home in backpacks; opening "boutiques" of new and donated clothing; partnering with local food banks to host a branch; opening health clinics; providing mental health services; providing laundry facilities; and promoting wellness through partnership with organizations and agencies, such as the YMCA and Parks and Recreation departments. In addition, they provide school supplies, yearbooks, and school uniforms, and they eliminate fees for athletics, band instrument rentals, and field trips.

In addition to addressing basic needs, equity-focused educators examine their mental maps. For example, consider how they ensure safety in HP/HP schools. They should ask, "For whom is our approach to discipline working—and for whom is it not?" In another example, as they attempt to engage parents, equity-focused educators may ask, "Which parents are able to attend parent-teacher conferences—and for which parents is attendance a hardship?"

Conducting the following activity could spark a conversation among faculty about inequities school policies and procedures too often perpetuate.

Activity: How Much Does School *Really* Cost?

Step 1: Brainstorm fees: Ask each individual to make a list on a sticky note of all the associated costs and fees charged to parents for their children to fully participate in school.

Step 2: Share and compare: Ask individuals to compare their list with a partner or small group of colleagues, with participants adding any costs not included on their list. Ask each individual to total the costs of their list.

Step 3: Display the data: Place the sticky notes on wall-mounted poster paper to form a graph. (Note: The poster paper has been divided into columns, and each column has been labeled in increments of $100—e.g., $100, $101–$200, $201–$300.)

Step 4: Extend the discussion: Talk about the range of responses. What does the range mean? What was surprising? What was confirming? Discuss the implications for the students and families the school serves. Conclude by discussing any actions that might be warranted to level the playing field for students and families living in poverty.

In this activity, there's no right answer to the question "What do you mean by 'fully participate in school'?" We tend to emphasize the importance of belonging as a basic need. Although it may be true that yearbooks, for example, are not "required" for students' academic learning, it can also be argued that yearbooks are intended to chronicle schooling experiences for the purpose of fostering a sense of belonging. For students who live in poverty, not being able to purchase a yearbook can be a painful reminder that they don't belong. This activity may engender a discussion about "providing scholarships" for students to purchase a yearbook. But we would caution educators to be sensitive to the research that has demonstrated that people who live in poverty often experience schooling as a series of shaming encounters (Beegle, 2006). Putting students (or parents) in the position of asking for a scholarship contributes to those encounters. Consider reading "How School Taught Me I Was Poor" by Jeff Sapp (2009) to continue the discussion.

The Principal's Role

Principals, working with teacher leaders and staff leaders from various vantage points within the school, are positioned to address the wide spectrum of environmental needs that confront high-poverty schools. Figure 6.3 describes the actions that principals in HP/HP schools take to ensure that every student is surrounded by the positive supports and scaffolds necessary to ensure his or her success.

Figure 6.3   The Principal's Role in Fostering a Healthy, Safe, and Supportive Learning Environment in HP/HP Schools

The principal—
- Relentlessly ensures the school is safe.
- Initiates conversation and supports professional learning about the influence of poverty.
- Organizes collaborative efforts to address student mobility and other poverty-related factors that negatively influence learning.
- Initiates and promotes policies, structures, and practices that link students and families with medical, dental, and mental health services, as well as other sources of support in the community.
- Promotes the development of positive relationships and a bond between students and school by doing the following:
  » Modeling caring;
  » Facilitating strategies that strengthen the student-adult connections, such as advisories and small learning groups; and
  » Examining data related to barriers to student participation in extracurricular activities and leading collaborative efforts to address them.
- Initiates and promotes policies, structures, and practices that develop trust between school and family, such as hiring a school-home liaison and visiting homes.
- Initiates and promotes policies, structures, and practices that connect schools to families and the community, such as service learning and using the school as a community center.
- Ensures effective, frequent communications between school staff, students, families, and the community.

High-performing, high-poverty schools don't go it alone—and they don't reinvent the wheel. They access support, resources, and guidance whenever and wherever they can to foster a healthy, safe, and supportive learning environment. The resources and organizations listed in Figure 6.4 can guide a school's efforts to build strong relationships with parents and families.

Many HP/HP schools belong to organizations that help to support their work. One of the most widely respected and accessed of these organizations is the National Network of Partnership Schools (NNPS) at Johns Hopkins University (http://nnps.jhucsos.com). Founded in 1996, this network "invites schools, districts, states, and organizations to join together and use research-based practices to organize and sustain excellent programs of family and community involvement that will increase student success in school." The network originated from the work of the Center on School, Family, and Community Partnerships and of its founder and senior scholar, Joyce Epstein. She explains,

> The way schools care about children is reflected in the way schools care about the children's families. If educators view children simply as students, they are likely to see the family as separate from the school. That is, the

Figure 6.4   Online Resources for Connecting Parents, Families, and Schools

Academic Parent Teacher Teams	aptt.wested.org
Boys and Girls Clubs of America	https://www.bgca.org/
Coalition for Community Schools	http://www.communityschools.org/
Communities in Schools	www.communitiesinschools.org
Families in Schools	www.familiesinschools.org
Larry Ferlazzo's Engaging Parents in School Blog	engagingparentsinschool.edublogs.org
Flamboyan Foundation	www.flamboyanfoundation.org
Harvard Family Research Project	www.hfrp.org
National Association for Family, School, and Community Engagement	http://nafsce.org
National Network of Partnership Schools	http://nnps.jhucsos.com
Parents as Teachers	www.parentsasteachers.org
Parent Teacher Home Visit Project	http://www.pthvp.org/
Parent Teacher Association (PTA) Family Engagement Tools	www.pta.org
Teaching for Change	https://www.teachingforchange.org/parent-organizing/our-approach
YMCA/YWCA Programs	https://www.ymca.net/ https://www.ywca.org

family is expected to do its job and leave the education of children to the schools. If educators view students as children, they are likely to see both the family and the community as partners with the school in children's education and development. (Families and School Together, August 2016)

Guided by more than three decades of research and practice, NNPS offers what Epstein calls "a new way" to incorporate parent and community involvement into a school's improvement process. The network helps member schools, districts, sites, and other organizations organize and implement action teams within their communities, with the goal of increasing quality partnerships.

 ## Taking Action

- *Create and act with a sense of urgency.* Do you understand the needs of your students who underperform, and are you addressing those needs?
- *Relentlessly monitor data* related to ensuring a safe learning environment. Are you making sure every student is always safe?
- *Build a commonly held understanding of the influences of poverty on learning* among the adults in the school. Do all staff members understand how living in poverty may negatively influence the ability of students to catch up?
- *Plan for mobility.* Are you ready for mobile students' arrival—that is, ready to provide welcome packets, diagnostic testing, and appropriate placements? Do you develop "catch-up" plans if needed? Do you provide built-in opportunities for new students to make friends with peers? Do you make it a practice to communicate with parents during the first six weeks after enrollment? Do you address transportation issues if a student is mobile within your district? Have you marshaled schoolwide support from staff?
- *Make sure all students are connected to a caring adult.* Do you know which students come to school without the support of a caring adult?
- *Start student advisories.* Is every secondary school student connected to an adult at school who regularly monitors his or her progress?
- *Personalize relationships* through creating small learning environments and communities of practice. Is the size of your school presenting problems for some students and preventing them from forming caring relationships?
- *Provide opportunities for all students to participate in extracurricular activities.* Do all your students have an equitable opportunity to participate?

- *Work to engage every family with school.* Do you have a plan in place to guide your efforts to build trust and connect with your families?
- *Personalize the connection between school and the student's home.* Who among your staff visits the homes of your kids?
- *Initiate an effective adult mentoring program.* How are you connecting students with caring adults and positive role models?
- *Offer community-based learning and service-learning opportunities* to all students. Are you connecting students with the community? Are you teaching students about the value of giving back? Are you providing opportunities for students to explore career options in the local community?
- *Visit every student's home.* Do you have a plan in place to guide you in conducting productive home visits?
- *Ensure two-way communication* between homes and school characterized by the following:
  - » Language-appropriate written and verbal contacts
  - » Translation assistance when needed
  - » Respectful and clear communications
  - » Frequent contact through the most effective mode
  - » Authentic requests for feedback and response
  - » Willingness to help with requests and family needs
  - » Personal invitations to participate in school conferences
  - » Timely invitations to activities and events
- *Open the school to the community.* Have you created a plan to provide welcomed and needed services to your community?
- *Join a network* to enhance school, family, and community relationships. Can you improve your connections with your families and communities?

7 Focusing on Student, Professional, and System Learning

> When I was a teacher, I remember working in an environment that needed a lot of love. By that I mean the children were awesome; they were craving knowledge. I felt lonely. I didn't have a team. I didn't see any structure. I didn't see a plan for children to have long-term success. I saw there was great disparity in how we taught and in our belief systems and in what each child was receiving each year.
>
> —*Alexa Sorden, principal, Concourse Village Elementary School, New York, NY*

When Alexa Sorden became principal of Concourse Village Elementary School, she was given access to the school on July 1. From then until August 9, when school registration began, she focused on transforming the physical learning environment. Much of the school had been painted black. Sorden explains, "We had to repaint everything. New York Cares [a large volunteer organization in New York City] was an amazing partner in painting classrooms and murals, so that when kids came, they had positivity everywhere they went."

Sorden then set up every classroom in a uniform manner. She told teachers who weren't accustomed to having the principal determine the physical layout of their classrooms that it wasn't about them, that she just wanted the rooms to all be structured in the same way, "the same format, the same colors, the same message." Here's how she explains it:

> Everything will be located in the same way because when our children walk into a classroom year after year, they should not have to relearn anything. They should just be able to fall right into place and know what the classroom looks like, feels like, how it works so they can start learning on the very first day of school.

Her aim is to ensure not only predictability for "scholars" (students) but also excellence in every classroom so that such consistency extends to the curriculum, instruction, and professional development, too. Using an approach they call Collaborative Reading, which is a blend of choral reading and close reading, scholars chorally read challenging grade-level and above-grade-level texts daily. Following the choral reading, in small groups scholars answer questions using a process known as MACAS (main idea, annotation, comprehension, author's purpose, and summary) before they attempt to do so independently. Literacy skill development is integrated into all other disciplines through close reading and reflective writing to develop scholars' critical thinking skills.

Learning in math is focused on conceptual understanding. For example, scholars use a standard five-step process to solve word problems: annotate the problem, think of a plan to solve it, use a strategy to solve it, describe how it was solved using labels and math language, and make connections by identifying patterns and rules. This process is illustrated on a Thinking Map that hangs in classrooms. Thinking maps are routinely used to make scholars' learning visible. As students work independently or in small groups, classical music plays in the background of every classroom.

Sorden's experience in high-poverty urban schools, where she witnessed great disparity in the quality of teaching, guides her theory of action as a leader. "I vowed that if I ever had the courage to lead," she explains, "I would create a place where children—no matter what teacher they ended up with that year—would have a great year of learning, and they would feel safe, respected, and loved."

Students aren't the only people who feel safe, respected, and loved at Concourse Village. Obtaining a job at Concourse Village is now competitive. As one teacher says, "Coming here was a brand new experience for me. I had to learn everything and unlearn a lot. It's a school where collaboration is key. We do everything as a community of one. It's an all-hands-on-deck type of school."

Is your school focusing on student, professional, and system learning? Are you making the most of the links among the three? Use the self-assessment rubric shown in Figure 7.1 to guide your reading and help you reflect on the current situation in your school.

Five questions can support educators as they make student, professional, and system learning agendas the focus of their actions:

1. How are we employing a pedagogy of possibility?
2. How are we ensuring every student can read proficiently?
3. How are we providing targeted interventions for students who need them?
4. How are we providing job-embedded opportunity for professional learning?
5. How are we ensuring equity?

Figure 7.1 Focusing on Student, Professional, and System-Level Learning: Assessing Our Structures and Processes for Enhancing Learning at All Levels

Progress Indicators or Evidence	No Action Yet	Getting Started	Gaining Momentum	Sustaining Gains, Refining
		• Urgency is apparent. • School status is understood. • A vision for improvement is shared. • Implementation strategies are selected. • Staff is prepared to begin.	• People are empowered. • Barriers are being removed. • Implementation is becoming routine. • Commitment is increasing. • Progress is monitored. • Initial gains are being made and celebrated. • Support for improvement continues.	• The improvements are embedded in daily practice. • Collaboration continues. • Refinements are made. • Gains continue to be made and sustained.
What is my school's progress?	0	1	2	3
Using a "pedagogy of possibility" (pp. 135–150)				
Unpacking standards (p. 139)				
Aligning curricula to standards (pp. 139–140)				
Developing a common understanding of excellence in teaching (pp. 140–141)				
Using practices that engage and empower students (pp. 141–142)				
Developing assessment literacy in teachers and students (pp. 142–147)				
Using formative and common assessment to analyze student work and collectively improve teaching (pp. 142–147)				
Understanding the importance of the teachers' dispositions (pp. 148–150)				

Progress Indicators or Evidence	No Action Yet	Getting Started	Gaining Momentum	Sustaining Gains, Refining
		• Urgency is apparent. • School status is understood. • A vision for improvement is shared. • Implementation strategies are selected. • Staff is prepared to begin.	• People are empowered. • Barriers are being removed. • Implementation is becoming routine. • Commitment is increasing. • Progress is monitored. • Initial gains are being made and celebrated. • Support for improvement continues.	• The improvements are embedded in daily practice. • Collaboration continues. • Refinements are made. • Gains continue to be made and sustained.
Ensuring all students read proficiently (pp. 150–152)				
Providing targeted interventions for students who need them (pp. 153–155)				
Using research-based models for professional learning (pp. 155–156)				
Encouraging reflective practice (p. 156)				
Ensuring equity in student, professional, and system learning (pp. 156–157)				

Let's now look at each of these questions in depth.

Are We Employing a Pedagogy of Possibility?

Concourse Village Elementary, located in the poorest congressional district in the United States, District 7 in the South Bronx, employs a pedagogy of possibility. Unpacking standards, aligning curriculum to those standards, creating a common vision of what excellent teaching looks like, using research-based instructional practices focused on student engagement and empowerment, integrating SEL objectives into academic learning and the learning environment, and developing and using common assessments are all part of creating a pedagogy of possibility that brings coherence to teachers' professional practice and positively influences the instructional core.

Too often, schools continue to use ineffective curricular approaches and instructional practices with students who live in poverty. Such practices are described as a "pedagogy of poverty" (Haberman, 1991; Padrón, Waxman, & Rivera, 2002), which is characterized by overuse of teacher-controlled discussions and decision making, lecture, drill and decontextualized practice, and worksheets. Researchers have documented differences in the intellectual quality of tasks required of students in high-poverty schools in contrast to schools where most of the students are middle- or upper-middle class (Anyon, 1981; Finn, 1999). This contrast can be seen within a single school when students are tracked into courses such as Consumer Math or Opportunity Math, which are often designated for students who are thought to be "unable" to learn algebra.

Rather than a pedagogy of poverty, students who live in poverty need "powerful pedagogy"—powerful instruction resulting in powerful (or deep) learning. Such pedagogy is consistent with a large body of research related to how people learn (Bransford, Brown, & Cocking, 2000). Powerful pedagogy has been conceptualized in various ways—as relevant to the learner (Brandt, 1998); meaning centered (Knapp & Adelman, 1995); supporting the development of various kinds of understanding (Wiggins & McTighe, 2005); accelerated, strength based, and empowering (Levin, 1989); as well as encompassing higher-order thinking, deep knowledge, and connections beyond classrooms (Newmann, Marks, & Gamoran, 1996). When a powerful pedagogy is employed, students are actively engaged in meaning making and developing understanding not only of content but also of one's self as a learner. Problem solving, reasoning, critical and creative thinking, and inquiry are integral. Lessons and units access and build on students' prior knowledge and focus on understanding and constructing new knowledge. Students are empowered through choice and given a voice in decision making.

UNCOMMON SENSE Educators at Henderson Collegiate Middle School point to the team of instructional coaches and the coaching model they use as key to their ability to maintain their growth in academic achievement. In the words of one coach, "We're not just adding great teachers who have experience—we're multiplying [excellence]." They not only intentionally push their "rookie" teachers to grow but also identify exemplar teachers by studying "their excellence and codifying what they're doing to continue to multiply" excellence in others. Using a model they learned from the Relay Graduate School of Education, which they describe as "see it, name it, do it," they work with teachers to help them see what "exemplary" looks like by giving them "real clear visuals." Teachers then name and codify what makes a particular practice a best practice, after which they're provided with authentic chances to practice, coupled with in-the-moment feedback. This coaching model focuses on improving the repertoire of teacher moves to get the most out of their students. ●

Jump-Starting a Pedagogy of Possibility

Comprehensive school reform models. When we studied schools for the first edition of this book, we discovered that about half of the schools had adopted a comprehensive school reform (CSR) model. Use of these models was a reflection of policy in the late 1990s that provided federal grants administered through state departments of education for the adoption of such approved models. In our current study, two schools, Pugliese West and East Garfield, both in Steubenville, Ohio, have used Success for All (SFA), a CSR model, as the foundation of their pedagogy of possibility, and both schools have had tremendous success with the model for two decades.

The CSR models are developed using a research-based rationale for the suggested instructional practices. Some models include curricular materials and formative and summative assessments. Most require specific professional development. This level of structure can be advantageous in jump-starting improvement. Over time, based on data, educators often tweak these models to best meet the needs of their students. Although educators at times have suggested to us that such models are too scripted and limit teachers' ability to exercise professional judgment, this does not appear to be the case in the Steubenville schools. Teachers pointed to SFA as foundational to their success. One teacher says, "At the end of the day, not only do we believe in SFA—we believe in our kids." Although SFA is highly structured, every grade level at Pugliese West and East Garfield engages students in complex project-based learning activities, some of which take an entire semester or a year to complete.

UNCOMMON SENSE Pugliese West 4th graders are engaged in project-based learning to learn about, and give back to, their community. The project is called Steubenville Past, Present, and Predicted Future. Students work with business and community leaders to improve the community, gain an appreciation for their community, and learn to contribute. As one teacher says, "It empowers the students. They feel like, 'Oh, my gosh, these adults are listening to my ideas . . . they think I'm important.'" Students take multiple field trips, visiting new and established businesses, engaging with the business owners. They discuss where they'd like their community to be in 10 years. A new focus in this project-based learning activity is entrepreneurism, where students create their own businesses. The teacher explains, "They come up with a unique product they want to sell, develop a business plan, open their business on our community night, and sell their products there." ●

Other paths and models. Other schools in our current study developed their pedagogy of possibility from models other than CSR. Evergreen Elementary adopted the No Excuses University Model, and Henderson Collegiate's development was informed by several models, including the Uncommon Schools Network, Achievement First, Teach For America, and the Relay Graduate School of Education. Still, most schools in our study didn't adopt a particular model; rather, they used a more homegrown, eclectic best-practices approach.

To varying degrees, pedagogy in all of the schools we studied was influenced by the policy push of the past decade, which mandated the adoption of more rigorous, college-ready standards. Even in elementary schools, talk of going to college was not uncommon, and it was not unusual to see bulletin boards with college themes, classrooms named for colleges, and field trips to college campuses at all levels of schooling.

At Henderson Collegiate Middle School, students get to visit college campuses early on; that includes kindergartners and 1st and 2nd graders. As Caitlin Terranova, the school's chief of staff explains,

> You have to make it a concrete thing, right? You have to make it a tangible thing that's a real place; it's not a lofty dream. They've been there. They've walked around. They deserve to be there. This is about normalizing the culture of college going and making it part of the daily fabric.

In 2018, the staff at Pass Christian High School looked at their student scores on the ACT assessment, Mississippi's required state assessment. As a result, they targeted those students who were just a point or two away from meeting the benchmark in math and English language arts. This wasn't just about accountability; it was more about getting students scholarship money to continue their educations. The district reimburses all students for dual-credit courses if they earn a *C* or above and for advanced placement (AP) test fees if they score 3 or better. The district also pays the tuition for students who qualify for the free and reduced-price meal program and who earn university credits.

Unpacking the Standards

In the years between our studies, most states adopted more rigorous academic standards. Educators in many of the schools described their work of unpacking the new standards as a way to clarify what they needed to teach and what their students needed to learn. Unpacking the standards was often a team effort, with grade levels or departments working together. Teachers focused on understanding the cognitive demand or depth of knowledge outlined in the standard, as well as the sequence of the standards from grade level to grade level.

After North Carolina switched to more rigorous standards, Henderson Collegiate experienced a 40 percent drop in their performance. Yet two years after that, the school met or exceeded the benchmarks. Celeste Olsen, dean of curriculum and instruction, explains how they met the challenges:

> We talked a lot about taxonomies of rigor. We recognized we had the ability to internalize the standards and revamp what we were doing across our classrooms because we were pretty small to start with. And, as a small staff, we were really motivated. By creating Classworks [our own curriculum] instead of buying materials and creating lesson plans or relying on something you've inherited from a former teacher, we built the curriculum from the ground up, and we knew it aligned.

Aligning the Curriculum

Findings from almost every study of HP/HP schools indicate that their staffs intensively focus on the curriculum as part of creating coherence in the instructional program. This work includes aligning the written curriculum with state and district standards, articulating the curriculum across subjects and grade levels through vertical and horizontal planning, identifying benchmarks and developing common assessments, planning collaborative units and lessons, differentiating curriculum and instruction, and monitoring the taught and tested curriculum through some form of instructional walk-throughs.

Describing their work aligning their curriculum, teachers at Lillian Peterson Elementary noted the importance of understanding when you should supplement your adopted curricular materials. Their discussions around curriculum alignment also surfaced the need for using a common mathematical language. Moreover, they described the benefit of not only "knowing and owning" what they teach at their grade level, but also what is taught at the preceding grade level and the grade level to follow. One teacher explained how learning what students struggled with in 3rd grade inspired her to introduce the "cube strategy" in 2nd grade, which ended up helping the next crop of 3rd graders move forward in solving two-step story problems.

Krista Barton-Arnold, principal of Parkway Elementary, describes instructional leadership as "Job No. 1" for her. Focusing on alignment of instruction with standards was important for developing consistency in the quality of instruction from classroom to classroom. When asked about Parkway's success, she says, "I was visible instructionally and did learning walks constantly, [where] we focused just on alignment—and the teachers knew that."

Developing a Common Understanding of Excellence in Teaching

Charlotte Danielson published the first edition of *Enhancing Professional Practice: A Framework for Teaching* in 1996. Her rationale for developing the framework was to address an important problem facing the teaching profession—the lack of a well-established body of knowledge to provide guidance and standards. She stated, "Indeed, other professions—medicine, accounting, and architecture among many others—have well-established definitions of expertise and procedures . . . such procedures are the public's guarantee that the members of a profession hold themselves and their colleagues to the highest standards" (p. 2). Ten years later, Danielson published a second edition of the Framework for Teaching (2006).

She was not alone in her claim or her quest. Robert Pianta (Wiltz, 2008), who had conducted studies of thousands of classrooms in hundreds of schools across the United States at the time, asserted the profession's definition of good teaching was "all over the map" (p. 1). Is this still the state of the teaching profession today? It is our observation that good teaching is more well defined now than it was 10 years ago, at least in the HP/HP schools we've studied.

Research into the assessment of teaching quality has proliferated in the past decade. Pianta and his colleagues developed the Classroom Assessment Scoring System (CLASS). CLASS is designed to assess the quality of teaching and "creates a common language about effective teaching practices across subject areas and grade levels" (https://curry.virginia.edu /classroom-assessment-scoring-system). Additionally, faculty at the Center for Educational Leadership (CEL) at the University of Washington created the 5 Dimensions of Teaching and Learning (5D) to both define and measure excellence in teaching (http://info.k-12leadership.org /5-dimensions-of-teaching-and-learning?_ga=2.136823280.114813081.156 9976088-1107909016.1569976088), and experts at the Learning Science Marzano Center (Carbaugh et al., 2017) also designed a model to define good teaching and measure it. Moreover, the Gates Foundation recently completed the Measures of Effective Teaching Project, which sought to answer two questions: (1) Is it possible to identify and measure effective teaching, and (2) can we pinpoint what works in the classroom? (https://k12education.gatesfoundation.org/blog/measures-of-effective -teaching-met-project/). Clearly research and development in this area has advanced our understanding, as a profession, of good teaching; thus, it could be argued we are no longer "all over the map."

Nonetheless, "knowing more" doesn't always result in "doing more" or "doing differently." Jeffrey Pfeffer and Robert I. Sutton, the authors of *The Knowing-Doing Gap: How Smart Companies Turn Knowledge into Action,* say "knowledge that is actually implemented is much more likely to be acquired from learning by doing than from learning by reading, listening, or even thinking" (p. 6). Although a richer knowledge base is a step in the right direction, it does not mean the "new science" has reached individual teachers or that those teachers have had a chance to "learn by doing" through job-embedded opportunities. Even more, in any given school developing a *common* understanding of that knowledge base, let alone consistent implementation of it, remains a significant challenge.

Even in schools employing a CSR model where the notion of what constitutes good teaching is, at least partially, conscribed by the model itself, the time spent on topics, the focus on skill development, and the use of instructional practices vary greatly from classroom to classroom. Further, such variation is often not linked to students' needs, such as to their socioeconomic background or prior achievement (Correnti & Rowan, 2007).

This is an area in which HP/HP schools appear to stand in stark contrast to the norm. Educators in these schools endeavor as a community of practice engaged in personal and collective reflection cycles to develop a common understanding of what good teaching looks like; establish clear expectations for students and teachers; use research-based instructional strategies; and monitor what happens in the instructional core through coaching, classroom walk-throughs followed by specific feedback, and a variety of other means.

Using Research-Based Practices to Engage and Empower Students

Decades of studies have demonstrated that specific pedagogical practices are effective in engaging and empowering students. These include service learning, internships, entrepreneurism, community-based learning, place-based education, outdoor education, student activism, and even well-planned field trips. Some HP/HP schools use programs or models that have a sound research base, such as the work of Russ Quaglia at the Quaglia Institute (quagliainstitute.org), which focuses on giving students greater voice and tapping into their interests and aspirations. Another, Talents Unlimited (https://talentsunlimited.schoolinsites.com), provides teacher training in how to nurture specific "talents" that prompt students to apply critical and creative thinking. Other schools turn to specific resources, such as Peter Johnston's book, *Opening Minds: Using Language to Change Lives* (2012) or *The Power of Our Words* (2013) by Paula Denton, which is part of the Responsive Classroom model. Both books support teachers in learning how to talk to students in ways that empower students to self-regulate and hone their decision-making skills.

Many schools have found student-led conferencing to be a highly effective structure for increasing students' metacognition and ownership in the learning process. Others have found that simply asking better questions can engage and empower students. "Understanding how using higher-level questions inspires kids is something I'm really passionate about," notes Dean Olsen at Henderson Collegiate. "If kids are given low-rigor material, they're going to be disengaged. They're not going to feel excited about the content, and they're not going to be as excited when they succeed." Figure 7.2 provides a synthesis of practices, supported by empirical evidence, that appear to work because they mitigate the poverty-related factors that adversely affect learning. Many of the studies included in this synthesis examine the effectiveness of the practice not only with students living in poverty but also with culturally and linguistically diverse populations of students.

Developing Assessment Literacy and Using Benchmark and Common Formative Assessments

Another important aspect of creating a coherent pedagogy of possibility is using high-quality assessments. A balanced and effective assessment system includes three levels of assessments: classroom, school, and district. Each level of assessment can serve multiple purposes, including both formative and summative purposes (Stiggins & DuFour, 2009). It's crucial that principals and teachers become assessment literate so they can use assessment to truly gauge learning and make appropriate instructional and programmatic decisions.

Figure 7.3 describes five elements of sound classroom assessments, the competencies necessary for teachers to develop and use high-quality classroom assessment to measure learning, and recommendations to support students in developing assessment literacy. Figure 7.4 lists 10 competencies educators need to develop to improve the quality of assessment practices schoolwide. Although these 10 competencies were intended to describe "a well-qualified principal," in HP/HP schools these competencies are present in teachers and teacher leaders as well.

Figure 7.2   10 Effective Practices for Developing a Pedagogy of Possibility

1. Teach, model, and provide experiences that develop creative and critical thinking skills.
   - Create maker spaces
   - Teach innovation design protocols
   - Ask open-ended questions
   - Use problem-based learning scenarios
   - Employ Socratic seminars
   - Develop multidisciplinary units
   - Integrate technology
   - Integrate the arts throughout the curriculum
   - Emphasize both STEM and STEAM

   See these resources for more information: Barton, Tan, & Greenberg (2017); Eisenman & Payne (1997); Johannessen (2004); Langer (2001); Ornelles (2007); Pogrow (2005); Schlichter, Hobbs, & Crump (1988); Sheridan et al. (2014); Wagner & Dintersmith (2015)

2. Prioritize literacy development.
   - Preteach vocabulary
   - Engage in word study
   - Access and build on prior knowledge
   - Embrace the reading and writing connection
   - Teach, model, and practice academic discourse
   - Focus on meaning making
   - Integrate literacy across the curriculum

   See these resources for more information: Edmondson & Shannon (1998) [in Milner]; Johannessen (2004); Kameenui & Carnine (1998); Knapp & Adelman (1995); Lareau (1987); Milner (2015); Rockwell (2007); Routman (2014)

3. Foster belonging and create a bond between students and school.
   - Conduct morning or class meetings
   - Facilitate team-building activities, particularly at the beginning of the year
   - Intentionally build relationships with students
   - Provide positive behavior supports
   - Facilitate cooperative learning, peer tutoring, and mentoring

   See these resources for more information: Benner, Nelson, Sanders, & Ralston (2012); Boss & Larmer (2018); Budge & Parrett (2009); Comer (1993); Craig (2016); Lalas (2007); Langer (2001); Luthar & Becker (2002); Milner (2015)

4. Personalize instruction based on learning needs, interests, and aspirations.
   - Mediate and scaffold learning experiences through
     » think-alouds
     » reciprocal teaching
     » visual organizers and models
     » guided practice
     » sheltered instruction
   - Differentiate instruction
   - Foster multiple intelligences
   - Provide for student choice in all phases of the learning process
   - Connect students' aspirations to learning
   - Integrate arts throughout the curriculum

   See these resources for more information: Campbell & Campbell (1999); Echevarría, Vogt, & Short (2004); Honigsfeld & Dunn (2009); Johannessen (2004); Kallick & Zmuda (2017); Palinscar & Brown (1985); Pogrow (2006); Quaglia & Fox (2003); Tomlinson et al. (2003)

5. Actively engage students in learning experiences for authentic, relevant purposes, which can help them envision their futures and foster hope.
   - Engage in project-based learning
   - Engage in place-based learning (service learning, environmental education, community-based learning, outdoor education, indigenous education, internships, apprenticeships, entrepreneurial activities)
   - Teach concepts and use formative assessment focused on deep levels of understanding
   - Employ student-led conferencing
   - Engage in expeditionary learning

   See these resources for more information: Bailey & Guskey (2000); Boaler (2002); Bodilly et al. (1998); Furco & Root (2010); Kinsley (1997); Newmann, Bryk, & Nagaoka (2001); Smith & Sobel (2010); Williams (2003)

(continued)

Figure 7.2 (*continued*)

6. Use teacher language that supports academic learning, develops self-control, and builds community.
   - Encourage a growth mindset in students
   - Provide feedback that encourages students to "own" their learning
   - Help students self-monitor their behavior
   - Teach and practice social skills
   - Positively redirect students
   - Help students identify their strengths
   - Promote positive identity development
   - Develop a sense of efficacy and agency in students

   See these resources for more information: Anderson (2019); Denton (2013); Johnston (2004, 2012)

7. Teach, model, and practice social and emotional skills.
   - Develop skills in conflict resolution, collaboration, communication, and adaptability
   - Develop the ability to recognize, express, and manage emotions
   - Teach and practice the ability to see others' perspectives
   - Use trauma-sensitive strategies
   - Employ mindfulness practices and other stress-reducing techniques
   - Emphasize a growth mindset
   - Develop character and citizenship

   See these resources for more information: Anderson (2019); Black & Fernando (2014); Buckner, Mezzacappa, & Beardslee (2009) | CASEL.org/impact; Claro, Paunesku, & Dweck (2016); Craig (2016)

8. Develop executive-functioning skills.
   - Use multisensory instruction
   - Provide memory aids such as mnemonic devices
   - Teach brainstorming, forecasting, and planning
   - Use graphic organizers
   - Use semantic mapping
   - Teach study skills
   - Chunk information
   - Build habits of mind

   See these resources for more information: Costa & Kallick (2009); Fogarty (2009); Hyerle (2009); Jensen (2009); Schlichter, Hobbs, & Crump (1988)

9. Integrate physical activity, exercise, and movement into teaching and learning.
   - Set fitness goals and monitor progress
   - Focus physical education on lifelong sports and fitness
   - Preserve recess time
   - Integrate movement into the teaching of academic subjects
   - Use stress reduction techniques such as time-out, breathing, yoga

   See these resources for more information: Armstrong (2019); Dariotis et al. (2016); Lindt & Miller (2017); Pellegrini & Bohn (2005); Sibley & Etnier (2003)

10. Develop students' awareness of bias, discrimination, and injustice.
    - Preserve social studies and civic education in the schedule
    - Teach about the history of poverty and classism
    - Read picture books and novels about empowered working-class families and those living in poverty
    - Use an anti-bias curriculum
    - Participate in poverty simulations
    - Engage in problem-based learning to address local issues

    See these resources for more information: Gorski (2012); Lalas (2007); Milner (2015); www.teachingtolerance.org

Figure 7.3   Sound Classroom Assessment Practice

1. Clear purposes Assessment processes and results serve clear and appropriate purposes.	a. Teachers understand who uses classroom assessment information and know their information needs. b. Teachers understand the relationship between assessment and student motivation and craft assessment experiences to maximize motivation. c. Teachers use classroom assessment processes and results formatively (assessment *for* learning). d. Teachers use classroom assessment results summatively (assessment *of* learning) to inform someone beyond the classroom about students' achievement at a particular point in time. e. Teachers have a comprehensive plan over time for integrating assessment *for* and *of* learning in the classroom.
2. Clear targets Assessments reflect clear and valued student learning targets.	a. Teachers have clear learning targets for students; they know how to turn broad statements of content standards into classroom-level learning targets. b. Teachers understand the various types of learning targets they hold for students. c. Teachers select learning targets focused on the most important things students need to know and be able to do. d. Teachers have a comprehensive plan over time for assessing learning targets.
3. Sound design Learning targets are translated into assessments that yield accurate results.	a. Teachers understand the various assessment methods. b. Teachers choose assessment methods that match intended learning targets. c. Teachers design assessments that serve intended purposes. d. Teachers sample learning appropriately in their assessments. e. Teachers write assessment questions of all types well. f. Teachers avoid sources of mismeasurement that bias results.
4. Effective communication Assessment results are managed well and communicated effectively.	a. Teachers record assessment information accurately, keep it confidential, and appropriately combine and summarize it for reporting (including grades). Such summary accurately reflects the current level of student learning. b. Teachers select the best reporting option (grades, narratives, portfolios, conferences) for each context (learning targets and users). c. Teachers interpret and use standardized test results correctly. d. Teachers effectively communicate assessment results to students. e. Teachers effectively communicate assessment results to a variety of audiences outside the classroom, including parents, colleagues, and other stakeholders.
5. Student involvement Students are involved in their own assessment.	a. Teachers make learning targets clear to students. b. Teachers involve students in assessing, tracking, and setting goals for their own learning. c. Teachers involve students in communicating about their own learning.

Source: From *Classroom Assessment for Student Learning: Doing It Right—Using It Well* by R. Stiggins, J. Arter, J. Chappuis, & S. Chappuis, Portland, OR: Pearson Assessment Training Institute, 2010. Reprinted with permission.

Figure 7.4   10 Assessment Competencies for School Leaders

1. The leader understands the attributes of a sound and balanced assessment system, as well as the conditions required to achieve balance in local systems.

2. The leader understands the necessity of clear academic achievement standards, aligned classroom-level achievement targets, and their relationship to the development of accurate assessments.

3. The leader understands the standards of quality for student assessments, helps teachers learn to assess accurately, and ensures that these standards are met in all school/district assessments.

4. The leader knows assessment *for* learning practices and works with staff to integrate them into classroom instruction.

5. The leader creates the conditions necessary for the appropriate use and reporting of student achievement information and can communicate effectively with all members of the school community about student assessment results, including report card grades, and their relationship to improving curriculum and instruction.

6. The leader understands the issues related to the unethical and inappropriate use of student assessment and protects students and staff from such misuse.

7. The leader can plan, present, and/or secure professional development activities that contribute to the use of sound assessment practices.

8. The leader knows and can evaluate the teacher's classroom assessment competencies and helps teachers learn to assess accurately and use the results to benefit student learning.

9. The leader analyzes student assessment information accurately, uses the information to improve curriculum and instruction, and assists teachers in doing the same.

10. The leader develops and implements sound assessment and assessment-related policies.

Source: From *Assessment Balance and Quality: An Action Guide for School Leaders* (p. 98), by S. Chappuis, C. Commodore, & R. J. Stiggins, 2009, Portland, OR: Educational Testing Service. Copyright 2009 by ETS. Reprinted with permission.

Pass Christian School District has developed assessment literacy throughout the system. Students in grades 4–12 take benchmark tests every three weeks each semester in English language arts and math. These 3-6-9–week assessments were developed by teachers and administrators in house. Test items are aligned to state standards but were not drawn from standard item banks, so they took more than a year to develop. As former principal Killebrew explains, "We labeled the standard by the question so we were able to run reports to see what percentage of our students had mastered what standards."

Pugliese West and East Garfield both administer frequent formative assessment as part of the Success for All model. The results are used for grouping and regrouping students, along with guiding instructional decisions. Parkway gives benchmark tests three times each year. Test results are displayed and analyzed using a data wall. At Evergreen Elementary, as part of the No Excuses University model, common assessment results are aggregated and displayed in the hallway.

In many HP/HP schools, students actively participate in using assessment to support their learning. Teachers set clear learning targets and engage their students in activities that help them acquire assessment literacy. These include selecting individual learning benchmarks, compiling portfolios, making public presentations of work, completing reflective revisions, and participating in student-led conferences. In some schools, the initiation of student-led conferences not only improved students' understanding of their own learning but also significantly improved parental attendance rates at school conferences.

UNCOMMON SENSE   At Parkway Elementary, students in grades 3–5 engage in goal setting and develop a data portfolio to track their progress. Students use the following sentence completion frame to establish their goals: "To get better at _____, I could _____. One thing I am going to start doing is _____. I'll start doing this on _____ and work on it until _____. One way I'll know I'm getting better is _____." Students set goals in language arts, math, and citizenship. Teachers conference with students regularly, and Principal Barton-Arnold meets with each student individually once a year and more if needed. According to Barton-Arnold, each year students have become more metacognitive and more engaged in their learning. ●

Rick Stiggins (2017) argues that our current obsession with standardized testing has led to a neglect of classroom assessment. He and others have pointed to the use of classroom assessment as vital to the improvement of teaching and learning, particularly the development and use of common assessments within a professional learning community structure (DuFour & Marzano, 2009; Stiggins & DuFour, 2009).

Nearly all the HP/HP schools we studied developed and used common assessments. This high-leverage strategy enables teachers to use their collective wisdom and expertise to (1) address the learning needs of individual students, (2) refine instructional practices, (3) increase the clarity of the learning targets they are attempting to reach, (4) enhance the quality of their assessments, and (5) support the development of a common vision of powerful teaching and learning (Stiggins & DuFour, 2009). High-performing, high-poverty schools connect curriculum and instruction to assessment. In turn, developing and using benchmark and formative common assessments contribute to the schools' success with students in poverty who underachieve.

A Pedagogy Update

In the 10 years between our two studies, some aspects of the pedagogy used in HP/HP schools have changed. The use of technology has become ubiquitous, and one-to-one mobile device initiatives are quite common.

Of late, with federal policy emphasis on social-emotional learning, many of the schools have come to realize, by necessity, that their pedagogical approach had always included social and emotional learning. Many of their efforts—for example, integration of academic learning with social and emotional learning, supportive discipline, healthy and safe learning environments, youth engagement and empowerment, professional learning focused on introspection and reflection, and authentic partnerships with parents—align with the competencies identified by the Collaborative for Academic, Social, and Emotional Learning (see www.casel.org).

It is our observation that data-based decision making has also become commonplace. Data walls, data days, data retreats, and data consultations are strategies noted by those we interviewed. In addition, the use of common assessments and well-developed communities of practice (Wenger, 1998) are more the norm than was true 10 years ago. These two practices greatly enhance instructional coherence, as teachers collaboratively analyze student work and discuss teaching practices.

Developing communities of practice, in particular, enables schools to create, implement, continuously improve, and sustain a pedagogy of possibility. Communities of practice are groups of people who work together over a period of time to hone their professional practice. They have a common sense of purpose and a real need to expand their understanding by sharing their expertise with and learning from their peers. We use the term *communities of practice* to describe the structures and processes observed in the HP/HP schools we studied because it emphasizes *practice*, a term that describes the work of professionals. Physicians practice medicine. Attorneys practice law. Education is also a profession, and those who work in HP/HP schools are consummate professionals. They draw on and contribute to a core body of knowledge, hone their skills in collaboration with one another, hold themselves accountable for student learning, and view their work as much more than a job. As one teacher told us, "I could work in another school, a more affluent school. Most of us could. But we work here. Why? Because every day I know I make a difference. A lot of people don't feel that way about what they do every day."

Something That Hasn't Changed: The Importance of the Teacher

Aligning curriculum, selecting research-based instructional practices, and using high-quality classroom assessments are only part of the picture. The school-related factor that makes the most difference in the lives of students who live in poverty (or all students, for that matter) is the quality of teaching that occurs in the classroom. Moreover, leaders and successful teachers know that high-quality teaching includes attributes well beyond technical knowledge and skills.

Sara Fry and Kim DeWit (2010) conducted a study of teachers who had struggled in school and asked them to identify, based on their experiences in K–12 schooling, what they believed to be the characteristics of effective teachers. Four characteristics emerged. Effective teachers (1) have caring relationships with students, (2) set high standards and help students reach them, (3) connect the curriculum to students' lives, and (4) participate in ongoing professional development. Fry and DeWit state, "These qualities reflect the belief that all children can learn. This disposition comes naturally to the teachers we interviewed because they know exactly what it is like to be the student who can—and did—learn despite facing challenges" (p. 71).

In *What Makes a Star Teacher: 7 Dispositions That Support Student Learning* (Hill-Jackson, Hartlep, & Stafford, 2019), the authors elaborate on the seven dispositions identified by Martin Haberman (1995) as characteristics and behaviors demonstrated by effective teachers:

1. **Teacher persistence**. Star teachers relentlessly search for what works best with each student.

2. **Protecting learners and learning**. Star teachers make children's involvement in productive work more important than curriculum rigidities and uneven school rules.

3. **Putting theory into practice**. Star teachers understand how teaching behaviors support ideas about effective teaching. This dimension predicts the teacher's ability to benefit from professional development and grow as a practitioner.

4. **Approaching learners who are at risk**. Star teachers assume personal accountability for their students' learning and form productive relationships with students to seed educational breakthroughs.

5. **Orienting to learners: Professional versus personal**. Star teachers respect and care about children, even when learners do things they dislike.

6. **Surviving in a bureaucracy**. Star teachers are able to survive in a school environment that is depersonalized, bureaucratic, and impersonal. Ultimately, they're more effective than other teachers in the classroom.

7. **Accepting and admitting fallibility**. Star teachers are willing to admit mistakes and correct them. This dimension of teacher behavior establishes the classroom climate for how students respond to their mistakes in the process of learning. (pp. 202–208)

We consistently found attributes in the teachers and other educators we have studied that were similar to Haberman's seven dispositions. These educators incorporate into their professional practice a particular ideology related to working with students who live in poverty that is foundational to all they do.

As Pete Selleck, vice principal of The Preuss School, points out,

> One realization I had when I came to Preuss was that we could have people who were really dedicated educators—really have great expertise—but then they worked with kids in poverty, and they weren't always equipped for that. It goes more to your worldview and to the core of what you believe about people. We have to have people who are dedicated to the mission first.

SCHOOL CULTURE ALERT   These educators know that their students who live in poverty are capable of learning to high standards; thus, they hold high expectations for them, insist they will learn, and provide the support they need to succeed. What was most striking among those educators with whom we talked was an unwavering professional accountability for learning. Teachers in HP/HP schools are confident in their ability to teach every child and do not make excuses for or blame students and families for their students' performance. ●

How Are We Ensuring Every Student Can Read Proficiently?

Second only to safety, ensuring that all students develop literacy skills is a core priority in HP/HP schools. As EJ Martinez, principal of Stillman Middle School, says, "We start with reading and end with reading. There's a lot of content and important stuff in between, but if our kids can't read at grade level, they'll never do as well as they could or should with the rest." Designing a comprehensive approach to reading improvement entails conducting an analysis of students' unique needs (e.g., those of English language learners); developing an understanding of the influence of poverty on reading achievement (Neuman, 2008); and examining the research base, especially concerning adolescent literacy (see Slavin, Cheung, Groff, & Lake, 2008.)

Teaching Kids to Read

The goal of many elementary schools is to ensure that all students are reading well by 3rd grade. At East Garfield and West Pugliese, students receive 90 minutes of instruction in reading—referred to as "holy time"—using the SFA model. In addition, students who need extra time are provided with tutoring or have an opportunity to read with students from a local university's teacher preparation program. Reading is the gateway skill to other knowledge, as well as to self-confidence and self-efficacy, and when students don't learn to read by 3rd grade or develop reading difficulties after 3rd grade, as is disproportionately the case for students living in poverty (Kieffer, 2010), they will likely struggle in every class thereafter. Once in secondary school, a student with reading difficulties might need to supplant an elective to provide the explicit instruction they need, which can present a dilemma for high schools. Requiring a student who is likely to be disillusioned about reading to take a reading course as an elective might not be his or her first choice. Nonetheless, all of the secondary schools we studied continue to teach students to read using various strategies and structures, some of which require tough choices for students.

UNCOMMON SENSE   All students at Stillman Middle School take reading as part of their regular coursework, in addition to a separate course in English. Although it's been suggested that the two courses be blended, EJ Martinez, principal, says, "We push reading. We want kids to read because reading is in every subject. It's in math, science, and social studies. That was also one of the big pushes to get our library updated and our kids in there." In addition to the reading course, students actively participate in the Accelerated Reader program, in which students are supported and held accountable for reading a specific amount of time each week. ●

In the middle grades, 4 through 8, Henderson Collegiate incorporates several intervention strategies to further develop students' literacy skills. Caitlin Terranova, chief of staff, explains,

> In grades 4 and 5, students take three separate classes that focus on different subsets of literacy skills: reading, writing, and nonfiction studies. Additionally, at these grades, students benefit from intervention blocks in which they receive targeted small-group instruction at their specific reading levels using data from the STEP assessment. As students advance to grades 6, 7, and 8, they take an English class that targets the full range of traditional literacy skills. In the 7th and 8th grades, students also receive instruction in a technology class curriculum that includes instruction around conducting research and writing essays. In grades 4 through 8, after-school tutoring is also provided for students who need extra practice and support.

Scott Barton, principal of The Preuss School, told us, "For the past 10 years, we have been doing a better job of identifying where each student is academically, including reading." When students enroll at Preuss, they are given a diagnostic test before they start, which includes an assessment of reading. Students who need additional support are given advisory classes and tutoring during the school day. Tutoring is also offered after school and on Saturdays. All 6th graders take an extra English class called

Literacy Enrichment. Beginning in 7th grade, students who still need extra support may be enrolled in a literacy support class in lieu of an elective or Spanish class. These support classes continue into high school.

At Pass Christian High School, literacy development is also a priority. Robyn Killebrew, principal, says,

> With regard to supporting our struggling readers, we work hard to meet them where they are while continuing to address grade-level standards. Our interventionist and special education teachers are included in [the district-sponsored] early reading skill training such as Orton Gillingham, LETRS, and Association Method. The multisensory approach, coupled with high-interest, age-appropriate literature, seems to garner the most growth.

Motivating Kids to Read

Reading, like any other skill, requires practice to improve. Although it's not an easy undertaking, HP/HP schools find ways to motivate students to read. At the beginning of each school year, students at Henderson Collegiate Middle School "earn" their classroom library. Each class has a classroom library from which students can check out books. To build enthusiasm for reading, teachers cover the classroom library with large sheets of butcher paper; students "tear off bits at a time" every time the class "earns" the privilege until they've "unwrapped" the library, which results in a big celebration as students are taught to value and care for the books.

Learning to read changes the lives of students who have struggled. They gain new appreciation for learning and, most important, a sense of self-efficacy that extends to other areas of their lives. At Peterson Elementary, an unofficial motto is "Kids at Peterson do hard things." One teacher relays the following story:

> Last year I had a student who really struggled behaviorally. It wasn't uncommon to find her hiding under tables or have her run away. The first thing she said to me was, "I can't read—I just can't." So I said, "Let's see if we can read just this word; I bet you can do it." And, sure enough, she could read words like *see, bee, cat* . . . that kind of thing. We talked about being brothers and sisters [here at school] and helping one another; we're going to bicker, but we're still a family. Her struggle reminded me that learning to read is hard, but I watched the kids support her and help her and celebrate with her as she made milestones. At the end of the year, she didn't make it to grade level, but she had made huge growth. She read accurately, and it was slow, but she did it. I said, "I'm so proud of you; you read that!" She replied, "Yeah, I can read. I've always been able to read." It was just so cool to see that she didn't remember starting the year telling me she couldn't read—because now she was a reader!

How Are We Providing Targeted Interventions for Students Who Need Them?

In her book *White Teachers/Diverse Classrooms*, Julie Landsman writes,

> We cannot follow the statement "All children can learn" with conditionals. No matter where we teach, we will rarely have a classroom in which every student is motivated, has a full stomach, lives in a safe neighborhood, and has a relationship with both of his or her parents. We must teach the students we have before us, understanding the complexities of their lives and helping each student deal with these complexities. Teachers must be bearers of hope in places where there are depression and despair. (Landsman & Lewis, 2006, p. 26)

Even with well-developed core instruction designed to improve the quality of teaching and learning in the classroom, students who live in poverty may need additional support. Too often, for too many students in poverty, the need for additional support has resulted in referral and placement in special education programs (Howard, Dresser, & Dunklee, 2009). With the advent of Response to Intervention (RTI) and the multitiered system of supports (MTSS), many schools are becoming more systematic about the use of interventions. Based on comprehensive assessments, RTI models provide additional support for students at the Tier 2 level and Tier 3 interventions for those with exceptional needs. Our use of the term *targeted intervention* is in some instances synonymous with the RTI Tier 2 support; in other cases, targeted interventions are offered as extended learning opportunities outside the school day or year.

High-performing, high-poverty schools have long been systematically providing targeted support for students' academic, social, and emotional learning within and outside the traditional school day, week, or year. All HP/HP schools continually review data to identify students who need before-, during-, and after-school small-group and individual tutoring or counseling; trauma-responsive support; self-paced interventions using technology; one-on-one academic advising and coaching; homework support; or additional assessment time.

All the schools we studied provide extended learning opportunities. Students at Henderson Collegiate Middle School who need additional instruction take a course called No Shortcuts, which provides them more time to focus on reading in small groups during the school day. Many other schools offer tutoring during the day, with a majority offering it outside the school day. Parkway, Concourse Village, Pugliese West, East Garfield, and Murtaugh provide both preschool and full-day kindergarten. Henderson

Collegiate offers Saturday tutoring for students, as does Preuss, which also offers an online summer school.

Not all interventions are created equal. For example, most schools offer tutoring, but in some schools it has little positive impact on student learning. If an intervention is to be effective, the manner in which it is structured and implemented must be of concern to leaders. Figure 7.5 includes descriptions of four common interventions—before- and after-school programs, tutoring, early childhood readiness programs, and summer school—as well as tips for design and implementation.

Figure 7.5   Tips for the Design and Implementation of Four Common Interventions

1. **Before- or After-School Programs**
   Document the need for before- or after-school program.
   Assess financial capabilities.
   Determine the scope of the intended program.
   Hire a program director to oversee and coordinate.
   Involve parents, businesspeople, and other community members.
   Provide ongoing evaluation.
   Focus on strengthening academic skills: direct instruction, learning strategies and skills, peer/cross-age tutoring, homework assistance.
   Plan group time focused on building healthy relationships and on opportunities to solve problems and increase self-esteem.
   Provide opportunities to widen students' horizons: recreational and cultural activities, technology-related activities, involvement in community-based youth organizations.
   Establish parent resource centers: parents participate or volunteer in children's activities, offer parenting knowledge/skill development.
   Provide transportation.
   Spend time on project-based, experiential, and hands-on learning, challenging students to think.
   Encourage positive staff-child relationships and include opportunities for student voice and autonomy.

   Related research: Fischer (2018); Schwendiman & Fager (1999); Silverberg (2018)

2. **Tutoring**
   Find partner teachers; determine content.
   Determine methodology.
   Determine program length.
   Train and provide feedback for tutors.
   Prepare the tutees.
   Match tutors and tutees.
   Inform parents.
   Monitor and assess the program.
   Structure lesson plans for tutors to follow.
   Provide frequent tutoring sessions (two or three per week).
   Identify a framework to ensure quality control and participant autonomy.
   Incorporate district administrators, principals, and teachers into the program.
   Provide an avenue to network with other programs.
   Place emphasis on building the relationship between the tutor and tutee.

   Related research: Bond (2002); McClure & Vaughn (1997); Partelow, Brown, Shapiro, & Johnson (2018)

Figure 7.5 (*continued*)

3. **Early Childhood/Readiness Programs**
   Provide prekindergarten programs, 12 weeks in duration, housed in the school.
   Supply services two or three days per week.
   Staff with teachers who have kindergarten experience.
   Provide ongoing support for teachers, including coaching and mentoring, with program assessments that measure the quality of classroom interactions and provide actionable feedback for teachers to improve instruction.
   Use assessments that consider children's academic, social-emotional, and physical progress and contribute to instructional and program planning.
   Base curriculum on literacy and numeracy.
   Include programs that encourage meaningful family engagement.
   Support 10–15 child-parent dyads (20–30 total).
   Encourage parents to drop in and participate in circle time.
   Extend learning by having teachers spend time in individual or small-group interactions.
   Provide outreach to hard-to-reach families.

   Related research: Meloy, Gardner, & Darling-Hammond (2019); Pelletier & Corter (2005)

4. **Summer School**
   Identify potential summer school students early in the year.
   Separate behavior from academics.
   Align instruction to student needs.
   Develop a rubric to determine which students need summer school.
   Establish small class sizes, and focus on students who have shown a higher level of failure.
   Create a handbook for the summer to include policies and procedures for summer classes.
   Set up courses to fit the compressed schedule.
   Develop policies that maximize participation and attendance.
   Deal with complex topics early in the course.
   Maintain a positive site culture.
   Allow students to complete assignments more readily; break larger assignments into frequent short assignments.
   Maintain expectations and standards.
   Assign only one course per teacher.
   Make certain administrators and teachers are available to parents and students beyond class time.
   Ensure teachers aren't teaching the course for the first time in a compressed format.

   Related research: Kops (2010); McEachin, Augustine, & McCombs (2018); Rischer (2009)

How Are We Providing Job-Embedded Opportunity for Professional Learning?

Educators in HP/HP schools hold a view similar to the one expressed by a superintendent in a Northwest school district: "There is a bright red thread running from every student-learning problem to a problem of practice for teachers, and, finally, to a problem of practice for leaders." Professional learning and student learning are two sides of the same coin—they cannot be separated. Some of the schools have effective professional learning communities (PLCs); others use sophisticated and focused coaching models.

In addition to instructional coaches, many of the principals and assistant principals provide instructional leadership using classroom walk-throughs or instructional rounds.

UNCOMMON SENSE   At Concourse Village, students' learning agenda is tightly linked to teachers' learning. Principal Sorden has structured the school calendar to accommodate opportunities for job-embedded professional learning. She provides workshops for teachers focused on everything from expected routines, such as lining up and morning greetings, to curriculum, instruction, and assessment. In addition, teachers are paired based on complementary strengths and weaknesses as "growth partners" for six-week segments. They visit each other's classrooms for a 15-minute observation once each week. After the observations, they meet to provide feedback using the TAG process (tell something you liked, ask a question, and give a suggestion). Sorden explains how she strategically pairs teachers. "If I know one teacher is great at questioning," she explains, "and another is great at building community, but the first teacher needs help with that, I pair them so they can see glimmers of great teaching practice." Sensitive to teachers' time commitments, she gives the observing teachers 60 minutes for lunch instead of 50. "So you get an additional 10 minutes for lunch," she tells them. "[In return], you give me back a teacher observation, meaning you observe a colleague once a week [for 15 minutes] and you give that colleague written feedback within 24 hours, copying me." ●

Several other structures and processes are effective in supporting professional learning and promoting reflective practices. These include action research, lesson study, case-based learning, networks, journaling, portfolio development, and tuning protocols.

High-performing, high-poverty schools continually endeavor to enhance professional capacity to better meet student needs. The adults in these schools take their own learning as seriously as their students' learning. As one teacher explains, "When I learn to do something better, it helps a lot of my kids. We all know this, and we continually work to find the time it takes [to learn]."

How Are We Ensuring Equity?

This question is fundamentally concerned with providing equal opportunity for learning and closing opportunity gaps. As previously described, one high-leverage approach is employing a pedagogy of possibility, an approach that depends on several factors, the most vital of which are the quality of instruction occurring in each classroom and the theories of action underpinning that instruction. In other words, teachers' knowledge and skills, as well as their dispositions, are of equal importance. Here are two crucially important equity-focused questions for school leaders and for educators more broadly: Which teachers need more support to develop their knowledge base and skill level? Which teachers have the dispositions necessary to successfully work with students who live in poverty and to authentically engage in the school's mission?

In our book *Disrupting Poverty* (2018), we examine three potentially hot button classroom practices that we view as a classroom teacher's equity litmus test—homework, grading, and classroom assessment. Let's briefly look at homework because it can illuminate a host of issues related to equity. Despite an abundance of research on the limited effectiveness of homework and researchers' warnings to "tread carefully with its use" (Hattie, 2009, 2015; Vatterott, 2009, 2018), assigning homework persists. Homework was used in all of the HP/HP schools we studied, but it was carefully and equitably assigned. For example, teachers ensured all students had the necessary materials to complete the homework either by sending those materials home with students or by providing access to materials at school. Students were also provided space and time to complete homework at school when their home environment or family context made it difficult to complete their homework in their home.

For students in poverty, homework can present multiple challenges. These include limited parental support for a variety of reasons, not the least of which are long working hours; lack of a quiet space; limited or absent materials and supplies; lack of technology such as computers, mobile devices, and internet service; siblings to care for; part-time jobs and work commitments; and household chores and cooking responsibilities required to support the family.

Cathy Vatterott (2009, 2018), a noted scholar of homework, suggests that homework should be used for practice only and that it should not be graded. *If* homework is absolutely necessary for students to master the content and meet standards, then the equity question at hand is this: How will we ensure that all students have equal opportunity to complete the homework? If educators can answer that question, the use of homework is likely to be more productive.

The Principal's Role

In HP/HP schools, the gap is small between principals' theories *of* action (espoused theories) and their theories *in* action (the theories that *actually* underpin their professional practice). In other words, their actions are consistent with their message. They're clear about their course of action and can articulate the rationale for those actions.

Simplifying the message keeps the vision clear and in the forefront of the school's improvement efforts. Leaders in the schools we studied "cut to the chase." Their words reflect the theories that underpin system-level learning in their schools:

- "We make decisions based on what's best for kids. We treat them as our own."
- "It's all about community."
- "*Everyone*'s a reading and language arts teacher here."
- "We share the big picture with people and give them enough information; then they engage."
- "We don't throw it at the wall and hope it sticks; we build the wall so we *know* it will stick."
- "We control the controllable."
- "If we think we've arrived, then we need to leave. We can always get better. "
- "We dare to be different."

Figure 7.6 shows some actions principals can take to focus on learning in HP/HP schools.

Figure 7.6   The Principal's Role in Focusing on Learning in HP/HP Schools

The principal—

- Facilitates ongoing conversations about what is possible in a high-poverty school.

- Continues as chief steward of the school's vision.

- Controls the narrative about the school, ensuring the focus is on high expectations and what it means to have an impact on student learning.

- Works with teachers to establish a common understanding of powerful teaching and learning.

- Uses his or her formal authority to ensure school structures and processes are in place to develop communities of practice through which teachers do the following:
  » Align curriculum to state/district standards.
  » Ensure instructional quality.
  » Develop assessment literacy.
  » Use assessments to guide decision making at the classroom and school levels.
  » Grow as professionals.

- Manages human and material resources to ensure targeted interventions are provided to students who need them.

- Promotes and supports a culture of inquiry as a means for continual improvement in the classroom and schoolwide.

SCHOOL CULTURE ALERT   Leaders and educators in HP/HP schools act with a keen sense of urgency. Krista Barton-Arnold shares this reality from Parkway Elementary:

> The judgment calls have high stakes ... that alone can be tiring and exhausting. You're making decisions in the fierce urgency of now. The kids need this education. I don't have time to play, and I don't have time to make mistakes. They need all we can do for them now." ●

Taking Action

- *Create a sense of urgency and act on it.* Are the needs of your students who underperform known and being addressed?
- *Create coherence in the instructional program.* Is your curriculum aligned to state and district standards? Have you articulated the curriculum across subjects and grade levels? Have you identified benchmark standards?
- *Employ a powerful pedagogy.* Are students primarily engaged in meaning making, developing various kinds of understanding, problem solving, reasoning, inquiry, and critical and creative thinking?
- *Develop a shared vision of what good teaching looks like.* Can all teachers describe a community-held understanding of good teaching? Can they list a core set of things to look for related to what teachers do and what students do when good teaching is happening?
- *Use research-based teaching strategies that specifically address the needs of students living in poverty.* Do teachers know which instructional strategies have a solid research base? Do teachers have the required expertise to employ research-based strategies?
- *Develop assessment literacy.* Do teachers understand and employ sound assessment practices? Do principals have the competencies necessary to improve assessment practices schoolwide?
- *Involve students in assessing their learning.* Are students engaged in activities that help them assess and monitor their own learning?
- *Develop and use benchmark and common formative assessments.* Have benchmark standards been identified? Have teachers been provided opportunities to collaborate to both develop assessments and use the information gained to inform instruction?
- *Ensure teachers develop and demonstrate the dispositions that lead to success with students living in poverty.* Do teachers know which

teacher attributes and functions lead to success? Do teachers possess these attributes and fulfill such functions?

- *Develop reading proficiency in all students.* How many students are not proficient in reading by 4th grade? Is reading taught after the elementary years when needed?
- *Provide targeted interventions when needed.* Does your school use data to identify students who need additional support? Has time been scheduled during, before, or after the school day to provide extra help for students?
- *Commit to equity.* Are teachers assigned to courses in a manner that equitably serves all students? Is data disaggregated to determine for whom practices, strategies, and systems are and are not working? Are all students provided with equal opportunity to learn?
- *Link professional learning to student learning and employ research-based models.* Do students' learning needs drive the content for professional development? Do professional development models support the development of communities of practice and prompt reflection and inquiry?

8 Eliminating Practices That Perpetuate Underachievement and Inequity

"If this was my child, this would not be happening. If this was your child, this would not be happening. This is happening because it is an inner-city child at a school that is economically disadvantaged and 100 percent African American." These powerful words from a principal supervisor . . . succinctly express the moral imperative to confront uncomfortable truths about our public schools.

—*Coby V. Meyers, Lamar Goree, and Keith Burton,* Phi Delta Kappan, *2019*

Committing to equity in our public schools is fundamentally about providing all students equal opportunity to learn. That won't happen until we confront the low expectations that often stem from classist and racist beliefs. Such beliefs are foundational to the inequitable conditions and counterproductive practices found in far too many schools that continue to perpetuate underachievement.

High-poverty schools become high performing in part by *abandoning* what doesn't work and replacing those approaches with those that *do* work. Educators aggressively confront entrenched, counterproductive practices. They are relentless in this effort. They know that inaction perpetuates low achievement and undermines effective practices.

But where to begin? Because there's no one right answer to that question, we have designed the tools in this book to help you and your fellow educators tailor the information to your unique context. To guide learning and help you reflect on the current situation in your school, use the self-assessment rubric shown in Figure 8.1, which isolates nine practices that HP/HP schools have identified as perpetuating underachievement and achievement gaps by denying students the opportunity to learn.

Figure 8.1   Eliminating Mindsets and Practices That Can Perpetuate Underachievement: Assessing Your School's Progress

Progress Indicators/Evidence	No Action Yet	Getting Started	Gaining Momentum	Sustaining Gains, Refining
		• People are aware of counterproductive mindsets, policies, structures, or practices. • Urgency is apparent. • Staff acknowledges need for change.	• People are empowered. • Barriers are being removed. • Commitment to the elimination of barriers is increasing. • Support for change continues.	• Counter-productive mindsets, policies, structures, or practices have been eliminated. • New mindsets, policies, structures, and practices are evident.
Counterproductive Practices	**0**	**1**	**2**	**3**
1. Low Expectations (pp. 163–164)				
2. Inequitable Funding (pp. 164–166)				
3. Inequitable Teacher Assignments (p. 166)				
4. Ineffective Instruction (pp. 166–168)				
5. Retention (pp. 168–169)				
6. Tracking, Ability Grouping, and Misuse of Pullouts (pp. 169–170)				
7. Misuse of Multitiered Systems of Support (pp. 170–171)				
8. Misassignment to Special Education (p. 171)				
9. Suspensions and Expulsions (pp. 172–173)				

A common characteristic of public education in the United States is the tendency to rarely, if ever, abandon policies, structures, and practices that have become mainstream. In many respects, this reluctance to change has served our systems well by supporting what works. But when something doesn't work, even when that something has been refuted by overwhelming research, we often have a difficult time changing course or abandoning what we're used to doing.

One reason, of course, for the perpetuation of these practices may lie in the inertia found in bureaucratic systems. Still, organizations are composed of people, and people have to change before systems change. As one principal in an HP/HP high school notes,

> We had to get to a point where we were all on board with the belief that every kid was going to learn, that every family mattered, and that regardless of the condition of the home, this child would learn and reach proficiency. We would do whatever it took, all of us. Did it mean several teachers chose to transfer or leave? Did it mean it took a couple of years to get there? Yes, but now everyone's on the same page, and that makes all the difference.

HP/HP schools work to eliminate the pervasive and destructive outcomes for students that accompany nine specific practices: (1) tolerating low expectations; (2) inequitable funding; (3) inequitable teacher assignments; (4) ineffective instruction; (5) retention; (6) tracking, ability grouping, and misuse of pullouts; (7) misuse of multitiered systems of support; (8) misassignment to special education; and (9) suspensions and expulsions.

Tolerating Low Expectations

A toxic atmosphere of low expectations permeates everything in a low-performing school. No underperforming school that enrolls students who live in poverty will ever reverse trends of underachievement without explicitly addressing the expectations held by all staff. High expectations are simply paramount to success.

Leaders and educators in HP/HP schools model high expectations for themselves. To counter the existence of any mental maps that reflect less than the very best for every student, they tackle the insidiousness of low expectations head-on. They don't tolerate excuses for underachievement, including those made by the students themselves. They're relentless in their efforts to help all students feel safe and develop a sense of belonging at school, they honor the effort required of students, and they celebrate the students' accomplishments. This mindset of high expectations and resulting action often begins with the development of a common vision of what powerful and deep learning looks like for all students and a verbalized belief that every student can and will achieve at high levels and experience other types of success in school. A culture of high expectations appears to be fostered, in part, by building relationships with students and their families;

seeking to understand their needs, strengths, interests, and assets; and, in turn, accessing whatever support is needed for them to succeed.

The importance of high expectations, as noted author Rhonda Weinstein (2002) states, is crucial to our children's future:

> When we respond to the individual differences among students by lowering our expectations and providing inferior educational opportunities, we underestimate the capacity for all of our children to grow intellectually, and we fail to provide adequate tools for learning. In these ways, we confirm our own predictions. To prevent such educational tragedies—a particularly urgent goal given the growing diversity of our children attending our schools—we need to both embrace and support pedagogically a vision of possibility regarding the educational achievement of all our children. (p. 2)

SCHOOL CULTURE ALERT High expectations hold incredible power, often single-handedly determining the fine line or enormous chasm between success and failure. Schools routinely serve as a broker to parcel out both types of expectations, high and low, and student success follows accordingly. High-performing, high-poverty schools are places of high expectations. One principal of an HP/HP school pointed to a student at his school who was struggling mightily in math. "We're going to get him there," the principal said, "I don't know how, but we're going to work that out. We're going to plan, and we're going to get him there because that's what we expect." Creating and sustaining this element of the school's culture require educators to eliminate blaming, excuse making, and a host of other counterproductive practices that not only perpetuate low achievement but also serve as barriers to building leadership capacity within the school. ●

Inequitable Funding

At the top of the list of the villains that rob students of the opportunity to catch up with their more advantaged peers is inequitable funding. Although we acknowledge that the formulas used by states and districts to finance schools are complex, leveling the playing field for students in poverty comes down, in part, to this simple question: Do we provide equitable funding to our students who live in poverty?

The answer is more complex than merely calculating per-pupil or per-teacher expenditures, although such figures are indeed revealing. Through two decades of research, the Education Trust has continued to document the fact that high-poverty schools in the United States receive, on average, substantially less funding—approximately $1,000 less (or 7 percent)—in per-pupil funding than do low-poverty districts. For districts serving the largest populations of American Indian, black, and Latinx students, the gap is even larger. They receive approximately $1,800 less (or 13 percent) in per-pupil funding. When adjusted for the additional costs of educating students in high-poverty schools (wraparound services, various student supports, and high-quality early learning), the disparity between high- and low-poverty district funding jumps to approximately $2,000 less (or 16 percent). Such funding gaps have proven persistent and appear to be continuing in various degrees in all states (Morgan & Amerikaner, 2018).

Countless decisions related to the use of resources influence whether students in poverty will catch up and whether students from low-income homes (whether they underachieve or not) will have the opportunity to fully participate in school. Instead of arriving at schools that provide opportunities to accelerate their learning and catch up, too often these students are greeted by inexperienced teachers (often teaching out of their area of expertise) in schools that are substandard and sometimes unhealthy, unsafe, and full of chaos and disorganization. In her keynote address at the Taking Charge of Change Conference sponsored by the Education Trust in November 2010, Kati Haycock said,

> Far too many of our kids arrive at school with less . . . vocabulary, preschooling, educational learning experiences, books in the home, parents in the home, supplies and materials associated with learning and school, safe environments, and more. And what do we give them? They come with less and, in return, we give them less.

In addition, students living in poverty are confronted with a barrage of hidden costs that serve as reminders that they simply don't belong. For example, in one middle school, the background colors on students' ID cards (which students were required to wear on lanyards around their necks) were chosen by the photography company and depended on whether the student had purchased a photo package. Staff members didn't notice the difference in IDs until a student told one of his teachers, "You know who bought pictures and who didn't by the color of the background."

The hidden cost of attending school often includes fees for participation in athletics, band, choir, and various clubs, as well as materials related to homework assignments, athletic uniforms, yearbooks, school pictures, social activities, and school supplies. Students who are poor often do without these aspects of school, which many students consider standard. High-performing, high-poverty schools commit to the equitable use of resources. They create and maintain budgets that become moral documents intended to target support where it's needed most. The schools' priorities drive the budgeting process and are aimed at leveling the playing field for students from low-income families.

Inequitable Teacher Assignments

When teachers instruct outside their area of expertise, students are often shortchanged. Unfortunately, higher proportions of low-income students than their higher-income peers are taught by teachers who are not certificated in the subject they're called on to teach (Haycock, 2010). The same is true for years of teaching experience. This egregious injustice, seemingly entrenched in our system, perpetuates underachievement. As one principal explains it, "We do our best. We have to have teachers who can both teach their areas and take on these other jobs. The new ones bear the brunt of this, but that's part of getting your foot in the door here."

The Education Trust found that, unfortunately, out-of-field teaching continues to persist in high-poverty schools. "Core academic classes in high-poverty secondary schools are almost twice as likely to have an out-of-field teacher . . . and one in every four secondary math classes . . . is taught by a teacher with neither a math major nor certification in math" (Almy & Theokas, 2010, p. 2).

In contrast, the most effective teachers in HP/HP schools are routinely placed with the highest-need students. In these schools, a commitment to equity means kids who need more get more. But this assignment strategy does not happen at the expense of ensuring excellence for all students. The result of this practice is that HP/HP schools succeed in closing achievement gaps and raising overall achievement, central tenets of the mission of public schooling in the United States.

Ineffective Instruction

No student should be subjected to an ineffective teacher. Unfortunately, many students will experience poor instruction during their school years. For students who are low performing and live in poverty, ineffective teachers can have a particularly harmful effect because, in many cases, these students are more dependent on the quality of their educational experience than are their more affluent peers. Numerous studies indicate that when students are assigned an ineffective teacher for two consecutive years, dramatic gaps will develop and grow between these students and students assigned to competent teachers (Sanders, 1999).

Educators in HP/HP schools do not tolerate poor teaching—at least not for long. Collaborative efforts, coaching, and other forms of assistance are used to support underperforming teachers who appear to have the potential to improve. Nevertheless, if improvement does not occur, principals in HP/HP schools initiate appropriate processes to dismiss a teacher, regardless of tenure status.

Alexa Sorden, principal of Concourse Village Elementary in the South Bronx, explains:

> Historically, poor-performing teachers have hidden in poor-performing schools and districts, which is the reason they're poor performing. The excuses are predictable: "Well, you know, it's a low-income community; they're children from a shelter." "Well, you know, there's a lot of single-parent households." "Well, you know, they're not even being raised by mom and dad; the child is suffering from trauma."

Sorden acknowledges that these situations make it hard, but she persists, asking, "What are we going to do to create the best learning environments for our kids?" Regarding ineffective teachers, she asserts, "I'm very passionate. If you can't share my passion, I won't hold it against you. What you just have to understand is that I won't let you hide here."

The level of a teacher's expectations for students can typically be seen in the assignments they give. Kati Haycock (2001) studied the disparity in assignments given to students in poverty. She was stunned by how little is expected of them—how few assignments they get in a given week or month. She was further stunned by the low level of the few assignments they do get. "In high-poverty urban middle schools," she says, "we see a lot of coloring assignments, rather than writing or mathematics assignments. Even at the high school level. 'Read *To Kill a Mockingbird*,' says the 11th grade English teacher, 'and when you're finished, color a poster about it.'"

HP/HP schools set and keep the bar high for their students. To meet and exceed achievement standards requires high-quality instruction by teachers who work together to craft high-quality lessons and assessments. These schools are models of collective teacher efficacy, which has been identified by John Hattie (2018) as the most significant factor (out of 252 factors) in terms of its potential to positively influence student achievement. We repeatedly heard comments like this from a teacher in a HP/HP school in a southern state: "We can't do this alone; we simply have to collaborate and work together every day. It's the only way to successfully reach our students."

When confronting ineffective teaching, Pete Hall (2019) admonishes educators to avoid engaging in what he calls the "dance of the lemons" (p. 16). He urges schools to avoid the practice of shuffling off an ineffective teacher and recommends, instead, a five-step process of support, including (1) setting a clear level of what high performance is; (2) giving frequent, descriptive, and focused feedback; (3) naming a concern if one arises; (4) offering continual support and resources; and (5) trusting the process. Ineffective teaching can be addressed, but it requires courage, will, patience, and a commitment to equity emboldened by the belief that every child deserves to be well taught.

Retention

Devon dropped out of school at age 13. A year later, no one knows where he is. Most likely, he's not in school. Devon was going to be retained to spend another year in the 6th grade. He was embarrassed and felt alone. He didn't want to be with a new group of kids who were younger. Truth was, Devon had been passed along with low reading skills for years. Now, in the beginning of his adolescent years, he was told he was going back to 6th grade. He gave the class a try—for three weeks—and then disappeared. With good intentions, Devon's teachers had recommended an intervention—retention—that resulted in the opposite effect of what they had hoped.

In fact, retention of students who are low performing and who reside in low-income families seriously compromises the students' chances of ever catching up and graduating (Schilder & Dahlin, 2016). Retention as an intervention for underachievement doesn't work for most students. Currently, 16 states and the District of Columbia mandate retention for students who are not meeting some form of proficiency on state-required achievement tests—this despite decades of research that, at best, question the effectiveness of this practice and, at worst, condemn its use.

The Center on Enhancing Early Learning Outcomes (Schilder & Dahlin, 2016) reports, "Retention is not uniformly supported by research as a remedy to most children's learning difficulties. Receiving the same information using similar instructional strategies a second year is unlikely to yield significant results for many children" (p. 12). The report continues,

> The preponderance of research indicates that academic gains associated with retention were short term and not evident several years following the retention, while the likelihood of dropping out of school increased significantly. Also, concerns that retention disproportionately impacts minority groups of children suggest the contributing causes of school difficulties must be addressed to reduce the need for retention. (p. 12)

This and other research (Hattie, 2009, 2011) bear out our conclusion that retention is the poster child for entrenched practices that are commonly employed to enable a student to catch up or, at times, to punish the student for not keeping up but that in the end perpetuate underachievement.

High-performing, high-poverty schools typically do not employ traditional forms of retention. "When I arrived at Parkway, there had been 20 retentions," shares Principal Krista Barton-Arnold. "It was a common practice. Teachers would quit on them in January and say, 'We'll just retain you.' When I took retention off the table, it was like, 'Whoa, now we've got to do something because retention is not an option.'" When students fail to learn, these schools focus on the individual needs of their students, with a goal of catching them up. They're carefully assessed, and improvement plans are constructed and implemented around their individual needs. Daily and weekly monitoring of interventions takes place, and midcourse corrections are made as needed. As students begin to make progress, interventions are modified or eliminated as appropriate.

Tracking, Ability Grouping, and Misuse of Pullouts

HP/HP schools begin with the expectation that all students can and will achieve to standards. That mission stands in stark opposition to the practice of tracking students by ability or, far worse, by the perception of ability. Werblow, Urick, and Duesbery (2013) explain, "Academic tracking has been shown to limit the quality of student instructional opportunities, decrease students' perceptions of their abilities, and negatively influence student achievement. These factors . . . may also influence students in lower tracks to learn less and ultimately drop out of school." The authors offer further caution to educators and policymakers regarding this practice: "Academic tracking also appears to disadvantage students who are Latinos, have Individualized Education Plans, or have lower socioeconomic backgrounds."

Researcher John Hattie (2009) found that tracking had an effect size of .12, which is far below the "hinge" point of effective practice of .40, and therefore should be carefully considered before using. That said, the use of tracking and ability grouping are alive and well in public schools despite these and other cautions.

UNCOMMON SENSE   "We actually have a detracked curriculum," says Scott Barton, principal of The Preuss School. "One track that's designed to get every one of our students into and through college." The schedule does allow for variance in several electives, but otherwise one curriculum with high expectations, wraparound services, and support for the students is in place. The same is true for Henderson Collegiate Middle School: There's a single-track, college-prep curriculum for every one of their 610 4th through 8th grade students. "We get them ready to succeed in high school, get accepted into a 4-year college, and graduate," shares Principal

Frank Terranova. "They're all in the same track, and we support them to get through." In these two schools in which 95 percent of the students live in poverty, high expectations for each student, a detracked curriculum, and teachers who work closely together and who have a relationship with and care for every student all contribute to their success. ●

Like tracking, ability grouping often fails to yield the results educators hope for. HP/HP schools typically use skills-based grouping, which entails frequently releveling students. This is the case in both elementary schools in Steubenville, Ohio. Their two-decade experience with the Success for All approach continues to prove effective for their students.

Excessive use of pullout instruction, a form of ability grouping or tracking, is not in the best interests of low-performing students who live in poverty. Such grouping schemes are often based on and perpetuate low expectations and do not offer models or examples of students who are further along in the learning progression; therefore, low-performing students in these situations do not tend to catch up. The exception is carefully designed approaches that use pullouts for targeted "skill shots" of instruction, with the goal of frequent assessment and reassignment to appropriate groupings, together with minimal time away from classroom instruction and the student's higher-performing peers.

It's no surprise that these practices are virtually absent in HP/HP schools—and for good reason. One factor contributing to this difference is the curricular offerings provided to students. High-performing, high-poverty secondary schools eliminate courses that are, in essence, a repetition of the curriculum provided in lower grades. These courses, with titles such as Consumer Math, Opportunity Math, or Workplace English, often don't offer the curriculum and instruction students need to meet standards or ready themselves to continue their education after high school. In secondary schools, offerings such as honors, advanced placement (AP), dual-credit courses, actual college courses, and International Baccalaureate (IB) programs and courses are often only available to high-achieving students and not to any student who wishes to enroll. Ensuring a powerful curriculum for all students can remove traditional barriers to participation in such programs for students who live in poverty.

Misuse of Multitiered Systems of Support

Many public schools use some type of multitiered system of support (MTSS), also known as Response to Intervention (RTI). Although many schools have experienced satisfactory results for their students, a study

(Balu et al., 2015) of RTI practices in elementary schools cautions educators regarding its effectiveness. Administered through the National Center for Education, Evaluation, and Regional Assistance, the study looked at the progress of more than 200,000 students in 13 states; it found that non-RTI students outperform those receiving the intervention. The authors suggested four reasons for this: (1) schools are using RTI as a kind of general education substitution for special education, (2) schools are not adequately evaluating students for learning disabilities before initiating an RTI program, (3) schools implementing RTI are not clearly separating the broader goals of general education instruction and the more narrowly focused goals of RTI instruction, and (4) the RTI instruction in the study was found to be rigid and standardized for all students.

Misassignment to Special Education

How often are students from low-income homes referred for testing and assessment by teachers who believe some type of learning disability exists? Once diagnosed with a disability, how often are they removed from general education classrooms for their core instruction? And how often do they leave special education programs and succeed in general education?

The answers to these questions paint an often-bleak portrait of the school experience for far too many low-income children. If a student's family is poor, the chance of that student being referred to and placed in special education programs increases significantly. Having been placed in special education, these students rarely transition back into general education (Howard et al., 2009). As one college student explains,

> I was diagnosed with a learning disability in the 6th grade and was sent to the resource room every day for two hours . . . same for junior high and an hour a day through high school. I never got out of Special Ed, and now I've learned that I really don't have any disability . . . and never did. I just never was taught to read.

Educators in HP/HP schools recognize that far too many students living in poverty are misdiagnosed as "disabled" and are referred to and placed in special education programs. These educators prevent disproportionate placement in special education by (1) providing excellent core instruction and follow-up interventions as needed; (2) fostering healthy, safe, and supportive learning environments in the classroom and schoolwide; and (3) developing a culture of high expectations and support for every student. Many HP/HP schools report the frequent exiting of students from previous IEPs as a result of their students' success.

Suspensions and Expulsions

One of the most entrenched contradictions in our current system of schooling relates to the importance we place on attendance in contrast with our disciplinary decisions. On the one hand, we routinely tell students school attendance is crucial; on the other, when students misbehave, we suspend them. Most ironic, we have encountered schools that routinely suspend students for the benign offense of too many absences.

Suspensions serve as short-term responses to disciplinary problems, with little known benefit other than relieving the school of the challenge of dealing with behavior issues. According to Hattie (2009), the likelihood of suspension and expulsion positively influencing student achievement is nonexistent. The student's separation from the culture of the school, from friends, and, most important, from the place of learning results in a benefit for the adults but rarely, if ever, in a benefit for the student. Suspension removes the problem from the teacher's classroom and school campus and supposedly sets a public example from which other students are meant to learn. For lesser offenses, many schools use in-school suspensions (ISS), in which students are required to study on their own or sit quietly. For the most serious offenses, a district will exclude or expel a misbehaving student for a longer term or permanently. Suspensions can, however, cause indelible damage.

In schools where suspension is commonly used, we would urge the educators to discuss the purpose of discipline in general and suspension in particular. Is it to teach or punish? If suspensions are not changing student behavior, schools should abandon the practice and find alternative forms of discipline that *do* change behavior.

When Krista Barton-Arnold arrived as principal at Parkway Elementary, she discovered the school had a dedicated ISS classroom staffed by a full-time paraprofessional. She asked teachers whether the in-school suspensions were working, and they told her that, no, they were not. "When you have an ISS room with a staff member in it, it's easy to put kids in there and give them busywork," she explains. "I figured out pretty quickly that we had to get rid of that ISS room because that was making it too convenient. The kids need to be in class to be able to learn."

Although a common characteristic of HP/HP schools is a dramatic decline in behavioral problems, sometimes kids do act out. When they do so in HP/HP schools, a collective effort on the part of the adults and often the students has resulted in the establishment of a healthy, safe, and supportive environment in which the vast majority of individual disciplinary issues are proactively and productively resolved. Most HP/HP schools engage in a number of systemic interventions, which often prevent misbehavior or address it in a far more productive manner. Positive behavioral interventions and supports (PBIS); restorative justice; responsive classroom; social and emotional learning approaches; student courts; teaching self-regulation strategies; and, more recently, meditation, yoga, and mindfulness are some of the approaches HP/HP schools use.

Relationships of mutual respect between students and educators go a long way toward eliminating disruptive behavior, as does the development in all students of a sense of belonging to the school. In such a school culture, when behavioral problems arise, the students themselves often intervene. When adults take disciplinary action, it's focused on teaching new behaviors and does not deprive students of the opportunity to continue academic learning. As a teacher in an HP/HP school explains, "Ornery kids can do both—they can learn from their mistakes *and* stay in class and learn from us!"

9 Supporting School Transformation from the District Office

I think how you serve the most vulnerable says a lot about you. It really does. And we don't do that so well all the time in urban areas or in areas of high poverty. I mean, you literally can walk in and say, OK, the way this building looks or this classroom looks, kids aren't first. Or you can watch a teacher, and he's lecturing and kids are sleeping. They're not first. Or kids come to school and they're hungry. And so, it's pretty simplistic. It's this uncommon sense of putting students first.

—*Tiffany Anderson, superintendent, Topeka Public Schools Unified District 501, KS*

High-performing, high-poverty schools sometimes achieve remarkable success in spite of being nested in large systems that are driven by multiple focal points and priorities—a situation sometimes referred to as *mission creep*. These systems are often more reactive than proactive and tend to operate as though school-level leaders are to be of service to the district office rather than the other way around. This tendency, at best, inhibits a district's ability to successfully support schools that serve large percentages of students who live in poverty, and, at worst, actively works *against* their improvement.

A growing body of research points to the importance of district-level leadership and seeks to define the nature of the relationship between district- and school-level leaders in cases where entire systems are improving (Chandler & Frank, 2015; David & Talbert, 2012; Fullan, 2011; Honig et al., 2010; Hitt, Robinson, & Player, 2018; Lorentzen & McCaw, 2015). These studies provide models for transformation of district or central office functions and examples of system learning that address two questions we must consider if real strides are to be made in meeting the needs of students who live in poverty: Can HP/HP schools sustain their success? Can we take their success to scale?

Unless we rethink the work of district-level leaders, pockets of excellence will continue to be found within a school district in the form of individual high-performing, high-poverty schools, but the conditions necessary to bring such improvement to scale will simply not exist. And without transformation of the relationship among leaders throughout the system, the success achieved in individual schools will likely prove difficult to sustain.

Can HP/HP Schools Sustain Their Success?

In *The Moral Imperative Realized,* Michael Fullan (2011) asserts, "Individual schools cannot get on—or if they do, cannot stay on—the moral track unless the whole district is working on the problem" (p. 39). After studying four such districts, he describes the relationships between district and school leaders as "symbiosis." In these districts, he says, leaders at all levels focus "on a small number of goals and corresponding powerful strategies that they employ in concert" (p. 55). When such conditions exist, "Everyone takes pride in whole-system accomplishments and reaches out to help each other whenever it is called for" (p. 55).

As we look to our own research and experience, we see that Fullan's finding rings true. Some HP/HP schools do not maintain their gains over time. Moreover, many high-poverty schools with which we have worked over the years attempt to do what they do without the support of the central office, superintendent, or school board. One HP/HP principal told us, "We've made the gains we've made in spite of the central office. We just try to stay out of their way. They don't really get what we're doing over here."

10 Ways School Districts Fail HP/HP Schools

Our observations have led us to conclude that when HP/HP schools do not maintain their success, various systemic factors are at play that often stem from a failure of districts to support the school. The tool shown in Figure 9.1 can help you assess how well your district is addressing these counterproductive mindsets and practices.

Lack of succession planning. District leaders fail to have a plan for leadership succession when a principal who has been successful in leading transformation and significant improvement in student learning leaves the job.

Inequitable funding. District leaders fail to provide continued funding when a successful school has largely depended on temporary grant funding for instructional materials, personnel, and professional learning, all of which have contributed to the school's success. Likewise, the district might provide equal funding for each school rather than equitable funding based on schools' needs.

Counterproductive staffing. District leaders arbitrarily and frequently reassign principals. They move ineffective teachers from school to school rather than supporting principals in addressing the root problem. They agree to reduction-in-force policies in negotiation with teachers unions that favor teacher seniority over teacher quality. The district's hiring policies and procedures allow staff of high-poverty schools to be disproportionally composed of inexperienced or uncertified educators.

Willful maintenance of segregation. District leaders fail to consider demographic factors when establishing geographical boundaries for neighborhood schools.

Lack of accountability for learning in all schools. District leaders engage in blaming principals and teachers for underachievement rather than assuming responsibility and holding themselves accountable for learning in *every* school.

Benign neglect. District leaders protect the status quo and encourage mediocrity by being unwilling to encourage systemic learning from HP/HP schools' success out of fear of how that may make other schools look or feel—and to avoid questions from patrons or the press as to why other schools in the system are not equally successful, particularly those serving primarily middle-class students.

Place incongruity. District leaders fail to consider or are unaware of the assets and challenges that students, families, and the community served by particular schools bring to the table. They fail to provide opportunities that would help educators gain understanding of the adverse influence of poverty on lives and learning in their school and in the community it serves.

Failure to build instructional leadership capacity. District leaders abdicate their responsibility to be of service to the schools and, instead, expect the schools to be of service to the central office. The district bargains away core instructional leadership responsibilities, such as principal oversight or participation in professional learning communities. District leaders may also fail to develop the necessary expertise in instructional leaders (primarily principals and coaches) to provide the needed infrastructure for excellence in teaching and learning.

Failure to embrace equity in facilities and student assignment. District leaders fail to provide equally well-maintained facilities throughout the school district, and students who live in poverty are disproportionally assigned to schools whose facilities are substandard.

What the Research Shows

Robert Marzano and Timothy Waters's (2009) synthesis of studies conducted between 1970 and 2005 demonstrates the importance

Figure 9.1   10 Ways School Districts Fail High-Poverty Schools: Assessing Your District's Progress

Progress Indicators/Evidence	No Action Yet	Getting Started	Gaining Momentum	Sustaining Gains, Refining
		• People are aware of counter-productive mindsets, policies, structures, or practices. • Urgency is apparent. • Staff acknowledges need for change.	• People are empowered. • Barriers are being removed. • Commitment to the elimination of barriers is increasing. • Support for change continues.	• Counter-productive mindsets, policies, structures, or practices have been eliminated. • New mindsets, policies, structures, and practices are evident.
Counterproductive Mindsets and Practices	**0**	**1**	**2**	**3**
1. Lack of Succession Planning				
2. Inequitable Funding				
3. Counterproductive Staffing				
4. Willful Maintenance of Segregation				
5. Lack of Accountability for Learning in All Schools				
6. Benign Neglect				
7. Place Incongruity				
8. Failure to Build Instructional Leadership Capacity				
9. Failure to Embrace Equity in Facilities and Student Assignment				
10. School Board Disconnection to Student Achievement				

of district-level leadership in improving academic achievement. More recently, Lorentzen and McCaw (2015) have demonstrated the link between school board governance and academic achievement, pointing to specific school board actions that correlate with higher than average student achievement. Other scholars have conducted research on leadership at various levels of the system. In his book *The Case for District-Based Reform: Leading, Building, and Sustaining School Improvement,* Jonathan Supovitz (2006) points to research that "makes the case" for districtwide initiatives focused on the improvement of teaching and learning.

Meredith Honig, Mike Copland, and colleagues (2010) at the University of Washington conducted a Wallace Foundation–funded study that examined the daily practices and activities of district office personnel as they sought not only to become more efficient but also to transform the district office into a support system for school-based leaders who were trying to improve teaching and learning. Leaders in the three urban school districts that demonstrated steady gains in student achievement credit their improvement, in part, to their efforts to transform the role of the district office and its relationship with schools. Desiring to radically depart from business as usual, leaders in these districts, according to the study, did the following:

- They focused the work of the central office "centrally and meaningfully" on the improvement of teaching and learning. Moving beyond rhetoric about being of service to schools, leaders in these districts could demonstrate how their work supported schools in concrete ways.
- They engaged everyone in the effort, even personnel whose function had not been traditionally defined as connected to teaching and learning.
- They called on central office personnel to restructure their relationship with schools so that their daily work was in the service of schools' efforts to improve teaching and learning.
- They aimed to transcend programs or initiatives, as opposed to reforming the district office for the purpose of implementing a particular program.

Can We Take Their Success to Scale?

The study of improving whole districts rather than individual schools has received increased attention over the past decade. Success stories of turning around a high-poverty school district, such as Sanger Unified School District in California, were chronicled by scholars (David & Talbert, 2012; Fullan, 2010) and organizations such as the Broad Foundation—which awarded the Broad Prize for Urban Education ($1 million) to public school districts that had demonstrated the greatest overall performance and improvement in student achievement while narrowing achievement gaps among low-income students—recognized "whole district" improvement. Organizations and agencies such as the American Enterprise Institute (Zavadsky, 2013); the California Collaborative on District Reform (2011); the Center on School Turnaround at WestEd (Hitt, Robinson, & Player, 2018); and MI Excel, which is funded by the State Department of Education in Michigan (Chandler & Frank, 2015), have developed frameworks for improvement with district reform as the focus. Figure 9.2 shows that the core strategic actions called for in the frameworks are remarkably consistent.

Figure 9.2   Core Components of District Improvement and Turnaround Frameworks

American Enterprise Institute (Zavadsky, 2013)	The Center on School Turnaround at WestEd (Hitt, Robinson, & Player, 2018)	California Collaborative on District Reform (2011)	MI Excel (Chandler & Frank, 2015)
• Strategic staffing • Development of turnaround leadership • Strong performance management systems	• Turnaround leadership • Talent development	• Fostering and deploying strong leadership • Fostering and deploying strong teaching	• Talent management
• Improving instruction (common definition of excellence in teaching and high-quality learning) • Balancing coherence with flexibility	• Instructional transformation	• Piloting promising ideas	• Impactful learning-focused network
• Restructuring the central office to better serve schools		• Using data to identify effective and ineffective practices	• Instructional infrastructure
			• Intense student support network
			• Equitable allocation of resources
	• Culture shift	• Establishing a district culture that supports school turnaround	• Culture of collective responsibility
		• Involving the community	
			• Safe, orderly, and respectful environment

In the course of our current study, we were fortunate to interview district-level leaders in many of the communities we visited. These leaders described improvement or turnaround initiatives congruent with current research. Melinda Young, superintendent of Steubenville City Schools in Ohio, told us about the strong instructional leadership pipeline the district maintains largely by "growing their own." She described partnerships with the community that enabled the district to open a health clinic and the importance of equitable decisions, such as ensuring that high-poverty schools were smaller in terms of student population.

Mark Flatau, superintendent of Kalispell School District, the district in which Lillian Peterson Elementary is located, talks about the need to get past the reluctance to recognize and learn from other schools in the system. "We have to be able to have honest conversations, and we're not good at that in education when one school is doing better [than others]," he says. "The instructional coaches have really helped. They collaborate, and so the instructional coach at Peterson often shares their successes with other schools' instructional coaches."

In *Motion Leadership: The Skinny on Becoming Change Savvy* (2009), Michael Fullan describes what happens when district leaders create the conditions for school leaders to drop their guard and become willing to learn from other school leaders. As he explains, "once they see the slightly bigger picture and get to know each other in a common endeavor of great moral purpose, they thrive on 'competitive collaboration'" (p. 39).

Goal-oriented collaboration is what resulted when Warren Hoshizaki, director of the District School Board of Niagara in Ontario, together with Superintendent Marian Reimer Friesen, selected four high-poverty, underperforming elementary schools to form a focused improvement cluster. The board provided targeted support and additional resources, as Reimer Friesen worked with each school individually and joined the four principals as they worked together in their learning network. The purpose was, in part, to build capacity and collective efficacy to disrupt poverty's adverse influence on learning. Hoshizaki advised Reimer Friesen (and other superintendents in the district) to "avoid the noise"—that is, focus on a small number of things and buffer principals from anything that distracts from that focus.

Hoshizaki also cautions superintendents, "Don't be a cake eater," those administrators who fill their days with meetings, events, and celebrations rather than "being up to their elbows in student instruction"—a lesson he learned from his mentor, Keith Leithwood. Reimer Friesen doesn't have to worry about being called a cake eater. Her instructional leadership has been instrumental in improving four high-poverty schools, which over the past four years have *all* climbed from significant underperformance to becoming HP/HP schools.

Carla Evers had been the superintendent in the Pass Christian School District on the Gulf Coast of Mississippi for less than three years when we interviewed her. She was quick to point out that the district was excellent when she got there, and she credited the work that had been done at the high school for helping the district maintain its accountability grade of *A*. She then relayed a story of the challenge she and other leaders faced her first year in the district, a district that had recently been the top-performing district in the state for years.

During Mississippi's transition to a new state-mandated assessment, which had not been completely aligned with the more rigorous state-adopted standards, the U.S. Department of Education gave the state a waiver, which allowed them to hold all districts "harmless, so to speak," says Evers. In 2012, Pass Christian received a grade of *A*, which remained their accountability status until the waiver expired. Based on students' performance the first year the new test was administered, the district would have received a grade of *C* had the waiver *not* been in place. Evers explains,

> In my first year, I had to bring the first *B* to the community. That was hard . . . the community had only ever seen an *A*, probably for the last 12, 13 years. I thought I was going to get kicked out of town. I took evidence to the mayor that we were only three points from an *A*, and that year, the Super Bowl was decided by three points. The high school was formidable and could stand through all that. The high school teachers—well, they just continued doing all the things they had done. They continued teaching and let the test happen. In our K–8 program, we were struggling a little bit with making the adjustments.

Evers held "legacy meetings" with teachers who had been in the district more than 15 years. As a result of those meetings, the district began providing teachers with specific professional development and materials that would help them align their curriculum with the new standards, as well as more coaching and classroom walk-throughs for additional support. Explains Evers,

> The teachers said to me, "We need some training." So that's what we're doing. . . . We're reworking and redesigning our work in our foundational years. Our goal is not necessarily to be No. 1; that's not what we're going after. We're going after students who are college- and career-ready, critical thinkers, and contributing citizens. That's what we want for our children.

The success of a single school within a district can be the impetus needed to spur the remaining schools to improve. All of the schools in Pass

Christian are *A* or *B* schools based on the state's accountability system, and the district as a whole received a grade of *A* this past year.

Another remarkable educator is Tiffany Anderson, currently superintendent of Topeka Unified School District 501 in Kansas, who has initiated and led districts in Virginia, Missouri, and Kansas on their journeys to significant, sustained districtwide improvement. We have studied her approach and progress in her work in high-poverty districts for a decade. Tiffany credits a "students first" approach to rapidly garner improvements in student achievement, graduation rates, behavior, and attendance. She shares,

> There are some things very unique to districts where I've served, but really, that student-first philosophy is, I think, something that I have from teaching, from being a principal, from being a superintendent. Sometimes I scratch my head about the decisions that are made, whether policies by school boards or legislators or just things that we do in schools, when they just simply don't put kids first.

For Anderson, putting students first begins and ends with building authentic relationships among all students and adults, implementing a standards-based curriculum, deploying learner-focused pedagogy, and carefully using data to guide the teaching and learning process. She explains,

> Even our data are really about students first. We don't just look at numbers; every week, teachers give an assessment and then come together to really drive the conversation about "How did a student do on this problem or that problem?"

Monthly, Anderson and the school improvement data specialist meet with each building leader for a "data consult" to review progress toward improvement goals. These supportive sessions inspect, help maintain, and drive systemic progress at the school, grade, subject-area content, individual classroom, and teacher levels. Anderson says her most important job is to build capacity among adults and systemwide to serve *all* students by leveling the playing field for those in poverty. She further explains that they had to double the original number of counselors.

> To really make this happen, we've reprioritized how we spend our budget—our title budget—and our general operating budget to ensure that we have adequate wraparound support for students. There has to be a great deal of intentionality so that when a student says, "I'm done, and I choose to give up," there is someone ready to say, "I love you, and that is not an option. I'm going to make sure that you make it. We're going to walk through this together." We all work to see the individual and to connect to that student in a deeper way, so that we truly feel—"if you don't do well, I don't do well."

A Call to Action

It's only through systemic reform that improvement will be both sustained in individual schools and taken to scale at the district, state, and national levels. District leaders must be amenable to learning from the hundreds of high-performing, high-poverty schools in the United States and the increasing number of districts engaging in this work. Much of the historic function of the central office needs to be transformed if district leaders are to apply the lessons learned. For example, central offices need to move away from siloed programs, which function as if schools should be of service to the central office rather than the central office being of service to schools. District-level leaders need to act from a theory of reciprocal leadership (Elmore, 2000) and hold themselves mutually accountable for student outcomes in each school.

Such change requires courage—courage to challenge the status quo and courage to reinvent public schooling. In Superintendent Carla Evers's words, "We can't use our demographics as an excuse because we have proved that given the right instruction, our children will rise. And certainly the work is doable, but do you *want* to do it is the thing. *Will* you do it is the thing."

We can do this work. Over the course of the past decade, high-poverty schools across the United States, Canada, and the world have embarked on improvement journeys and have successfully transformed high-poverty schools into high-performing schools. And, they have learned how to sustain their gains. More than 40 years ago, eminent scholar Ron Edmonds (1979) penned these words:

> We can, whenever and wherever we choose, successfully teach all children whose schooling is of interest to us. We already know more than we need to do that. Whether or not we do it must finally depend on how we feel about the fact that we haven't so far. (p. 23)

Schools like those described in this second edition provide a roadmap for other schools and demonstrate high performance is both plausible and achievable. These schools, and many others, stand as exemplars of the possible. We implore you to visit high-performing, high-poverty schools, learn from them, and leverage their hard-earned lessons in your own setting.

The primary determinant in a HP/HP school's success is garnering and maintaining the collective will to ensure that *all* students succeed. We urge you to commit to embarking on your own transformational journey. Your students are worthy of nothing less.

Acknowledgments

This edition could not have been written without the ingenuity, courage, passion, and persistence of many educators and others whose lives are dedicated to supporting children and adolescents who live in poverty. To all of you, we owe our deepest respect and gratitude.

Heading the cast of many are principals and their colleagues who opened their doors to our questions and probing inquiries: Alexa Sorden, Concourse Village; Derek Harley, E.I. McCulley Elementary; Marian Reimer Friesen and Warren Hoshizaki, District School Board of Niagara; Jamie Burnett, Evergreen Elementary; Tracy Ketchum, Lillian Peterson Elementary; Mark Flatau, Kalispell Independent School District; Krista Barton-Arnold, Parkway Elementary; Lynnette Gorman, Pugliese West Elementary; Shawn Crosier, East Garfield Elementary; Melinda Young, Steubenville Independent School District; Michele Capps, Murtaugh K–12; EJ Martinez, Stillman Middle; Eric and Carice Sanchez, Frank and Caitlin Terranova, and Celeste Olsen, Henderson Collegiate Middle; Robyn Killebrew, Pass Christian High; Carla Evers, Pass Christian School District; and Scott Barton and Pete Selleck, The Preuss School. Our heartfelt appreciation goes to all of you. And to those leaders who shaped our first edition, we continue to appreciate all you did to inform this work: Andrew Collins, Teri Wagner, Randy Dalton, Valarie Lewis, Pat Swift, Wayne Roellich, and Susan Williamson. We stand in awe of your dedication and commitment to your students.

We continue to be grateful to the scholars and practitioners whose work informs, influences, and supports the belief that high-poverty schools can become high-performing schools. Specifically, we offer our respect and gratitude to Tiffany Anderson, Robert Barr, Karin Chenoweth, Michael Copland, Ron Edmonds, Richard Elmore, Michael Fullan, Paul Gorski, Kati Haycock, and Rick Stiggins.

We are particularly indebted to two special individuals at ASCD for their unwavering support: Genny Ostertag, whose gracious and ever-present encouragement was there for us from "invitation" to completion; and our favorite (and the best) editor on the planet, Darcie Russell, again masterfully managed the complex array of editorial and production details to shape this work. Darcie's talent, patience, and expertise have made this a far more accessible, useful, and compelling book for anyone interested in improving their school and district.

Many colleagues and friends at Boise State University supported us in this effort, including Diana Esbensen, Eva Horn, Richard Osguthorpe, Jennifer Snow, and Keith Thiede.

Invaluable assistance came from the staff of the Center for School Improvement and Policy Studies. In particular, we sincerely thank Abbey Montoya Denton, Michele Panacoast, Amanda Pearson, and Rachel Swindon. We would like to especially thank our post-doctoral research assistant, Liesl Milan, whose countless hours, energy, and relentless sleuthing helped support our research effort through the entire process. And as always, we are indebted to Larry Burke, our friend and editing wizard, who provided invaluable suggestions for organization, structure, and word choice that brought life to the book.

Finally, we are grateful for the love of our children, and grandchildren Jonathan, Elsa, Mia, Ahijah, Katrina, AJ, Adley Jo, Nathan, Lindsey, Lukas, and Kennedy. Thank you all so much for what you bring to our lives and for all we have as a family. We sincerely hope this book contributes in some small way to making the world a better place for all children and grandchildren.

References

Allington, R., & McGill-Franzen, A. (2008). Got books? *Educational Leadership, 65*(7), 20–23.

Almy, S., & Theokas, C. (2010). *Not prepared for class: High-poverty schools continue to have fewer in-field teachers.* Washington, DC: Education Trust.

Anderson, M. (2019). *What we say and how we say it matter: Teacher talk that improves student learning and behavior.* Alexandria, VA: ASCD.

Anyon, J. (1981). Social class and school knowledge. *Curriculum Inquiry, 11*(1), 3–42.

Argyris, C., & Schön, D. A. (1974). *Theory in practice: Increasing professional effectiveness.* San Francisco: Jossey-Bass.

Armstrong, T. (2019). *Mindfulness in the classroom: Strategies for promoting concentration, compassion, and calm.* Alexandria, VA: ASCD.

Azma, S. (2013). Poverty and the developing brain: Insights from neuroimaging. *Synesis: A Journal of Science, Technology, Ethics, and Policy, 4*(1), G40–G46.

Bailey, J. M., & Guskey, T. R. (2000). *Implementing student-led conferences.* Thousand Oaks, CA: Corwin.

Balfanz, R., & Byrnes, V. (2012). *Chronic absenteeism: Summarizing what we know from nationally available data.* Baltimore, MD: Johns Hopkins University Center for Social Organization of Schools. Retrieved from https://ccrscenter.org/products-resources /resource-database/chronic-absenteeism-summarizing-what-we-know-nationally

Ball, J. (2001). High-performing, high-poverty schools. *Leadership, 31*(1), 8–11.

Balu, R., Zhu, P., Doolittle, F., Schiller, E., Jenkins, J., & Gersten, R. (2015). *Evaluation of Response to Intervention practices for elementary school reading* (NCEE 2016-4000). Washington, DC: National Center for Education Evaluation and Regional Assistance, Institute of Education Sciences, U.S. Department of Education.

Bambrick-Santoyo, P. (2019). *Driven by data 2.0.* San Francisco: Jossey-Bass.

Bandura, A. (1993). Perceived self-efficacy in cognitive development and functioning. *Educational Psychologist, 28*(2), 117–148.

Banks, J. A. (1997). *Educating citizens in a multicultural society.* Multicultural Education Series. New York: Teachers College Press.

Barr, R. D., & Gibson, E. L. (2013). *Building a culture of hope: Enriching schools with optimism and opportunity.* Bloomington, IN: Solution Tree.

Barr, R. D., & Parrett, W. (2007). *The kids left behind: Catching up the underachieving children of poverty.* Bloomington, IN: Solution Tree.

Barton, A. C., Tan, E., & Greenberg, D. (2017). The makerspace movement: Sites of possibilities for equitable opportunities to engage underrepresented youth in STEM. *Teachers College Record, 119*(6), 1–44.

Beegle, D. M. (2006). *See poverty . . . . Be the difference! Discover the missing pieces for helping people move out of poverty.* Tigard, OR: Communication Across Barriers.

Benard, B. (1991). *Fostering resiliency in kids: Protective factors in the family, school, and community.* Portland, OR: Northwest Regional Education Laboratory.

Benner, G., J., Nelson, J. R., Sanders, E. A., & Ralston, N. C. (2012). Behavior intervention for students with externalizing behavior problems: Primary-level standard protocol. *Exceptional Children, 78*(2), 181–198.

Berger, W. (2014). *A more beautiful question: The power of inquiry to spark breakthrough ideas.* New York: Bloomsbury.

Berman, S., Chaffee, S., & Sarmiento, J. (2018). *The practice base for how we learn: Supporting students' social, emotional, and academic development.* The Aspen Institute. Retrieved from https://assets.aspeninstitute.org/content/uploads/2018/03/CDE-Commission-report.pdf

Bernhardt, V. L. (2005). Data tools for school improvement. *Educational Leadership, 62*(5), 66–69.

Berry, B. (2008). Staffing high-needs schools: Insights from the nation's best teachers. *Phi Delta Kappan, 89*(10), 766–771.

Billig, S. (2000a). *Educators' guide to collecting and using data: Conducting surveys.* Denver, CO: RMC Research.

Billig, S. (2000b). *Profiles of success: Engaging young people's hearts and minds through service-learning.* Berkeley, CA: Grantmaker Forum on Community and National Service.

Black, D. S., & Fernando, R. (2014). Mindfulness training and classroom behavior among lower-income and ethnic minority elementary school children. *Journal of Child and Family Studies, 23*(7), 1242–1246.

Boaler, J. (2002). *Experiencing school mathematics: Traditional and reform approaches to teaching and their impact on student learning.* Abingdon, UK: Routledge.

Bodily, S., Keltner, B., Purnell, S., Reichardt, R., & Schuyler, G. (1998). *Lessons from new American schools' scale-up phase: Prospects for bringing designs to multiple schools.* Santa Monica, CA: RAND.

Bond (2002). *Introductory guide for implementing and evaluating volunteer reading tutoring programs.* Greensboro, NC: SERVE (Southern Regional Vision for Education).

Borman, G. D., & Dowling, N. M. (2006). Longitudinal achievement effects of multiyear summer school: Evidence from the Teach Baltimore randomized field trial. *Educational Evaluation and Policy Analysis, 28*(1), 25–48.

Boss, S., & Larmer, J. (2018). *Project based learning: How to create rigorous and engaging learning experiences.* Alexandria, VA: ASCD.

Bradshaw, T. K. (2006). Theories of poverty and anti-poverty programs in community development. *Community Development, 38*(1), 7–25. Rural Policy Research Center. Retrieved from http://www.rupri.org/Forms/WP06-05.pdf

Brandt, R. (1998). *Powerful learning.* Alexandria, VA: ASCD.

Bransford, J. D., Brown, A. L., & Cocking, R. R. (2000). *How people learn: Brain, mind, experience, and school.* Expanded edition. Washington, DC: National Academies Press.

Brinson, D., Kowal, J., & Hassel, B. (2008). *School turnarounds: Actions and results.* Lincoln, IL: Center on Innovation and Improvement.

Brinson, D., & Steiner, L. (2007, October). *Building collective efficacy: How leaders inspire teachers to achieve.* Issue Brief. Center for Comprehensive School Reform and Improvement.

Brooks-Gunn, J., & Duncan, G. J. (1997). The effects of poverty on children. *The Future of Children, 7*(2), 55–71.

Brooks-Gunn, J., Duncan, G. J., Klebanov, P. K., & Sealand, N. (1993). Do neighborhoods influence child and adolescent development? *American Journal of Sociology, 99*(2), 353–395.

Brown, K. M., Benkovitz, J., Muttillo, A. J., & Urban, T. (2011). Leading schools of excellence and equity: Documenting effective strategies in closing achievement gaps. *Teachers College Record, 113*(1), 57–96.

Bryk, A. S., Bender Sebring, P., Allensworth, E., Luppescu, S., & Easton, J. Q. (2010). *Organizing schools for improvement: Lessons from Chicago.* Chicago: University of Chicago Press.

Bryk, A. S., & Schneider, B. (2002). *Trust in schools: A core resource for improvement.* New York: Russell Sage Foundation.

Buckner, J. C., Mezzacappa, E., & Beardslee, W. R. (2009). Self-regulation and its relations to adaptive functioning in lower income youths. *American Journal of Orthopsychiatry, 79*(1), 19.

Budge, K. M., & Parrett, W. H. (2009). Making refugee students welcome. Available: http://www.ascd.org/publications/educational-leadership/apr09/vol66/num07/Making-Refugee-Students-Welcome.aspx.

Budge, K. M., & Parrett, W. H. (2018). *Disrupting poverty: Five powerful classroom practices.* Alexandria, VA: ASCD.

California Collaborative on District Reform. (2011). Beyond the school: Exploring a systemic approach to school turnaround [Policy and practice brief]. Available: https://cacollaborative.org/publication/beyond-school-exploring-systemic-approach-school-turnaround-0

Calkins, A., Guenther, W., Belfiore, G., & Lash, D. (2007). *The turnaround challenge: Why America's best opportunity to dramatically improve student achievement lies in our worst-performing schools: New research, recommendations, and a partnership framework for states and school districts.* Boston: Mass Insight Education & Research Institute.

Campbell, L., & Campbell, B. (1999). *Multiple intelligences and student achievement: Success stories from six schools.* Alexandria, VA: ASCD.

Carbaugh, B., Marzano, R., & Toth, M. (2017). The Marzano focused teacher evaluation model, 1–25. Retrieved from https://www.learningsciences.com/wp/wpcontent/uploads/2017/06/Focus-Eval-Model-Overview-2017.pdf

CASEL (Collaborative for Academic, Social, and Emotional Learning). (2019). Overview of SEL. Retrieved https://casel.org/overview-sel/

Centers for Disease Control. (2019). Adverse childhood experiences (ACEs). Retrieved from https://www.cdc.gov/violenceprevention/childabuseandneglect/acestudy/index.html

Chandler, G., & Frank, J. (2015). The blueprint for systemic reconfiguration. Retrieved from www.miexcelresourcecenter.org

Chappuis, S., Commodore, C., & Stiggins, R. J. (2009). *Assessment balance and quality: An action guide for school leaders.* Portland, OR: Educational Testing Service.

Chenoweth, K. (2007). *"It's being done": Academic success in unexpected schools.* Cambridge, MA: Harvard Education Press.

Chenoweth, K. (2009a). *How it's being done: Urgent lessons from unexpected schools.* Cambridge, MA: Harvard Education Press.

Chenoweth, K. (2009b). It can be done, it's being done, and here's how. *Phi Delta Kappan, 91*(1), 38–43.

Chenoweth, K. (2017). *Schools that succeed: How educators marshal the power of systems for improvement.* Cambridge, MA: Harvard Education Press.

Ciaccio, J. (2000a). A teacher's chance for immortality. *Education Digest, 65*(6), 44–48.

Ciaccio, J. (2000b). Helping kids excel on state-mandated tests. *Education Digest, 65*(5), 21.

Claro, S., Paunesku, D., & Dweck, C. (2016). Growth mindset tempers the effects of poverty on academic achievement. *Proceedings of the National Academy of Sciences, 113*(31), 8664–8668.

Clement, M. C. (2009). Hiring highly qualified teachers begins with quality interviews. *Phi Delta Kappan, 91*(2), 22–24.

Coleman, J. S. (1966). *Equality of educational opportunity*. Washington, DC: U.S. Department of Health, Education, and Welfare.

Collins, J. (2001). *Good to great: Why some companies make the leap—and others don't*. New York: HarperCollins.

Comer, J. P. (1993). All children can learn: A developmental approach. *Holistic Education Review, 6*(1), 4–9.

Conrath, J. (1988). *Full-year prevention curriculum: Secondary dropout prevention*. Gig Harbor, WA: Author.

Conrath, J. (2001). Changing the odds for young people: Next steps for alternative education. *Phi Delta Kappan, 82*(8), 585–587.

Correnti, R., & Rowan, B. (2007). Opening up the black box: Literacy instruction in schools participating in three comprehensive school reform programs. *American Educational Research Journal, 44*(2), 298–339.

Costa, A. L., & Kallick, B. (2009). *Habits of mind across the curriculum: Practical and creative strategies for teachers*. Alexandria, VA: ASCD.

Craig, S. E. (2015). *Trauma-sensitive schools. Learning communities transforming children's lives, K–5*. New York: Teachers College Press.

Craig, S. E. (2016). *Trauma-sensitive schools: Learning communities transforming children's lives, K–5*. New York: Teachers College Press.

Danielson, C. (1996). *Enhancing professional practice: A framework for teaching*. Alexandria, VA: ASCD.

Dantley, M. E., & Green, T. L. (2015). Problematizing notions of leadership for social justice: Reclaiming social justice through a discourse of accountability and a radical, prophetic, and historical imagination. *Journal of School Leadership, 25*(5), 820–837.

Dantley, M., & Tillman, L. C. (2006). Social justice and moral transformative leadership. In C. Marshall & M. Oliva (Eds.), *Leadership for social justice: Making revolutions in education*. Boston: Pearson.

Danziger, S. K., & Danziger, S. H. (2008). Childhood poverty in economic and public policy. In S. B. Newman (Ed.), *Educating the other America: Top experts tackle poverty, literacy, and achievement in our schools*. Baltimore, MD: Paul H. Brookes.

Dariotis, J. K., Mirabal-Beltran, R., Cluxton-Keller, F., Gould, L. F., Greenberg, M. T., & Mendelson, T. (2016). A qualitative evaluation of student learning and skills use in a school-based mindfulness and yoga program. *Mindfulness, 7*(1), 76–89.

Darling-Hammond, L. (2010). Teacher education and the American future. *Journal of Teacher Education, 61*(1–2), 35–47.

David, J. L., & Talbert, J. E. (2012). *Turning around a high-poverty school district: Learning from Sanger Unified's success*. Palo Alto: Bay Area Research Group; and Stanford, CA: Center for Research on the Context of Teaching.

Delgado, B. M., & Ford, L. (1998). Parental perceptions of child development among low-income Mexican American families. *Journal of Child and Family Studies, 7*(4), 469–481.

Delpit, L. (1995). *Other people's children: Cultural conflict in the classroom*. New York: New Press.

Denton, P. (2013). *The power of our words: Teacher language that helps children learn*. Turners Falls, MA: Center for Responsive Schools.

Desilver, D. (2018, August 7). For most Americans, real wages have barely budged for decades. Pew Research Center. Retrieved from https://www.pewresearch.org/fact-tank/2018/08/07/for-most-us-workers-real-wages-have-barely-budged-for-decades/

Dill, V. (2015). Homeless—And doubled up. *Educational Leadership, 72*(6), 42–47.

Donohoo, J. (2017). *Collective efficacy: How educators' beliefs impact student learn-ing.* Thousand Oaks, CA: Corwin.

Donohoo, J., Hattie, J., & Eells, R. (2018). The power of collective efficacy. *Educational Leadership, 75*(6), 40–44.

Dryfoos, J. G. (1994). *Full-service schools: A revolution in health and social services for chil-dren, youth, and families.* San Francisco: Jossey-Bass.

Dryfoos, J. G., & Maguire, S. (2002). *Inside full-service community schools.* Thousand Oaks, CA: Corwin.

DuFour, R., & Marzano, R. (2009). High-leverage strategies for principal leadership. *Edu-cational Leadership, 66*(5), 62–68.

Duncan, J., & Murnane, R. J. (2014). *Restoring opportunity: The crisis of inequality and the challenge for American education.* Cambridge, MA: Harvard Education Press.

Echevarría, J., Vogt, M., & Short, D. (2004). *Making content comprehensible for English learners: The SIOP model* (2nd ed.). Boston: Allyn & Bacon.

Economic Policy Institute. (2002). *The state of working class America 2002–03.* Washing-ton, DC: Author.

Edmonds, R. (1979). Effective schools for the urban poor. *Educational Leadership, 37*(1), 15–18, 20–24.

Edmondson, J., & Shannon, P. (1998). Reading education and poverty: Questioning the reading success equation. *Peabody Journal of Education, 73*(3/4), 104–126.

Education Trust. (2002). *Dispelling the myth . . . over time.* Washington, DC: Author.

Eells, R. (2011). *Meta-analysis of the relationship between collective efficacy and student achievement.* Unpublished doctoral dissertation. Loyola University of Chicago.

Eisenman, G., & Payne, B. D. (1997). Effects of the higher order thinking skills program on at-risk young adolescents' self-concept, reading achievement, and thinking skills. *Research in Middle Level Educational Quarterly, 20*(3), 1–25.

Eklund, N. (2009). Sustainable workplaces, retainable teachers. *Phi Delta Kappan, 91*(2), 25–27.

Elmore, R. F. (2000). *Building a new structure for school leadership.* Unpublished paper for Albert Shanker Institute, Washington, DC.

Elmore, R. F. (2006, November/December). Three thousand missing hours: Where does all the instruction time go? *Harvard Educational Newsletter, 22*(6).

Families and School Together. (2016, August). *The importance of parent engagement: A list of research and thought leadership.* Retrieved from https://www.familiesandschools .org/blog/the-importance-of-parent-engagement/

Federal Register. (2018, May 8). Child nutrition programs; income eligibility guidelines *83*(89). Retrieved from https://www.govinfo.gov/content/pkg/FR-2018-05-08/pdf /2018-09679.pdf

Ferlazzo, L. (2011). Involvement or engagement? *Educational Leadership, 68*(8), 10–14.

Finn, P. J. (1999). *Literacy with an attitude: Educating working-class children in their own self-interest.* Albany, NY: State University of New York Press.

Fischer, A. (2018). Afterschool in rural America. Retrieved from https://www .afterschoolalliance.org/AfterschoolSnack/Afterschool-in-rural-America_05 -28-2019.cfm

Fogarty, R. (2009). *Brain-compatible classrooms.* Thousand Oaks, CA: Corwin.

Fry, S., & DeWit, K. (2010). Once a struggling student. *Educational Leadership, 68*(4), 70–73.

Fullan, M. (2009). *Motion leadership: The skinny on becoming change savvy.* Thousand Oaks, CA: Corwin.

Fullan, M. (2010). *All systems go: The change imperative for whole system reform.* Thou-sand Oaks, CA: Corwin.

Fullan, M. (2011). *The moral imperative realized.* Thousand Oaks, CA: Corwin.

Furco, A., & Root, S. (2010). Research demonstrates the value of service learning. *Phi Delta Kappan, 91*(5), 16–20.

Glatthorn, A., & Jailall, J. (2010). *The principal as curriculum leader: Shaping what is taught and tested.* Thousand Oaks, CA: Corwin.

Goddard, R., Hoy, W. K., & Hoy, A. W. (2000). Collective teacher efficacy: Its meaning, measure, and impact on student achievement. *American Educational Research Journal, 37*(2), 479–507.

Goldhaber, D., Lavery, L., & Theobald, R. (2015). Uneven playing field? Assessing the teacher quality gap between advantaged and disadvantaged students. *Educational Researcher, 44*(5), 293–307.

Gorski, P. C. (2007, Spring). The question of class. *Teaching Tolerance, 31,* 26–29.

Gorski, P. C. (2008). The myth of the culture of poverty. *Educational Leadership, 65*(7), 32–36.

Gorski, P. C. (2012). Perceiving the problem of poverty and schooling: Deconstructing the class stereotypes that mis-shape education practice and policy. *Equity & Excellence in Education, 45*(2), 302–319.

Gutman, L., & McLoyd, V. (2000). Parents' management of their children's education within the home, at school, and in the community: An examination of African-American families living in poverty. *The Urban Review, 32*(1), 1–24.

Haberman, M. (1991). The pedagogy of poverty versus good teaching. *Phi Delta Kappan, 73*(4), 290–294.

Haberman, M. (1995). *Star teachers of children in poverty.* West Lafayette, IN: Kappa Delta Pi.

Hall, P. (2019). The instructional leader's most difficult job. Retrieved from http://www.ascd.org/publications/educational-leadership/mar19/vol76/num06/The-Instructional-Leader's-Most-Difficult-Job.aspx

Harry, B., Allen, N., & McLaughlin, M. (1995). Communication versus compliance: African American parents' involvement in special education. *Exceptional Children, 61,* 364–377.

Hattie, J. (2009). *Visible learning: A synthesis of over 800 meta-analyses relating to achievement.* Abingdon, UK: Routledge.

Hattie, J. (2011). *Visible learning for teachers: Maximizing impact on learning.* New York: Routledge.

Hattie, J. (2015). The applicability of visible learning to higher education. *Scholarship of Teaching and Learning in Psychology, 1*(1), 79–91.

Hattie, J. (2018). What is "collective teacher efficacy"? [Video file]. Retrieved from https://vimeo.com/267382804

Haycock, K. (2001). Closing the achievement gap. *Educational Leadership, 58*(6), 6–11.

Haycock, K. (2010, November). Taking charge of change: Effective practices to close achievement gaps and raise achievement. [Keynote address]. Conference, National Education Trust, Arlington, VA.

Hill, N., & Taylor, L. (2004). Parental school involvement and children's academic achievement: Pragmatics and issues. *Current Directions in Psychological Science, 13*(4), 161–164.

Hill-Jackson, V., Hartlep, N. D., & Stafford, D. (2019). *What makes a star teacher: 7 dispositions that support student learning.* Alexandria, VA: ASCD.

Hirsch, E., & Emerick, S. (2006). *Teacher working conditions are student learning conditions: A report on the 2006 North Carolina Teacher Working Conditions Survey.* Chapel Hill, NC: Center for Teaching Quality.

Hitt, D. H., Robinson, W., & Player, D. (2018). *District readiness to support school turnaround: A guide for state education agencies and districts* (2nd ed.). Center on School Turnaround at WestEd. San Francisco: WestEd.

Holloway, S. D., Rambaud, M. F., Fuller, B., & Eggers-Piérola, C. (1995). What is "appropriate practice" at home and in child care? Low-income mothers' views on preparing their children for school. *Early Childhood Research Quarterly, 10*(4), 451–473. Retrieved from https://doi.org/10.1016/0885-2006(95)90016-0

Honig, M., Copland, M., Rainey, L., Lorton, J., & Newton, M. (2010). *How district central offices can help lead school improvement.* New York: Wallace Foundation.

Honigsfeld, A., & Dunn, R. (2009*). Differentiating instruction for at-risk students: What to do and how to do it.* Lanham, MD: Rowman & Littlefield Education.

Howard, T., Dresser, S. G., & Dunklee, D. R. (2009). *Poverty is not a learning disability: Equalizing opportunities for low SES students.* Thousand Oaks, CA: Corwin.

Hoy, W., & Miskel, C. (2008). *Educational administration: Theory, research, and practice.* Boston: McGraw-Hill.

Hubmer, J., Krusell, P., & Smith, A. (2016, December). *The historical evolution of the wealth distribution: A quantitative-theoretic investigation* [NBER working paper no. 23011]. Cambridge, MA: National Bureau of Economic Research. Retrieved from Introduction.tt.docxhttps://doi.org/10.3386/w23011

Hyerle, D. (2009). *Visual tools for transforming information into knowledge.* Thousand Oaks, CA: Corwin.

Jackson, Y. (2002). Mentoring for delinquent children: An outcome study with young adolescent children. *Journal of Youth and Adolescence, 31*(2), 115–122.

Jensen, E. (2009). *Teaching with poverty in mind: What being poor does to kids' brains and what schools can do about it.* Alexandria, VA: ASCD.

Jerald, C. (2007). Believing and achieving. *Issue Brief.* (ERIC Document Reproduction Service No. ED495708).

Johannessen, L. R. (2004). Helping "struggling" students achieve success. *Journal of Adolescent and Adult Literacy, 47*(8), 638–647.

Johnston, P. H. (2004). *Choice words: How our language affects children's learning.* Portland, ME: Stenhouse.

Johnston, P. H. (2012). *Opening minds: Using language to change lives.* Portland, ME: Stenhouse.

Jones, R. (2001). How parents can support learning: Not all parent involvement programs are equal, but research shows what works. *American School Board Journal, 188*(9), 18–22.

Jones, J. (2015, July 27). Drinking highest among educated, upper-income Americans. *Gallup News.* Retrieved from https://news.gallup.com/poll/184358/drinking-highest-among-educated-upper-income-americans.aspx

Jordan, G. (2004). The causes of poverty—cultural vs. structural: Can there be a synthesis? *Perspectives in Public Affairs, 1,* 18–34.

Joseph, T., Vélez, W., & Antrop-González, R. (2017). The experiences of low-income Latina/o families in an urban voucher, parochial school. *Journal of Latinos and Education, 16*(2), 143–155. Available: https://doi.org/10.1080/15348431.2016.1205992

Kallick, B., & Zmuda, A. (2017). *Students at the center: Personalized learning with habits of mind.* Alexandria, VA: ASCD.

Kameenui, E. J., & Carnine, D. W. (1998). *Effective teaching strategies that accommodate diverse learners.* Des Moines: Prentice-Hall.

Keller, J., & McDade, K. (2000). Attitudes of low-income parents toward seeking help with parenting: Implications for practice. *Child Welfare, 79*(3), 285–312.

Kieffer, M. (2010). Socioeconomic status, English proficiency, and late-emerging reading difficulties. *Educational Researcher, 39*(6), 484–486.

Kinsley, C. W. (1997). Service learning: A process to connect learning and living. *NASSP Bulletin, 81*(591), 1–7.

Knapp, M. S., & Adelman, N. (1995). *Teaching for meaning in high-poverty classrooms.* New York: Teachers College Press.

Knapp, M. S., Copland, M. A., & Talbert, J. E. (2003). *Leading for learning: Reflective tools for school and district leaders.* Center for the Study of Teaching and Policy (CTP) research report. Seattle, WA: University of Washington. Retrieved from https://eric.ed.gov/?id=ED482827

Koball, H., & Jiang, Y. (2018). Basic facts about low-income children. National Center for Children in Poverty. Retrieved from http://www.nccp.org/publications/pub_1194.html

Kops, B. (2010). Best practices for teaching in summer session. *Education Digest, 75*(9), 44–49.

Kozol, J. (1991). *Savage inequalities: Children in America's schools*. New York: Crown.

Ladson-Billings, G. (1994). *The dreamkeepers: Successful teachers of African American children*. San Francisco: Jossey-Bass.

Ladson-Billings, G. (2009). *The dreamkeepers: Successful teachers of African American children* (2nd ed.). San Francisco: Jossey-Bass.

Lalas, J. (2007). Teaching for social justice in multicultural urban schools: Conceptualization and classroom implication. *Multicultural Education, 14*(3), 17.

Lambert, L. (2005a). Leadership for lasting reform. *Educational Leadership, 62*(5), 62–65.

Lambert, L. (2005b). What does leadership capacity really mean? *Journal of Staff Development, 26*(2), 38–40.

Landsman, J., & Lewis, C. W. (Eds.). (2006). *White teachers/diverse classrooms: A guide to building inclusive schools, promoting high expectations, and eliminating racism* (1st ed.). Sterling, VA: Stylus.

Langer, J. (2001). Beating the odds: Teaching middle and secondary school students to read and write well. *American Educational Research Journal, 38*, 837–880.

Lareau, A. (1987). Social class differences in family-school relationships: The importance of cultural capital. *Sociology of Education, 60*(2), 73–85.

Larson, C. L., & Ovando, C. (2001). *The color of bureaucracy: The politics of equity in multicultural school communities*. Florence, KY: Taylor & Francis.

Leader, G. C. (2010). *Real leaders, real schools: Stories of success against enormous odds*. Cambridge, MA: Harvard Education Press.

Levin, H. M. (1989). *Accelerated schools: A new strategy for at-risk students*. Bloomington, IN: Indiana Education Policy Center. Retrieved from https://eric.ed.gov/?id=ED309534

Lindt, S. F., & Miller, S. C. (2017). Movement and learning in elementary school. *Phi Delta Kappan, 98*(7), 34–27.

Livingston, G. (2018, April 27). About one-third of U.S. children are living with an unmarried parent. Pew Research Center. Retrieved from https://www.pewresearch.org/fact-tank/2018/04/27/about-one-third-of-u-s-children-are-living-with-an-unmarried-parent/

Lorentzen, I. J., & McCaw, W. (2015). How board governance practices affect student achievement. In T. L. Alsbury & P. Gore (Eds.), *Improving school board effectiveness: A balanced governance approach* (pp. 53–64). Cambridge, MA: Harvard Education Press.

Lott, B. (2001). Low income parents and the public schools. *Journal of Social Issues, 57*(2), 247–259.

Lott, B. (2003). Recognizing and welcoming the standpoint of low-income parents in the public schools. *Journal of Educational and Psychological Consultation, 14*(1), 91–104.

Luthar, S. S., & Becker, B. E. (2002). Privileged but pressured? A study of affluent youth. *Child Development, 73*(5), 1593–1610.

Mapp, K. L., Carver, I., & Lander, J. (2017). *Powerful partnerships: A teacher's guide to engaging families for student success*. New York: Scholastic.

Marzano, R. J., & Waters, T. (2009). *District leadership that works: Striking the right balance*. Bloomington, IN: Solution Tree.

Marzano, R. J., Waters, T., & McNulty, B. A. (2005). *School leadership that works: From research to results*. Alexandria, VA: ASCD.

Mayer, M. J., & Cornell, D. G. (2010). New perspectives on school safety and violence prevention: Guest editors' preface. *Educational Researcher, 39*(1), 5–6.

McClure, J., & Vaughn, L. (1997). *Project tutor's "how to" guide: For implementing a cross-age tutoring program in your elementary school*. Rohnert Park, CA: California Institute on Human Services.

McEachin, A., Augustine, C. H., & McCombs, J. (2018, March 9). Effective summer programming. Retrieved from https://www.aft.org/ae/spring2018/mceachin_augustine_mccombs

McGee, G. W. (2004). Closing the achievement gap: Lessons from Illinois' Golden Spike high-poverty, high-performing schools. *Journal of Education for Students Placed at Risk, 9*(2), 97–125.

McWayne, C., Hampton, V., Fantuzzo, J., Cohen, H., & Sekino, Y. (2004). A multivariate examination of parent involvement and the social and academic competencies of urban kindergarten children. *Psychology in the Schools, 41*(3), 363–377.

Meloy, B., Gardner, M., & Darling-Hammond, L. (2019). *Untangling the evidence on preschool effectiveness: Insights for policymakers.* Learning Policy Institute. Retrieved from https://learningpolicyinstitute.org/sites/default/files/productfiles/Untangling_Evidence_Preschool_Effectiveness_REPORT. pdf

Merriam, S. B. (1998). *Qualitative research and case study applications in education.* San Francisco: Jossey-Bass.

Meyers, C. V., Goree, L., & Burton, K. (2019). Leading with a commitment to equity. *Phi Delta Kappan, 100*(8), 47–51.

Milner, H. R. I. (2015). *Rac(e)ing to class: Confronting poverty and race in schools and classrooms.* Cambridge, MA: Harvard Education Press.

Morgan, I., & Amerikaner, A. (2018). Funding gaps 2018. An analysis of school funding equity across the U.S. and within each state. Education Trust. Retrieved from https://edtrust.org/resource/funding-gaps-2018/

Mortenson, T. (1993). *Postsecondary education opportunity: The Mortenson report on public policy analysis of opportunity for postsecondary education.* Iowa City: American College Testing Program.

National Center for Children in Poverty (NCCP). (2018). Child poverty. Available: http://nccp.org/topics/childpoverty.html

National Center for Education Statistics. (2017). Preschool and kindergarten enrollment. Retrieved from https://nces.ed.gov/programs/coe/indicator_cfa.asp

National Center for Education Statistics. (2019). Public high school graduation rates. *The condition of education.* Retrieved from https://nces.ed.gov/programs/coe/indicator_coi.asp

National Center for Homeless Education. (2019). Federal data school years 2014–15 to 2015–16. Retrieved from https://nche.ed.gov/wp-content/uploads/2019/02/Federal-Data-Summary-SY-14.15-to-16.17-Final-Published-2.12.19.pdf

National Child Traumatic Stress Network. (2008a). Child trauma toolkit for educators. Retrieved from https://www.nctsn.org/resources/child-trauma-toolkit-educators

National Child Traumatic Stress Network. (2008b). Trauma facts for educators. Retrieved from NCTSN.org/resources/trauma-facts-educators

National Dropout Prevention Center. (2019). Mentoring/tutoring. Retrieved from http://dropoutprevention.org/effective-strategies/mentoring-tutoring/

National Head Start Association. (2018, November 5). Retrieved from https://www.nhsa.org/national-head-start-fact-sheets

Neuman, S. B. (2008). *Educating the other America: Top experts tackle poverty, literacy, and achievement in our schools.* Baltimore, MD: Paul H. Brookes.

Newmann, F., Bryk, A. S., & Nagaoka, J. K. (2001). *Improving Chicago's schools: Authentic intellectual work and standardized tests: Conflict or coexistence?* Chicago: Consortium on Chicago School Research.

Newmann, F. M., Marks, H. M., & Gamoran, A. (1996). Authentic pedagogy and student performance. *American Journal of Education, 104*(4), 280–312.

Ornelles, C. (2007). Providing classroom-based intervention to at-risk students to support their academic engagement and interactions with peers. *Preventing School Failure: Alternative Education for Children and Youth, 51*(4), 3–12.

Padrón, Y. N., Waxman, H. C., & Rivera, H. H. (2002). *Educating Hispanic students: Obstacles and avenues to improved academic achievement.* Santa Cruz, CA: Center for Research on Education, Diversity & Excellence.

Palinscar, A., & Brown, A. (1985). Reciprocal teaching: Activities to promote "reading with your mind." In T. L. Harris & E. J. Cooper (Eds.), *Reading, thinking, and concept development: Strategies for the classroom* (pp. 299–310). New York: College Board.

Palmer, P. J. (2007). *The courage to teach: Exploring the inner landscape of a teacher's life.* San Francisco: Jossey-Bass.

Parker, L., & Shapiro, J. (1993). The context of educational administration and social class. In C. A. Capper (Ed.), *Educational administration in a pluralistic society* (pp. 36-65). Albany: State University of New York Press.

Parrett, W., & Budge, K. (2012). *Turning high-poverty schools into high-performing schools.* Alexandria, VA: ASCD.

Partelow, L., Brown, C., Shapiro, S., & Johnson, S. (2018, March 28). 7 great education policy ideas for progressives in 2018. Center for American Progress. Available: https://www.americanprogress.org/issues/education-k-12/reports/2018/03/28/448156/7-great-education-policy-ideas-progressives-2018/

Pellegrini, A. D., & Bohn, C. M. (2005). The role of recess in children's cognitive performance and school adjustment. *Educational Researcher, 34*(1), 13–19.

Pelletier, J., & Corter, C. (2005). Design, implementation, and outcomes of a school readiness program for diverse families. *The School Community Journal, 15*(1), 89.

Pfeffer, J., & Sutton, R. (2000). *The knowing-doing gap: How smart companies turn knowledge into action.* Boston: Harvard Business School Press.

Pogrow, S. (2005). HOTS revisited: A thinking development approach to reducing the learning gap after grade 3. *Phi Delta Kappan, 87*(1), 64–75.

Pogrow, S. (2006). The Bermuda Triangle of American education: Pure traditionalism, pure progressivism, and good intentions. *Phi Delta Kappan, 88*(2), 142–150.

Putnam, R. D., & Feldstein, L. M. (2003). *Better together: Restoring the American community.* New York: Simon & Schuster.

Quaglia, R. J., & Fox, K. M. (2003). *Student aspirations: Eight conditions that make a difference.* Champaign, IL: Research Press.

Reed, E. (2019, April 16). Income inequality in America: Growth and statistics. *TheStreet.* Retrieved from https://www.thestreet.com/politics/income-inequality-in-america-14927750

Reinicke, C. (2018, July 19). U.S. income inequality continues to grow. CNBC.com. Retrieved from https://www.cnbc.com/2018/07/19/income-inequality-continues-to-grow-in-the-united-states.html

Rischer, A. D. (2009). Strategies for a successful summer school program. *Education Digest, 74*(9), 34–36.

Rist, R. C. (1979). On the means of knowing: Qualitative research in education. *New York University Education Quarterly, 10*(4), 17–21.

Rockwell, S. (2007). Working smarter, not harder: Reaching the tough to teach: Part I: Prior knowledge and concept development. *Kappa Delta Pi Record, 44*(1), 8–12.

Rodriguez, G. M., & Fabionar, J. (2010). The impact of poverty on students and schools: Exploring the social justice leadership implications. In C. Marshall & M. Oliva (Eds.), *Leadership for social justice* (pp. 55–73). Upper Saddle River, NJ: Pearson.

Rothstein, R. (2008). Whose problem is poverty? *Educational Leadership, 65*(7), 8–13.

Routman, R. (2014). *Read, write, lead: Breakthrough strategies for schoolwide literacy success.* Alexandria, VA: ASCD.

Sadowski, M. (Ed.). (2004). *Teaching immigrant and second-language students*. Cambridge, MA: Harvard University Press.

San Antonio, D. (2008). Understanding students' strength and struggles. *Educational Leadership, 65*(7), 74–79.

Sanburn, J. (2014, July 31). The rise of suburban poverty in America. *Time*. Retrieved from http://time.com/3060122/poverty-america-suburbs-brookings/

Sanders, E. (1999). *Urban school leadership: Issues and strategies*. Larchmont, NY: Eye on Education.

Sapp, J. (2009, Spring). How school taught me I was poor. *Teaching Tolerance, 35*. Retrieved from https://www.tolerance.org/magazine/spring-2009/how-school-taught-me-i-was-poor

Scheurich, J. J., & Skrla, L. (2003). *Leadership for equity and excellence: Creating high-achievement classrooms, schools, and districts*. Thousand Oaks, CA: Corwin.

Schilder, D., & Dahlin, M. (2016). *Center on Enhancing Early Learning Outcomes: Year 4 evaluation*. National Institute for Early Education Research. New Brunswick, NJ: Rutgers University.

Schlichter, C., Hobbs, D., & Crump, D. (1988, April). Extending talents unlimited to secondary schools. *Educational Leadership, 45*(7), 36–40.

Schwendiman, J., & Fager, J. (1999). *After school program: Good for kids, good for communities*. Portland, OR: Northwest Regional Educational Laboratory.

Sheridan, K., Halverson, E. R., Litts, B., Brahms, L., Jacobs-Priebe, L., & Owens, T. (2014). Learning in the making: A comparative case study of three makerspaces. *Harvard Educational Review, 84*(4), 505–531.

Sibley, B. A., & Etnier, L. (2003). The relationship between physical activity and cognition in children: A meta-analysis. *Pediatric Exercise Science, 15*(3), 243–256.

Silverberg, L. (2018). New resources: Implementing and expanding afterschool programs for principals. Retrieved from https://www.afterschoolalliance.org/afterschool snack/New-resources-Implementing-and-expanding-afterschool-programs_03-19-2018.cfm

Skrla, L., McKenzie, K. B., & Scheurich, J. J. (2009). *Using equity audits to create equitable and excellent schools*. Thousand Oaks, CA: Corwin.

Slavin, R. E., Cheung, A., Groff, C., & Lake, C. (2008). Effective reading programs for middle and high schools: A best-evidence synthesis. *Reading Research Quarterly, 43*(3), 290–322.

Smith, G. A., & Sobel, D. (2010). *Place- and community-based education in schools*. New York: Routledge.

Smith, S. (2013). Would you walk through my front door? *Educational Leadership, 70*(8), 76–78.

Smith, W. H., & Ternes, E. (2004). *The invisible soldiers: Unheard voices*. Sudbury, MA: WHS Media.

Sommeiller, E., & Price, M. (2018, July 19). The new gilded age: Income inequality in the U.S. by state, metropolitan area, and county. Economic Policy Institute. Retrieved from https://www.epi.org/publication/the-new-gilded-age-income-inequality-in-the-u-s-by-state-metropolitan-area-and-county/

Stark, P., & Noel, A. M. (2015). *Trends in high school dropout and completion rates in the United States: 1972–2012* (NCES 2015-015). U.S. Department of Education. Washington, DC: National Center for Education Statistics. Retrieved from http://nces.ed.gov/pubsearch.

Stiggins, R. (2017). *The perfect assessment system*. Alexandria, VA: ASCD.

Stiggins, R., Arter, J., Chappius, J., & Chappius, S. (2010). Classroom assessment for student learning: Doing it right—using it well [workshop materials]. Portland: Pearson Assessment Training Institute.

Stiggins, R., & DuFour, R. (2009). Maximizing the power of formative assessments. *Phi Delta Kappan, 90*(9), 640–644.

Suitts, S. (2015). A new majority research bulletin: Low income students now a majority in the nation's public schools. Southern Education Foundation. Retrieved from https://www.southerneducation.org/what-we-do/research/newmajorityreportseries/

Supovitz, J. A. (2006). *The case for district-based reform: Leading, building, and sustaining school improvement*. Cambridge, MA: Harvard Education Press.

Teddlie, C., & Stringfield, S. (1993). *Schools make a difference: Lessons learned from a 10-year study of school effects*. New York: Teachers College Press.

Theoharis, G. (2009). *The school leaders our children deserve: Seven keys to equity, social justice, and school reform*. New York: Teachers College Press.

Tomlinson, C. A., Brighton, C., Hertberg, H., Callahan, C., Moon, T. R., Brimijoin, K., & Reynolds, T. (2003). Differentiating instruction in response to student readiness, interest, and learning profile in academically diverse classrooms: A review of literature. *Journal for the Education of the Gifted, 27*(2/3), 119–145.

U.S. Bureau of Labor Statistics. (2014). *A profile of the working poor, 2012.* (Report No. 1047). Washington, DC: Author. Retrieved from https://www.bls.gov/opub/reports/working-poor/archive/workingpoor_2012.pdf

U.S. Bureau of Labor Statistics. (2019) A profile of the working poor, 2017. (BLS Reports). Retrieved from https://www.bls.gov/opub/reports/working-poor/2017/home.htm

U.S. Census Bureau. (2017). POV-14. Families by householder's work experience and family structure. Retrieved from https://www.census.gov/data/tables/time-series/demo/income-poverty/cps-pov/pov-14.html

U.S. Census Bureau. (2019, September 26). American Community Survey Data. Retrieved from https://www.census.gov/programs-surveys/acs/data.html

U.S. Department of Agriculture Economic Research Service. (2018). Key statistics and graphics. Retrieved from https://www.ers.usda.gov/topics/food-nutrition-assistance/food-security-in-the-us/key-statistics-graphics.aspx

U.S. Department of Education. (n.d.). *Full service community schools program*. Retrieved from https://www.2.ed.gov/programs/communityschools/index.html

Utti, C. (2016, October 24). Is there a correlation between income and drug and alcohol abuse? Retrieved from https://willingway.com/income-drug-alcohol-abuse/

Valencia, R. R. (1997). *The evolution of deficit thinking: Educational thought and practice*. London: Falmer Press.

Valenzuela, A. (1999). *Subtracting schooling: US-Mexican youth and politics of caring*. Albany, NY: State University of New York Press.

Vatterott, C. (2009). *Rethinking homework: Best practices that support diverse needs*. Alexandria, VA: ASCD.

Vatterott, C. (2018). *Rethinking homework: Best practices that support diverse needs* (2nd ed.). Alexandria, VA: ASCD.

Waanders, C., Mendez, J., & Downer, J. (2007). Parent characteristics, economic stress, and neighborhood context as predictors of parent involvement in preschool children's education. *Journal of School Psychology, 45*(619–636). doi:10.1016/j.jsp.2007.07.003

Wagner, T., & Dintersmith, T. (2015). *Most likely to succeed: Preparing our kids for the innovation era*. New York: Simon & Schuster.

Walsh, J. (1999). The role of area-based programmes in tackling poverty. In D. G. Pringle, J. Walsh, & M. Hennessy (Eds.), *Poor people, poor place: A geography of poverty and deprivation in Ireland* (pp. 279–312). Dublin: Oak Tree Press.

Wang, F. (2018). Social justice leadership—Theory and practice: A case of Ontario. *Educational Administration Quarterly, 54*(3), 470–498.

Warren, M. R., Hong, S., Rubin, C. L., & Uy, P. S. (2009). Beyond the bake sale: A community-based relational approach to parent engagement in schools. *Teachers College Record, 111*(9), 2209–2254.

Webster-Stratton, C. (1997). From parent training to community building. *Families in Society: The Journal of Contemporary Human Services, 78*(2), 156–171.

Weinstein, R. (2002). *Reaching higher: The power of expectations in schooling.* Cambridge, MA: Harvard University Press.

Wenger, E. (1998). *Communities of practice: Learning, meaning, and identity.* New York: Cambridge University Press.

Werblow, J., Urick, A., & Duesbery, L. (2013). On the wrong track: How tracking is associated with dropping out of high school. *Equity & Excellence in Education, 46*(2), 270–284. https://doi.org/10.1080/10665684.2013.779168

Wiggins, G. P., & McTighe, J. (2005). *Understanding by design* (2nd ed.). Alexandria, VA: ASCD.

Williams, D. T. (2003, November). Rural routes to success. *Educational Leadership, 61*(3), 66–70.

Wiltz, S. (2008). Neither art nor accident. *Harvard Education Letter, 24*(1).

Winter, V. E., & Cowie, B. (2009). Cross-cultural communication: Implications for social work practice and a departure from Payne. *Journal of Educational Controversy, 4*(1).

Zavadsky, H. (2013). Scaling turnaround: A district-improvement approach. *American Enterprise Institute, 70*(1), 16.

Index

Note: Page numbers followed by f and b refer to figures and boxes respectively.

About the Authors

William H. Parrett has received international recognition for his work in school improvement related to children and adolescents who live in poverty. He has coauthored 11 books; three recent books are best sellers. The award-winning and best-selling book, *Turning High-Poverty Schools into High-Performing Schools*, with Kathleen Budge, has provided a Framework for Action that has been adopted throughout the United States to guide lasting improvement and student success in high-poverty schools. He is also the coauthor, with Kathleen Budge, of *Disrupting Poverty: Five Powerful Classroom Practices*. As director of the Boise State University Center for School Improvement and Policy Studies (since 1996), Parrett coordinates funded projects and school improvement initiatives that currently exceed $5 million a year and in excess of $80 million over the past 25 years. He is a frequent speaker at international and national events, and his work with state and regional educational organizations, districts, and schools spans 46 states and 17 nations. Throughout his career, Parrett has worked to improve the educational achievement of all children and youth, particularly those less advantaged. These efforts have positively affected the lives of thousands of young people, many of whom live in poverty. Contact Parrett by e-mail at wparret@boisestate.edu or follow him on Twitter @WHParrett.

Kathleen M. Budge brings 26 years of practical experience as a teacher and administrator combined with 14 years of work dedicated to bridging the gap between the university and the teaching profession. She is an associate professor of Educational Leadership and former chair of the Curriculum, Instruction, and Foundational Studies Department at Boise State University, where her research focuses on poverty, rural education, school improvement, and leadership development. Budge is coauthor (with William Parrett) of the 2012 award-winning and best-selling book, *Turning High-Poverty Schools into High-Performing Schools,* and *Disrupting Poverty: Five Powerful Class-room Practices,* and the video series, *Disrupting Poverty in Elementary and Secondary Classrooms.* She has conducted numerous presentations at international, national, and state conferences and served as guest speaker for webinars, podcasts, and symposiums related to the topic of poverty and the "whole child." Budge's work includes state departments, boards of education, education associations, state and regional service providers, and schools in 26 states and 8 nations. She earned her doctorate from the University of Washington in 2005. Budge continues to maintain that her most important and significant work has been teaching 1st graders to read. Contact her at kathleenbudge@boisestate.edu or follow her on Twitter @KathleenBudge.

Related ASCD Resources: Educating Students Living in Poverty

At the time of publication, the following resources were available (ASCD stock numbers in parentheses).

Online Course

Turning High-Poverty Schools into High-Performing Schools (Reimagined) [PDO] with Kathleen M. Budge, William H. Parrett, and Margo Healy (#PD16OC006S)

DVDs

Disrupting Poverty in the Elementary School Classroom (DVD) with William H. Parrett and Kathleen M. Budge (#616044)

Disrupting Poverty in the Secondary School Classroom (DVD) with William H. Parrett and Kathleen M. Budge (# 616071)

Print Products

Creating a Trauma-Sensitive Classroom (Quick Reference Guide), by Kristin Souers and Pete Hall (#QRG118054)

Disrupting Poverty: Five Powerful Classroom Practices, by Kathleen M. Budge and William H. Parrett (#116012)

Engaging Students with Poverty in Mind: Practical Strategies for Raising Achievement, by Eric Jensen (#113001)

Fostering Resilient Learners: Strategies for Creating a Trauma-Sensitive Classroom, by Kristin Souers and Pete Hall (#116014)

The Handbook for Poor Students, Rich Teaching, by Eric Jensen (#319078)

Relationship, Responsibility, and Regulation: Trauma-Invested Practices for Fostering Resilient Learners, by Kristin Van Marter Souers and Pete Hall (#119027)

Teaching Students from Poverty (Quick Reference Guide), by Eric Jensen (#QRG118041)

Teaching with Poverty in Mind: What Being Poor Does to Kids' Brains and What Schools Can Do About It, by Eric Jensen (#109074)

Your Students, My Students, Our Students: Rethinking Equitable and Inclusive Classrooms, by Lee Ann Jung, Nancy Frey, Douglas Fisher, and Julie Kroener (#119019)

For up-to-date information about ASCD resources, go to www.ascd.org. You can search the complete archives of *Educational Leadership* at www.ascd.org/el.

ASCD myTeachSource®

Download resources from a professional learning platform with hundreds of research-based best practices and tools for your classroom at http://myteachsource .ascd.org/

For more information, send an e-mail to member@ascd.org; call 1-800-933-2723 or 703-578-9600; send a fax to 703-575-5400; or write to Information Services, ASCD, 1703 N. Beauregard St., Alexandria, VA 22311-1714 USA.

WHOLE CHILD
TENETS

1 HEALTHY
Each student enters school healthy and learns about and practices a healthy lifestyle.

2 SAFE
Each student learns in an environment that is physically and emotionally safe for students and adults.

3 ENGAGED
Each student is actively engaged in learning and is connected to the school and broader community.

4 SUPPORTED
Each student has access to personalized learning and is supported by qualified, caring adults.

5 CHALLENGED
Each student is challenged academically and prepared for success in college or further study and for employment and participation in a global environment.

THE WHOLE CHILD

The ASCD Whole Child approach is an effort to transition from a focus on narrowly defined academic achievement to one that promotes the long-term development and success of all children. Through this approach, ASCD supports educators, families, community members, and policymakers as they move from a vision about educating the whole child to sustainable, collaborative actions.

Turning High-Poverty Schools into High-Performing Schools relates to the **safe**, **supported**, and **engaged** tenets.

*For more about the ASCD Whole Child approach, visit **www.ascd.org/wholechild**.*